The Filmmaker's Guide to Final Cut Pro Workflow

The Filmmaker's Guide to Final Cut Pro Workflow

Dale Angell

AMSTERDAM • BOSTON • HEIDELBERG • LONDON
NEW YORK • OXFORD • PARIS • SAN DIEGO
SAN FRANCISCO • SINGAPORE • SYDNEY • TOKYO

Focal Press is an imprint of Elsevier

Acquisitions Editor: Dennis McGonagle
Publishing Services Manager: George Morrison
Project Manager: Mónica González de Mendoza
Assistant Editor: Chris Simpson
Marketing Manager: Marcel Koppes
Cover Design: Eric DeCicco

Focal Press is an imprint of Elsevier
30 Corporate Drive, Suite 400, Burlington, MA 01803, USA
Linacre House, Jordan Hill, Oxford OX2 8DP, UK

 Recognizing the importance of preserving what has been written, Elsevier prints its books on acid-free paper whenever possible.

Library of Congress Cataloging-in-Publication Data
Angell, Dale.
   The filmmaker's guide to Final cut pro workflow / Dale Angell.
      p. cm.
   Includes index.
   ISBN 978-0-240-80986-1 (pbk. : alk. paper)   1. Motion pictures—Editing—Data processing.
2. Final cut (Electronic resource)   I. Title.
   TR899.A584 2008
   778.5′350285—dc22

                                                                    2007024309

British Library Cataloguing-in-Publication Data
A catalogue record for this book is available from the British Library.

ISBN: 978-0-240-80986-1

For information on all Focal Press publications
visit our website at www.books.elsevier.com

Transferred to Digital Printing 2010

Contents

A Letter from the Author   vii

Introduction   ix

The Kodak 35 mm Project   xv

1   When Shooting on Film   1

2   When Shooting Digital Video   23

3   Initial Audio Workflow, Importing Production Audio, and Syncing   35

4   Editing Picture to Lock   51

5   Finishing on Film   57

6   Finishing on Digital Video, the Online Edit   81

7   Sound Edit Workflows   93

8   Titles for Digital Video and Film   119

9   Color Timing and Color Grading   133

10   After the Film Is Finished: Distribution   143

Appendix 1   Understanding the NTSC Video Format and Digital Video   151

Appendix 2   Understanding the PAL Video Format   163
Jaime Estrada-Torres

Appendix 3   Current Video Formats   167

Appendix 4   Current Film Formats   177

Appendix 5   Understanding Time Code   181

Appendix 6   Aspect Ratios, Anamorphic Image, and Wide-screen   183

Appendix 7   Understanding File Architecture   189

Appendix 8   Conforming Negative   197

Appendix 9   Deconstructing Several Films' Workflows   209

Appendix 10 Example Workflows   225

Index   241

A Letter from the Author

I edited my first film in 1974 on rewinds and a viewer. I also had a mag reader that could interlock three tracks of sound. My focus shifted to sound editing and mixing, but for the next ten years I continued editing on film using Steenbeck, Movieolla, and Kem flatbed editors. The vast majority of my editing was done on the ubiquitous Movieolla upright, rewinds, and several good film bins. I still bear the physical scars from runaway reels and inattentive use of my cherished Revis splicers. To this day, I thrill when entering an old editing room that still has the smell of a "real" editing room, that wondrous mix of acetate, acetone, and stale coffee.

But time marches on. In the eighties, I was back editing picture and sound, only now on nonlinear Sony video systems. Mine was a glorious system: linear time code, A-B playback with digital effects switcher, with GPI trigger and interlock to an eight-track audio system. But just when I thought it couldn't get any better, along came Avid.

I learned nonlinear editing on the Avid Media Composer Express. It was a bare bones, stripped-down system with composite video input from a U-Matic, three-quarter-inch video deck. The price, not including the video recorder, was $35,000. Keep in mind that this was at a time when you could buy a small house for $50,000.

But it was awesome. It could do anything the nonlinear system could do. Plus, I could make any complicated effect or edit, change anything whenever I wanted to, and I could do all of it with the click of a mouse. The interface was easy to understand and the learning curve rather flat.

It had some serious limitations, though. It still only had eight audio tracks. It was expandable to more, but this was part of an expensive upgrade. It only had 20 Gig of video storage, so I was always out of space. It could only use Avid media drives, so I couldn't simply plug in a couple of extra drives. And everything from Avid was wickedly expensive.

The best part was I didn't pay for it. While I always thought of any editing system I was using as mine, I had never owned any editing system. I could design the layout and suggest what equipment I wanted to use, but my employer always bought it; I simply used it.

Then, in the late nineties, I decided I needed my own editing system. Much of the work I was doing at the time was my own work and this was becoming a problem at work. I had also bought a home out in the desert and wanted to edit right there, in the middle of nowhere, amid the scorpions and jackrabbits. What I wanted was a simple Avid capable of capturing DV from firewire-component video and serial digital interface (SDI) with serial deck control. I needed to be able to edit film and video and I wanted a good Pro Tools 32-channel system with an 8-channel audio interface. I was also very interested in DVD authoring and burning, and I was hoping to be able to add this as well. Add high-speed Internet access and I would be all set to edit to my heart's content right there in the literal middle of nowhere.

So, like anyone in my situation I headed for NAB. I have long held that both depression and elation are the result of expectation colliding with reality. There was no Avid that could capture from firewire. You could only configure the Avid hardware to capture from SDI or component, but not both. Every AVR codec for every format cost money. In order to edit film, you needed the Film Composer or the Film Cutter and the Film Cutter couldn't edit video. The Avid rep suggested it would be more affordable if I bought two Avids, one for film and one for video. The Pro Tools interface was a piece of cake, but it was not compatible with the Avid AVR video codec so I would need an expensive machine control setup. Total cost, around $150,000, without any video and audio recorders.

I could add DVD authoring and burning for about another $10,000. The good news was I found I could get high-speed Internet with a wireless UHF setup shooting to a distant mountain in Arizona for $39.95 per month. This was more in line with by budget.

So this was depression. I now knew why they held the NAB conference in Las Vegas. I figured, if I took the amount I was planning to spend and put it on a roulette number, I'd be editing if it hit.

Fortunately, instead of heading for the casino, I wandered into the Apple booth. I thought this would cheer me up because I've always been an Apple nerd. I bought my first Mac literally right off of the delivery truck in 1984. I'd heard about Final Cut Pro but had not actually seen it yet. I convinced one of the Apple reps to let me take a turn at the controls of one of the Final Cut Pro demo machines and found it easy to understand and rather Avid-like. It did lack some of the cool tools, but it had a feature I really loved: I could afford it.

I also found that with second-party software called Film Logic, I could edit film. It could capture DV from FireWire, and SDI and component video boards were available as well. I could configure it to do anything I wanted to do.

So this was elation. I made the switch to Final Cut Pro and never looked back. It's taken seven years for technology and prices to catch up with my desires back then, but I now have that dream system. Film Logic became Cinema Tools, Avid released the Pro Tools LE software able to play Final Cut Pro's Quick-Time video as its reference video, and DVD authoring and burning became simple and affordable.

True, in that same time, Avid has become more affordable and flexible, but Avid still likes to do only one thing on each hardware configuration. It's a great system when your goal is to simply edit in one format on one system, be it film, HD video, or DV, and still manages to dominate the film industry, at least for now. But with Final Cut Pro, I was able to work at home amid the scorpions and jack-rabbits. This book is about what I learned, although I have left out the information on keeping scorpions out of the edit room and how to deal with a flash flood.

Introduction

Overview

There was a time, not long ago when, if someone asked how motion pictures were edited, you could hand them a book. It was a fairly short and straightforward book explaining the process of work printing, syncing, editing, and conforming. All films were shot and edited in, more or less, the same way. The editors all knew what was expected of them, the lab knew what their role was, and the costs were simply the costs.

Those days are gone with the dinosaurs and the ten-cent cup of coffee. That well-worn path through the woods is now overgrown with brush, and filmmakers can be seen stumbling blindly through the trees and undergrowth in search of the fastest and cheapest route between here and there. Now and then, someone shouts that they have found a shortcut, a new and clever way through, only to have someone else shout them down saying that their way is faster still and cheaper to boot.

The path through postproduction is now called workflow, the ordering of the steps that takes the film from shooting to distribution. The problem is not that there are no good workflows, but that there are so many. And each has options, variations in when to zig and when to zag. An examination of one-hundred films will likely reveal one-hundred workflows.

The starting and ending points are shifting as well. Shooting on digital formats, digital intermediates, and digital projection all complicate the problem. What worked this year may not work next year because the technology moved on, or the new and revolutionary thingamajig that you just bought for half a million dollars may have turned out to be a digital Edsel.

This book is intended to direct motion picture editors through the complicated maze of postproduction workflow using Final Cut Pro Studio with Cinema Tools, Adobe graphics applications, and Pro Tools. While there are many other paths through this maze, this book focuses on workflows using only these software packages. This is not because this is the most common or simplest way of editing motion pictures, but precisely because it is not the most common. The advantages of these workflows are cost savings, flexibility, and freedom. Freedom to edit on a laptop in a cabin at Lake Tahoe or the red sandstone cliffs of Utah, flexibility to edit 35 mm film, high-definition digital, or digital video all from the same system. And the cost savings can slash equipment costs by as much as 95 percent. It is also a system that can evolve with changing demands and new technologies.

Because this book is dedicated to these concepts, there are chapters on such diverse subjects as improving digital titles on National Television Standards Committee (NTSC) video, conforming negative, digital intermediates, and even sound design, all with an eye on cost savings.

The question comes up, if these workflows are that much cheaper and more flexible, why doesn't the mainstream Hollywood industry use them? The answer is that sometimes they do, but Hollywood has never done anything they perceive as risky in the name of cost savings. It's not an industry that looks to anything new except to sell more tickets.

There was an old adage back in the eighties that said, "Nobody ever got fired for buying IBM." When clones and Macs were first coming out, an executive was not risking criticism for sticking with mainstream thinking and buying the expensive IBM system. But ask yourself this, when was the last time you were in a business and they were using an IBM PC? Cost savings and efficiency have always won out.

These workflows are here to stay, and can perform any task or achieve the end result as well as any other system. When criticisms come up, they are usually based on lack of information, rarely on actual limitations in the workflow or software. Add to that, the workflows and software are changing and evolving almost daily and it becomes obvious: this is the future.

This book is not intended to be a how-to guide on software. It is assumed that the reader has a good working knowledge of basic digital video editing using Final Cut Pro and Pro Tools.

Final Cut Pro, Final Cut Studio, and Cinema Tools

Final Cut Pro is a resolution-independent, software-based, nonlinear editing system for the Macintosh. In many ways, it is no different than a dozen other such systems. What sets it apart is its ability to interface with almost any hardware or video system. Because it is totally resolution in-dependent, it can be used to edit any video format from streaming Web video to HD cam. It uses a host of frame rates and can convert many to 29.97 video for display in real time. And, yet, it requires no hardware interface at all. It works fine on a laptop without any video or audio monitor. It is one soft-ware package that is equally at home in a backpack or running a million-dollar HD online edit suite.

But what really pushes it over the top is Cinema Tools. This software was originally an expensive add-on package. Now, it comes bundled with Final Cut Pro and many of its features have been inte-grated directly into FCP. Cinema Tools allows management of film key code information, audio time code, edit decision lists (EDLs), cut lists, and even film opticals. It allows telecined film to be reversed back to the original frames for frame-accurate editing and audio syncing. It can even pull the frame rate back up to 24 for true 24-frame film editing without pull-up and pull-down issues. When these applications first came out, they cost $1,000 each, a bargain compared to systems that did less and cost more than $100,000. Today, you can buy both as a bundle for less than the original cost of just one.

Final Cut Studio includes many software add-ons for advanced color grading, motion graphics and compositing, sound editing and DVD authoring. When used with second party io devices, these programs can be used with any digital format including 2 K and 4 K as well as Apple's new Pro Res 422 and Red Camera's Redcode.

Final Cut also exports a variety of audio formats, including open media framework (OMF), making a seamless transition into the audio edit smooth and problem free. Or for the die-hard audio onliners, Cinema Tools can manage a complete audio EDL for reimport of time code audio.

Pro Tools

Pro Tools is the old man on the block, a well-respected and widely used audio edit and mixing system. Like other digital audio workstations, Pro Tools is an audio-only editing system. It does, however, provide for video playback from either machine control or movie files, and supports most video and film frame rates. The newest versions, 6 and above, support portable firewire drives and firewire video playback. Pro Tools always requires a hardware interface, but these are, for the most part, compatible with each other. Integration with Final Cut Pro requires an expensive ($500) software plug-in, but then the seam between Final Cut Pro and Pro Tools all but disappears.

Pro Tools comes in two basic versions: the HD systems, which require expensive and often extensive hardware interfaces, and LE systems that use simpler and more affordable interfaces. The good news is that the two systems are compatible with each other. As long as the editor avoids using the extreme sample rates available on the HD systems and keeps to the basic sample rates and bit depths used in Final Cut Pro, the Pro Tools session can be opened on any Pro Tools system and seamlessly integrates back into the Final Cut Pro edit. Many of the LE hardware interfaces are also compatible with Final Cut, and can be used for audio recording or output.

This is great news for editors. It means that for about $900, they can add Pro Tools to their Final Cut Pro edit system. They are now free to edit their sound design on their own system, with real-time monitoring of levels and effects. They can take their project on a firewire drive to thousands of sound houses for automatic dialogue replacement (ADR), Foley (a special kind of sound effect), and scoring, and they can make temp dubs back on their own edit system. And, if they choose, they can mix at almost any expensive, high-end dub stage in Los Angeles. Or, for the no-budget gorilla film-maker, they can edit and mix right on their edit system for the cost of coffee and doughnuts.

DigiDesign division of Avid, the makers of Pro Tools, even offers a new Internet solution where the entire project can live on a server in Los Angeles, voice work can be done in Sidney and London, effects cut in Bali, and the editor can be temp-mixing right in their own living room, all at the same time.

Other Software

Final Cut Pro also comes with Sound Track Pro and Live Type. In their first version, they were little more than fun toys. However, Sound Track Pro is perhaps the simplest music loop editor ever created. New workflow design in Final Cut Pro allows a seamless transition between Final Cut Pro and Sound Track Pro. Sound Track Pro has greatly expanded the audio capabilities of Final Cut Pro with expanded plug-ins, previewing, and an interactive programmable mixer that can even be interfaced with many control surfaces.

And, if you have an overwhelming desire to have your titles turn into flames and go up in smoke, Live Type may provide the answer. While it is definitely a special effects titler, it makes the wild and crazy, easy and fun. Graphics and titling can also be greatly improved with the addition of the

Adobe applications: After Effects, Photoshop, and Illustrator or a good titling system such as Boris FX. So, we look at working these applications into your workflow as well.

The Final Cut Studio bundle also comes with Color, Compressor, DVD Studio Pro, and Motion. We will also look at integrating these applications into your finishing workflow.

Basic Editing Workflows

Workflows can be divided into two basic types, depending on the shooting and finishing formats. Projects shot on film, which will be finished on film, can follow several unique workflows. In this camp are the projects that will be cutting the camera negative to make film prints for distribution. Other projects will make digital intermediates for printing to 35 mm film. This is the realm of the big-budget, feature film, Hollywood's lifeblood.

In the other camp are digital video and film shooting with digital video finishing; with these workflows, projects can be shot on digital video or film in any format. Film is transferred to digital video and edited and finished as video. This is not to say that Hollywood blockbusters on film are not found here as well. The finished digital video can be used to create 35 mm film prints, and with the increase in theaters that have digital projection, soon film prints may not be necessary. But the workflow here is different; it is a video-based workflow, more often used to make television shows, music videos, and commercials.

The Basic Workflow Elements

There are many steps in workflow, and these elements must fall in a reasonable and workable order. They may be preformed in different orders or not preformed at all, depending on the workflow and the type of media being edited.

Processing, Printing, and Syncing

Historically, this was the developing and printing of the camera film as well as the transfer of audio from the original recording to an editable format and syncing to the picture.

Processing may still be the developing of the film, but it may also be processing 2 K or 4 K data into a digital video format for editing. It may be moving media from memory cards to drive or even tape, or it could be rendering virtual elements into digital video.

The printing may still include work printing of the camera original for projection. But, more likely, printing may be telecine or datacine (transcoding one media form into another or "cloning" high-definition tapes to a lower resolution format) of the film to a digital video format for editing, and capture of digital video to drive.

Audio may be dubbed from the original tape to another format, captured or recorded into the editing system, or it may be simply copied to drive on the editing system ready for syncing. This transfer may include a speed change to the audio to match the video, or it may be in sync with the original audio.

Syncing can happen in telecine or on the editing system prior to editing. It can be done with the time-honored system of matching the image of the clapper closing to the sound of the clapper, or it may be done with time code or smart slate.

Organizing and Editing

Historically, the work print was logged as it was syncing (also known as sunc), and the edit logs were related to the original camera reports, sound reports, and lab reports so that the editor and assistant editors could tell where the shot they were editing came from, what camera roll, what lab print roll, what sound roll as well as adding comments into this information about the shot. Such information as problems (i.e., misslates, scratches, focus problems, printing problems, sound problems, and any other issues with the footage) were logged. This way, if a problem is seen with the shot, the editor should be able to tell if the camera original has the problem or if the problem is only in the print.

Today, this data can be compiled as a database in Cinema Tools and even amended and printed in other software such as Microsoft Excel or Text Edit. The footage can be organized into bins and subbins in Final Cut. Computers are definitely in their element when managing a database. The hours once spent finding footage, shots, trims, and making reports has been virtually eliminated. But this data is still critical, especially when finishing on film. Good editing has, and always will, go hand in hand with good organization.

Color Correction

Even the best footage requires major color correction. Historically, this was done by labs like Deluxe and Technicolor as they printed the camera negative. Today, color correction is done in many different ways and in many different places in the workflow. Some projects will go through several corrections while some will color correct all at one time.

Color correction may be done in telecine, as the shots are edited, after the shots are edited using Final Cut's tools, in online editing, after editing on a tape-to-tape color correction system, as part of a digital intermediate, or as a film print is being made. Or a project may use several or even all of these.

Color correction tools within Final Cut have come a long way since the release of Version 1. With the release of Version 6 and Final Cut Studio 2 with Color, these tools do a truly outstanding job of color correction and many projects will not need to color correct outside of Final Cut.

Sound Editing and Mixing

While it is entirely possible to edit and mix sound ("sweeten") in Final Cut, most workflows will require editing and mixing outside of Final Cut. Sound can be edited in Soundtrack Pro, and even moved seamlessly back and forth between Sound Track and Final Cut. But, the better choice is Pro Tools. Pro Tools allows for editing and mixing of 32 tracks without rendering, using the LE version, and virtually unlimited tracks in the HD system depending on the hardware configuration.

Because sound is always handled as separate media files in Final Cut, the steps for separating and recombining these media are simple and effective.

Finishing

Beyond color correction, there are several aspects to finishing the project. This may include conforming work print and camera negative, online editing, scanning to digital intermediate and conforming the digital intermediate, bumping up standard definition to high definition, outputting digital video to film, and making master tapes. It can also include encoding audio to AC3 and compressing the video to a DVD-compliant codec for mastering DVDs.

The remainder of this book focuses on these workflows in depth. We also study several projects and take their workflow apart looking for problems and solutions, shortcuts, and pitfalls.

How to Use This Book

While most of this book deals with workflow theory, where specific examples of menu commands are listed, they are listed by the name of the software or the word go > the name of the menu > the menu selection.

The chapters in this book assume a high level of knowledge of film and video formats, time code, and use of the software packages. While there is some step-by-step information on Cinema Tools, this book is directed at understanding workflow. As mentioned earlier, it is not a how-to book on software. If you find some of the expressions or terms confusing, there are several in-depth appendices on film and video as well as on time code, aspect ratios, conforming, and file structure.

If you find the expressions and information confusing, read the corresponding appendix and, hopefully, this will help clarify the information. Also, because of the book's thickness, it is ideally suited for raising the front of a 16 mm projector that is sitting on a coffee table so that it projects the image exactly four feet up on the wall. But I'm sure you already noticed that.

The Kodak 35 mm Project

The Kodak 35 mm project is a program of Kodak's Student Filmmaker Program. The project gives student filmmakers the opportunity to create a 35 mm motion picture using the same tools used by filmmaking professionals. Kodak sponsors The 35 mm Project in conjunction with Mole Richardson, Clairmont Camera, FotoKem Laboratories, Dolby Laboratories, Laser Pacific, Mix Magic, NT Audio, and FPC.

The sponsors provide 35 mm motion picture film, film processing, camera package, lighting, grip and generator equipment, surround sound and audio mixing, front and end titles, optical sound transfers to film, telecine, and answer printing. Students are also mentored by top filmmakers, including members of the American Society of Cinematographers such as Laszlo Kovacs, ASC, and Richard Crudo, ASC, various members of the American Cinema Editors, and professional sound mixers. The sponsors also provide workshops and demonstrations on the use of cameras and equipment. The concept for The 35 mm Project was developed in 2001 by Lorette Bayle of Kodak. The pilot schools included Chapman University and the California Institute for the Arts. The 35 mm Project was extended to include the University of California, Los Angeles; Loyola Marymount University; California State University of Long Beach; University of Arizona; California State University of Northridge; the University of California Santa Barbara, and the Brooks Institute. Figure i.1 shows students from Brooks working on their film.

The sixty-year-old Brooks Institute of Santa Barbara, California, has become a regular participant in the 35 mm project. Brooks Institute graduates are visible nationally and internationally, working for distinguished organizations including National Geographic, Smithsonian, *Los Angeles Times*, and other national media outlets, including Hallmark Publishing, Cousteau Society, HBO, Kodak, and other industry leaders in visual media fields. Brooks has brought in several sponsors to support its annual project, including The Santa Barbara International Film Festival, Fisher Light, T and T Effects, Match Frame Video, and Chapman Leonard.

Brooks' Professors Tracy Trotter and Dale Angell enlist the help of a who's who list of industry experts. Students work under the mentorship of professionals, including producer Steve Traxler, whose credits include *Legally Blonde* and *Out of Time*; actor John Cleese of Monty Python's Flying Circus; Chuck Minsky, director of photography on *Pretty Woman, Almost Famous*, and *The*

Figure i.1 Student's work on film project, *Lost Hope and More* at the Santa Barbara courthouse. Brooks student Ben Kim slates the shot

Producers; Bill Butler, director of photography on more than eighty films, including *Jaws, The Conversation*, and *Biloxi Blues*; director Perry Lang of *Alias, Dawson's Creek*, and *NYPD Blue*; and photographer Wayne Goldwyn whose credits include *CSI, Jeopardy*, and *Nixon*. The list of professional mentors numbers in the dozens and changes every year.

The Kodak 35 mm Project at Brooks involves a 150-person film crew, more than thirty vendors, rental equipment valued at more than $1,000,000, and an estimated 24,000 hours of labor from students, faculty, and volunteers. Figure i.2 is a shot of some of the student crew for *Lost Hope and More*.

Figure i.2 Members of the student crew and production support vehicles in front of the Santa Barbara courthouse for the Kodak 35 mm project, *Lost Hope and More*

Lost Hope and More

Directed by Carmon Cone and Isaiah Mcamini

Written by Jessie Griffith

Figure i.3 shows the poster from the movie *Lost Hope and More*, which was the second student film made by students at the Brooks Institute as part of the Kodak student filmmaker program. It was shot and finished on Kodak 35 mm with a Dolby LCRS and Dolby 5.1 sound track. Production audio was recorded on a PD4 digital recorder with smart slate. The planned workflow was a standard Final Cut Pro/Cinema Tools film-to-film workflow with cut work print, Pro Tools sound design and mixes, conformed negative, A-B rolls, and 35 mm release prints.

We follow this film as it moves through its workflow in the chapters that follow.

Like all films, the project started with a script—in this case, a submission of student scripts. Certain elements were required to be in every script submitted: each project had to be an action comedy, have a scene at a party, a scene at the Santa Barbara Film Festival, and a SWAT team. The script

Figure i.3 *Lost Hope and More*

selected was written by Jessie Griffith and went into development only eight weeks before principal photography was scheduled to begin.

A crew was selected from resumes and reels submitted by students who were vying for one of the forty coveted major crew positions. Six weeks before production, Cameron Cone and Isaiah Mcamini were selected to direct and joined the development, budgeting, casting, and location scouting.

Only two weeks before production was scheduled to begin, a major flood hit the sound stages at Brooks' Ventura campus, which can be seen in Figure i.4. The area had received more than twenty-four inches of rain and the Canada Larga creek left its banks and brought with it millions of tons of mud and debris. There were hundreds of landslides in the area, closing all roads into the campus. Santa Barbara students were cut off by a huge slide that closed Interstate 101 and destroyed a dozen homes in the seaside village of La Conchita. Tragically, ten people were killed and several Brooks students were left homeless.

Figure i.4 Flood in Casitas Canyon above the Brooks Studios. Three weeks before production of *Lost Hope and More*, Southern California was hit with massive flooding after 24 inches of rain fell

Undaunted, the production pressed forward, as shown in the set construction shot in Figure i.5. Santa Barbara students were shuttled to the campus by sea using a water taxi. Set construction was only delayed by several days, in spite of bulldozers and front loaders removing truckloads of mud and debris from the campus and stages.

The sets were designed and constructed, costumes and props located, and the production schedule put together. Student producers arranged insurance, permits, equipment deals, housing for mentors, and a thousand and two last-minute changes.

The shooting schedule was three days. Two crews were used to cover scenes at two locations, simultaneously. A student crew mans the spy truck in Figure i.7. At times, one crew acted as a first unit

Figure i.5 Students work on set construction

Figure i.6 Executive Producer Tracy Trotter explains the use of the portable generator on location in Santa Barbara California

with the other crew getting second-unit coverage. More often, both crews were working within several hundred feet of each other on different scenes so that the directors and actors could move from one set to the other in minutes.

With the exception of the flood, everything from the equipment to the schedule and the strange requirements on the script were meant to create a real model of a Hollywood feature. All union requirements were also met whenever possible. The project truly gave the students knowledge of what goes on when making a modest-budget feature, plus real world, on-set experience.

Figure i.7 The "spy truck" set on stage 2b. The set was built in an old panel van that could be driven into the sound stage

The students also attended various workshops in Los Angeles on the camera systems to be used, lighting systems, generators, sound gear, and support systems. They were also guided in scheduling, getting insurance, working with municipalities gaining permits, and arraigning transport and housing.

Most of the student crew members had an industry mentor working directly with them during production. At times, the mentors would move from one set to the other checking on progress. A sound team works together in the shot in Figure i.8.

Figure i.8 Students and mentors recording sound and recording video from the video tap on the 35mm camera. By using a video tap on the film camera, video can be viewed and re-viewed on set in the area known as "video village"

The project was shot in conjunction with the Santa Barbara International Film Festival. Several scenes were shot at the historic Santa Barbara courthouse (see Figure i.9) and were open to the festival attendees.

Figure i.9   Films were shown on a giant video screen outside of the Santa Barbara Courthouse while filming was going on inside. The project is produced in conjunction with the Santa Barbara international Film Festival and the public is able to tour the set during breaks in production

The production came off without any more significant problems, and was on time and on budget. The film was delivered to Foto Kem for processing and work printing. Next, it was time to start down the winding path of a film finish workflow, which is outlined in the chapters that follow.

1 When Shooting on Film

The Film Format

Film provides the highest quality image currently available in motion pictures. Even with high-definition (HD) digital formats and new digital cameras coming out every day, film still provides the highest definition, best colors, and broadest contrast range. While there will likely come a day when digital surpasses film, that day has not yet arrived. And film has "legs." As video formats have come and gone, and digital formats will come and go, there has always been film. It is high quality, it can be scanned into any video or digital format, blown up to another film format, or adapted to whatever exotic format is created. It has always been and will always be marketable because of this universality. And with new scanning systems being created for film, it fits any workflow and keeps looking better. While digital cameras are becoming a real alternative to film, film will be around for quite a while.

Film is expensive. A ten-minute roll of 16 mm film can cost more than one hundred and fifty dollars. The same ten-minute roll of 35 mm film can cost almost eight hundred dollars. And the film still needs to be developed and transferred via telecine to digital video. High quality comes with a high price tag.

Telecine

In telecine, the film is transferred to digital video, usually to tape, but it can also be done directly to drive at some postproduction houses.

The film negative is threaded on a telecine machine, in Figure 1.1, a Quadra at Laser Pacific in Hollywood. Several different optics "heads" can be mounted on the device for transfer of different film formats and aspect ratios.

The telecine machine can also read "key code" numbers. These are a series of numbers and machine-readable bar codes visible on the edge of the film. Each key code is a unique number and can be used to identify any film frame in the project. (For more detailed information on key code, read Chapter 5 on film finish.)

Figure 1.1   Quadra telecine machine

The telecine machine is controlled remotely from the "telecine bay." Figure 1.2 shows this, which is a control room where the video image is displayed and color correction can be performed using very powerful, digital, color-correction systems. The system can be interlocked with time code sound recorders that can be locked to the picture so that the production sound can be synchronized with the picture or "sunc up" during telecine. The system can also export a "telecine log," a record of

Figure 1.2   Telecine bay

everything that was done during telecine, including key code information from the negative as well as video and audio time codes. (For more information on syncing in telecine, see Chapter 3 on audio capture and syncing.)

The footage undergoes several changes during this process besides the obvious change from film to video. The colors are manipulated, sound can be added, the frame rate is changed and the playback speed is slowed down by .1 percent.

The Conversion of 24 FPS Film to 29.97 FPS Video with 3:2 Pull Down

The process whereby 24 FPS film is converted to 29.97 FPS digital video is telecine using 3:2 pull down. The 3:2 pull down and its related issues are a problem in the United States and Japan where video and digital systems are derived from the National Television Standards Committee (NTSC) standards. There is also the "advanced" pull down pattern of 2:3:3:2 that can be captured in real time that is used by some digital video cameras, This is not available in telecine.

For the most part, film is shot at 24 frames per second (FPS) in the United States. Film is also normally projected at 24 FPS. This is true of both 16 mm and 35 mm. While there are digital video formats that record and play at 24 and 23.98 FPS, often referred to as "24P" or 24-frame progressive, standard definition video normally records and plays at 29.97 FPS.

One part of the 3:2 pull down process involves adding extra frames. In NTSC, video frames actually consist of two interlaced "fields." (For further explanation, see Appendix 1, on understanding video formats.) The 3:2 process, which really should be called the 2:3 process as the cadence starts with two fields, is shown in Figure 1.3. It takes the first frame of film, let's call it the A frame, and copies

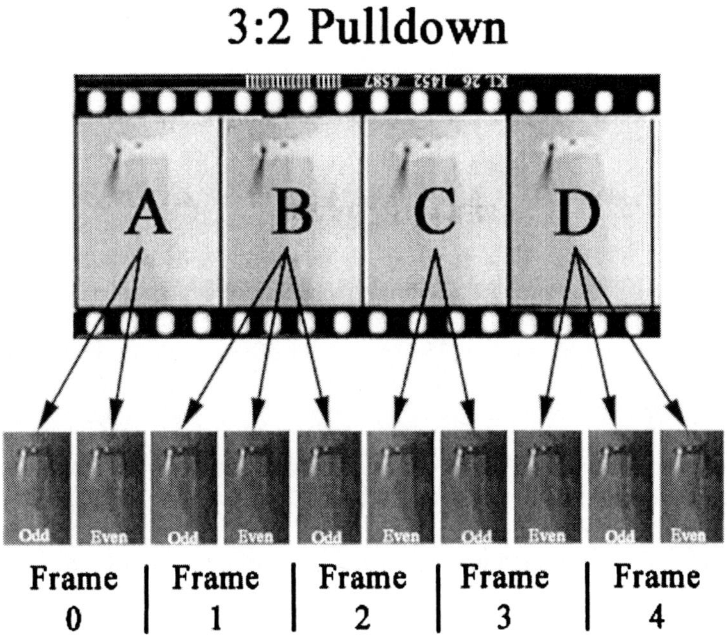

Figure 1.3   3:2 pull down pattern or "cadence"

it into the odd field and the even field on the first video frame. Let's call this frame zero. The next film frame, B, is copied in the odd and even field in video frame one and into the odd field on video frame two. The next film frame, C, is copied into the even field in frame two and the odd field in frame three. The last film frame, D, is copied into the even field of frame three and both the odd and even fields of frame four. At this point the whole process repeats, starting with a new A frame being copied into the odd and even fields of frame five. In this way, 24 frames of film become 60 fields, which is to say 30 frames of video. But video plays at 29.97 FPS, not 30 FPS. In order to achieve the proper frame rate, the film is not run in the telecine machine at 24 FPS but rather at 23.976 FPS, or .1 percent slower (usually called 23.98). For anyone finishing on film or 24P, this whole process is very important to understand. For someone finishing on video, it's enough to know that the film was slowed by the telecine .1 percent.

Speed changes are not a big issue, per se. Films shot at 24 FPS are often projected at 25 FPS and no one is the wiser. However, if the sound and picture are being recorded and/or played separately, it is critical that they each play at the proper speed or the sound will go out of sync with the picture. Digital systems often record sound on the same tape as the picture (single system). But, in film production, the sound is always recorded on a separate recorder (double system).

So, slowing the film to 23.98 FPS will cause the sound to slowly move out of sync. It will be one full frame out of sync after thirty-three seconds. When syncing up film either in telecine or after it has been telecined, it is necessary to also slow the audio by the same .1 percent and this process must be exact.

For purposes of this discussion, *film speed* refers to any film or digital video or audio that plays at 24 FPS or 30 FPS. *Video speed* refers to film, video, or digital that plays at 29.97 FPS or 23.98 FPS. It is best to think of it in these terms, even if the film or digital was shot at 23.98, it's still video speed. If you are changing from film speed to video speed, you are pulling down. If you are changing from video speed to film speed, you are pulling up.

Anamorphic Telecine

Film shot for 2.35, 1.85, or 16 × 9 can use an "anamorphic" process in telecine to pack the most resolution onto the digital video. (For more information on aspect ratios, see Appendix 6 on aspect ratios and letterboxing.) A 16 × 9 CCD head can be mounted on the telecine, and then, if necessary, masked later in Final Cut Pro to an even wider aspect ratio. Super 16 is shot in 1.66:1 and therefore loses a tiny amount of picture top and bottom as it is clipped to 16 × 9 (1.78:1). Masking to 1.85 shows a small amount of letterboxing; 2.35 shows a lot of letterboxing. However the squeezing to 16 × 9 is done in telecine, and no scan lines of picture will be lost.

Except for working copies, it is highly ill advised to letterbox to 4 × 3 when making a show in any widescreen aspect ratio. Letterboxing uses almost a third of the scan lines recording nothing but two black bars that can automatically be created in playback when needed. If the film is telecined letterboxed, these scan lines are forever lost. The best choice is to telecine to 16 × 9 anamorphic and add any other masks in final postproduction. Only 4 × 3 shows should be telecined at 4 × 3.

The telecined "anamorphic" digital video is no different than native 16 × 9 video shot on a 16 × 9 digital camera, however the digital camera "flags" this media telling Final Cut Pro that it is anamorphic. The telecined video is not flagged, so you will need to set that yourself. The anamorphic flag resizes the windows on the computer screen and flags of exported video to 16×9 for QuickTime or DVD. The flags do not make the video anamorphic, it already is. You are only flagging it so that Final Cut Pro recognizes it as 16×9. The image on the video monitor is not affected by the anamorphic flagging. If a 16×9 monitor is used in editing the image will be normal with the flags set or not.

Many people who are planning to only record back to tape and not export don't set the anamorphic flags. The image will look stretched on the computer screen, but it will look normal on a 16×9 video monitor.

The flag (check) is set in the browser window in Final Cut Pro. Scroll over to a column labeled anamorphic and check all the anamorphic clips. It is important that the sequence settings match the flagging, so in this case you also need to set the anamorphic check in the sequence. There are anamorphic presets in the capture settings and the sequence settings; however, all this does is set these flags while capturing or creating a new sequence.

Telecine Logs and Databases

A database is necessary in order to cut and print the negative or even go back and retelecine at a higher definition or with better color correction. You need a map to find your way back to the exact film frame you are seeing on the computer in editing; see Figure 1.4 as an example.

```
|000 Manufacturer Evertz      No. 016 Equip Tracker      Version 1.6.001   FLEx 1005
010 Title KODAX STUDENT FILMMAKER
011 Client                          Facility TELECINE-5
012 Shoot Date 01/28/05 Transfer Date    - -   Opr      Asst      Bay
013 Notes

100 Edit     1 to V1234       Field A1 NTSC Split V1234        Delay 00:00:00:00.0
110 Scene 22        Take 1        Cam Roll A1        Sound 1A        15:22:07:04.0
120 Scrpt
200 ACMAD 35 23.98 000       000175+10 000394+14 Key EASTM EH540833 008195+06 p
300 Video Assemble    VT001     At 01:00:00:00.0 For 00:03:24:10.0 Using
400 Sound          1A         At 15:22:07:04.0 For 00:03:24:10.0 Using

100 Edit     2 to V1234       Field A1 NTSC Split V1234        Delay 00:00:00:00.0
110 Scene 22        Take 2        Cam Roll A1        Sound 1A        15:34:22:06.0
120 Scrpt
200 ACMAD 35 23.98 000       000484+01 089798+05 Key EASTM EH540833 008592+03 p
300 Video Assemble    VT001     At 01:03:25:05.0 For 00:04:16:20.0 Using
400 Sound          1A         At 15:34:22:06.0 For 00:04:16:20.0 Using

100 Edit     3 to V1234       Field A1 NTSC Split V1234        Delay 00:00:00:00.0
110 Scene 22        Take 3        Cam Roll A3        Sound 1A        15:48:13:18.0
120 Scrpt
200 ACMAD 35 23.98 000       000872+02 000212+08 Key EASTM EH064172 008393+09 p
300 Video Assemble    VT001     At 01:07:42:20.0 For 00:02:21:20.0 Using
400 Sound          1A         At 15:48:13:18.0 For 00:02:21:20.0 Using

100 Edit     4 to V1234       Field A1 NTSC Split V1234        Delay 00:00:00:00.0
110 Scene 22        Take 4        Cam Roll A3        Sound 1A        15:59:25:05.0
```

Figure 1.4 Telecine log

Information contained in the telecine log includes: camera roll number, lab roll number, sound roll number, the time code being read from the audio player (if syncing in telecine), the scene number, the take number, the format of the video recorder or recorders, the time code recorded onto the videotape(s), and the key code information from the film. Other information and comments can be added after the fact and can be used as a cutting log. It is indispensable for a film or 24P finish when shooting on film.

Telecine logs come in several formats, FLX, TLC flex, FTL and others. Final Cut Pro and Cinema Tools work with these three formats.

Take-by-Take

If film is telecined on a take-by-take basis, a telecine log can be created. The film can be transferred as whole rolls and a database can be still created after the fact from scratch, but it's much easier when done in telecine. While slower and therefore more expensive, take-by-take telecine also allows for syncing time code-referenced sound as part of telecine. Even if you are not planning to go back to the film negative, if you create a database, then this option is still open. And the database can be used to batch capture and as a cutting log, saving time and work.

Another advantage of take-by-take transfer is color correction. Each scene is adjusted for color and exposure and the scene and take information entered into the telecine log. If the camera roll is transferred in one pass, there is no way to create a log or do anything other than finding the best light for the entire roll.

Window Burns

Any work copies on video should be recorded with one or more window burns. The window burn is a great way to check time codes against the original accuracy of the pull down and especially the reverse telecine. The most common format of window burn places the video time code in a window on the lower left, edge code in a window on the lower right, and audio time code, if any, in a window in the upper left or directly above the video time code. This is normally used only on work copies; you would never want these windows on the finished project.

If you pulled "selects," in other words, the best takes, and had the lab print them for screening dailies, they cut the best takes out of the original camera rolls so there are splices in the rolls of negative you are telecining. It is critical that the telecine operator knows the negative has been cut and to look out for splices. Splices affect the key code information and can cause major problems later if they are not noticed in telecine. (See the following section on deconstructing several film workflows for the film *Lost Hope and More*.) Also, if you are using short ends and, for some reason your negative was rewound before exposure, the key codes will be on the wrong side of the negative and they will run in descending order. The bar code reader on the telecine machine cannot read the bar code backwards and you will get no key code information. To find out if the film was rewound, develop a short test strip. Rewinding the film again before exposure can solve this problem.

Creating and Working with the Cinema Tools Database

The telecine logs are usually delivered on a 3.25 inch floppy disc. Someday telecine may join the twenty-first century and deliver these logs on nonarchaic media; in the meantime, the hardest part of working with the database is finding a computer that can copy the file onto your computer or portable drive. Ask before the telecine if they can burn the log to a CD. Some places can. You can also often get them to e-mail it to you. Either way, also get the mini floppies as a backup.

Before doing anything with the telecine log, make a backup copy. Never work with the original. Cinema Tools writes directly to the drive all the time. There is no undo. The telecine log can be opened in Cinema Tools.

Launch Cinema tools. When asked for the database, click cancel. Choose: Database > New Database. You can set the parameters of your film and telecine. However, this information is part of the Telecine Log and should overwrite and set itself, but any information not in the log will not be automatically set. Be thorough and set it right. Remember, if your time code is drop frame, there is a semicolon before the frames, NDF, colon. (For and explanation of time code, see Appendix 4 on time codes.)

Name your database and save.

Choose File > Import > Telecine log.

Locate your copy of the telecine log. Cinema Tools will tell you how many events were imported. If you know how many shots you have, this number should match. It is possible for a shot to not import because of a file problem in the log, but it is not common.

The Cinema Tools list and detail window should open (see Figure 1.5). From here you can add comments to any shot. You may have no comments until you see the video, but you can always come back here and add comments. Be very cautious when working in these windows, there is no undo and everything you do is saved to disc. Always keep backups. And don't close the window by clicking delete. It deletes the shot from the database!

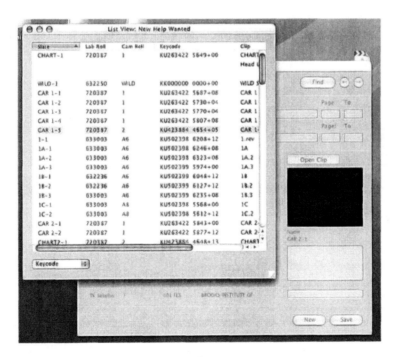

Figure 1.5   The Cinema Tools interface and event list

Navigation of the list is strange, but manageable. Use the Database > Find and Replace Existing to reduce the scope of the list or find one shot. To restore use Find All.

In the list, you can check the accuracy of the telecine. Switch the key code setting at the bottom left to Video. Because all shots should have a zero A-frame reference, when the key code pull down cycle identifier shows an A, the video time code should end in 0 or 5. If not, there is a problem with the telecine that will cause major problems later if you are reversing the telecine. Call the telecine people and have them fix it. (You can't.) Fortunately such problems are rare.

You are ready to export the batch list and capture video. Select File > Export > Batch Capture. Final Cut Pro Video. Name and save your batch list (see Figure 1.6).

Name	Duration	In	Out	Media Start	Media End	Tracks	Good	Log N
1	00:00:03:11	01:41:52:12	01:41:55:22	01:41:49:05	01:42:11:25	1V, 2A		
1	00:00:22:17	Not Set	Not Set	01:41:49:04	01:42:11:20	1V, 2A		
1A	00:00:04:19	01:42:19:01	01:42:23:19	01:42:11:16	01:43:00:17	1V, 2A		
1A	00:00:49:02	Not Set	Not Set	01:42:11:16	01:43:00:17	1V, 2A		
1A.2	00:00:28:13	Not Set	Not Set	01:43:00:05	01:43:28:17	1V, 2A		
1A.2	00:00:28:10	Not Set	Not Set	01:43:00:04	01:43:28:13	1V, 2A		
1A.3	00:00:00:28	01:43:58:12	01:43:59:09	01:43:28:00	01:44:17:10	1V, 2A		
1A.3	00:00:49:09	Not Set	Not Set	01:43:28:00	01:44:17:08	1V, 2A		
1B	00:00:01:10	01:36:30:23	01:36:32:02	01:36:09:08	01:36:59:17	1V, 2A		
1B	00:00:50:10	Not Set	Not Set	01:36:09:08	01:36:59:17	1V, 2A		
1B.2	00:00:07:09	01:37:43:01	01:37:50:09	01:36:59:04	01:38:11:06	1V, 2A		
1B.2	00:01:12:03	Not Set	Not Set	01:36:59:04	01:38:11:06	1V, 2A		
1B.3	00:00:02:15	01:45:14:10	01:45:16:24	01:44:16:25	01:45:33:00	1V, 2A		
1B.3	00:01:16:11	Not Set	Not Set	01:44:16:20	01:45:33:00	1V, 2A		
1C	00:00:03:14	01:45:44:00	01:45:47:13	01:45:32:12	01:46:01:16	1V, 2A		
1C	00:00:29:05	Not Set	Not Set	01:45:32:12	01:46:01:16	1V, 2A		
1C.2	00:00:07:15	01:46:04:07	01:46:11:21	01:46:01:12	01:46:29:06	1V, 2A		

Figure 1.6 Final Cut Pro batch list imported from Cinema Tools

Launch Final Cut Pro. Make sure you are set up for DV video at 29.97. Go to Final Cut Pro > Audio Video Settings > Capture settings and confirm you are in 29.97. Select: File > Import > Batch List 29.97. Find your batch list and click Choose.

All of your shots should appear in the browser off line and ready for Batch Capture, and you should be in a very familiar place. Go to batch capture and insert whichever tape Final Cut Pro asks for.

New telecine logs can be imported into the existing database. New batch lists can also be imported into the Final Cut Pro project. This way, daily telecine sessions can be integrated into the edit during production.

If you did not sync in telecine, you will need to sync at this point. If you need information on transferring audio and pulling the audio down, refer to Chapter 7 on audio workflow.

You will now want to return to your Cinema Tools database and link your video to the database. Select: Database > Connect Clips and select one clip from your Final Cut Pro capture folder.

Verify the accuracy of the clips by clicking on Open clip, as shown in Figure 1.7. This opens the clip in a playable window with options. If you are finishing on film or 24P, click on the Identify button.

Figure 1.7 Detail view in Cinema Tools with captured video linked to the database

This opens a window with time codes and key code information. Check that the time code and edge codes match your burn windows. If not, edit in the right information. Always trust the burn windows.

In the key code window burn, the first frame of each shot should be a complete A frame, and so the time code in the window burn should end in 0 or 5. If the numbers in the database don't match the windows, this error can be corrected here in Cinema Tools. The window burn should be correct; reenter the numbers in the database to match the window burn. Such errors are rare, but they do happen.

Notice in the example shown in Figure 1.8 that the slate shows a different time code from the audio time code window burn (upper left window). The window is displaying the time code from the audiotapes. This can be off because the two time code generators used in production—the one in the slate and the one in the audio recorder—were drifting and had not been "jammed" in several hours.

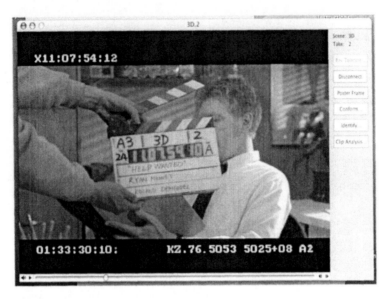

Figure 1.8 Clip window in Cinema Tools

Periodically during production, the time code generator in the slate needs to be synchronized to the time code coming from the recorder. In this case, the two are off because the telecine machine is still finding sync. They will match at sticks close.

Notice also, we are parked on a time code ending in 0 and so we should be on an A frame. The pull down cycle identifier shows A with the 1 and 2 overprinted. This is exactly what we should be seeing. As this is 29.97 video and has not been reversed to 23.98, the key code information will not move forward in a smooth or readable way. There will be a clear A followed by a clear B followed by a B and C overprinted, followed by a C and D overprinted, and then a complete D. If you refer back to Figure 1.3 of 3.2 pull down pattern or cadence, you will see why this is so. Because of the 3:2 cadence, you will never see a complete C frame; they are always overprinted this way unless the video has been reverse telecined. This is a simple way to identify reversed video: look for the C frames. This is also why the C frame is underlined.

If you are going to finish in 24P or on film, you have more work to do here and you will be coming back often. If you are finishing on video, you are ready to start editing.

Inked Edge Code Numbers

Before computer editing, film was cut with sound recorded onto magnetic film, simply film with magnetic oxide for recording sound. Before magnetic film, these tracks were photographic film with optical sound. Once the sound was in sync with the work print (which is a noncolor-corrected positive print of the camera original; see Chapter 5 for more detail), both were "inked" with matching edge numbers. This way, if the sound was moved out of sync, the numbers could guide the editor in putting the sound back into sync.

As there are no magnetic sound tracks in computer editing, there is no reason to ink edge numbers, yet Cinema Tools supports this. This is simply for ease of use with some workflows for finishing on film.

Some editors like to perform final editing to the work print, and the ink numbers can help with this workflow. Where an optical key code number can be rather hard to read, an inked number is easy to see and read. Work print can be inked at the lab and the inked numbers entered into the Cinema Tools database. As these numbers are not machine-readable, the ink numbers are entered manually by reading them directly from the work print. They can be entered at any time, even after the work print is conformed to the cut list. ("Conforming" is accomplished by matching "key code" numbers located on the edge of the film. We look more closely at this in Chapter 5, on finishing on film.)

Edit Logs

It is simple to turn your database into an editing log, where the editor can add comments or look up needed information. You can export a new batch list from your Cinema Tools database or from Final Cut Pro, only, instead of using it as a batch list, open it in a text editor like TextEdit or even Microsoft Word.

You can add comments in the text editor and reprint as needed (see Figure 1.9). Your text editor may change the type of file when you save it to a Word or other file. This is fine, as long as you don't try

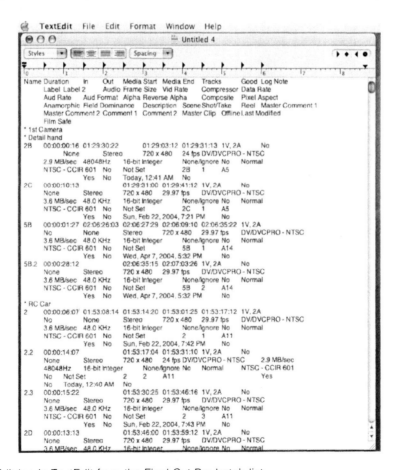

Figure 1.9 Edit log in TextEdit from the Final Cut Pro batch list

to use it in the future as a batch capture list. Final Cut can't work with the odd file types. In the example shown in Figure 1.10, we are working in TextEdit, displaying rich text. Any of the tabs or information not needed in the cutting log can be deleted.

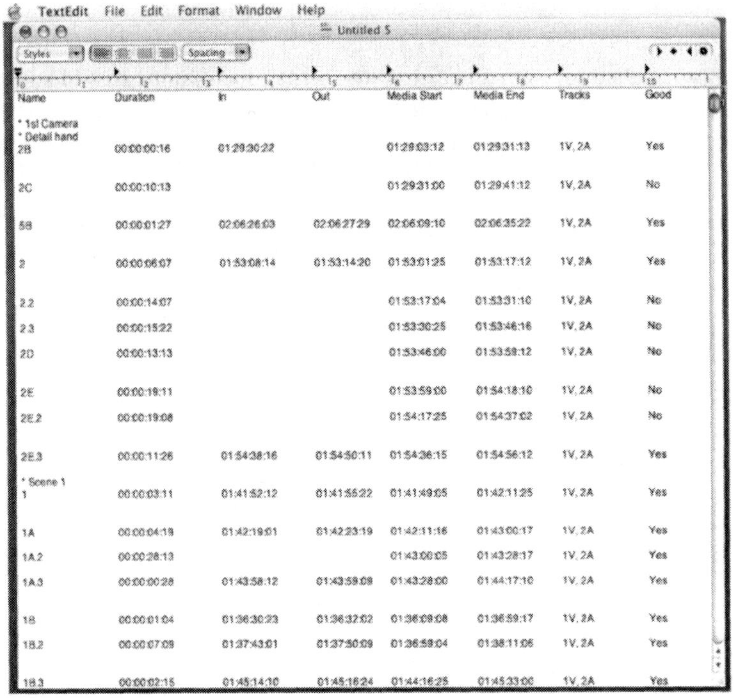

Name	Duration	In	Out	Media Start	Media End	Tracks	Good
* 1st Camera * Detail hand 2B	00:00:00:16	01:29:30:22		01:29:03:12	01:29:31:13	1V, 2A	Yes
2C	00:00:10:13			01:29:31:00	01:29:41:12	1V, 2A	No
5B	00:00:01:27	02:06:26:03	02:06:27:29	02:06:09:10	02:06:35:22	1V, 2A	Yes
2	00:00:06:07	01:53:08:14	01:53:14:20	01:53:01:25	01:53:17:12	1V, 2A	Yes
2.2	00:00:14:07			01:53:17:04	01:53:31:10	1V, 2A	No
2.3	00:00:15:22			01:53:30:25	01:53:46:16	1V, 2A	No
2D	00:00:13:13			01:53:46:00	01:53:58:12	1V, 2A	No
2E	00:00:19:11			01:53:59:00	01:54:18:10	1V, 2A	No
2E.2	00:00:19:08			01:54:17:25	01:54:37:02	1V, 2A	No
2E.3	00:00:11:26	01:54:38:16	01:54:50:11	01:54:36:15	01:54:56:12	1V, 2A	Yes
* Scene 1 1	00:00:03:11	01:41:52:12	01:41:55:22	01:41:49:05	01:42:11:25	1V, 2A	Yes
1A	00:00:04:18	01:42:19:01	01:42:23:19	01:42:11:16	01:43:00:17	1V, 2A	Yes
1A.2	00:00:28:13			01:43:00:05	01:43:28:17	1V, 2A	Yes
1A.3	00:00:00:28	01:43:58:12	01:43:59:08	01:43:28:00	01:44:17:10	1V, 2A	Yes
1B	00:00:01:04	01:36:30:23	01:36:32:02	01:36:09:08	01:36:59:17	1V, 2A	Yes
1B.2	00:00:07:09	01:37:43:01	01:37:50:09	01:36:59:04	01:38:11:06	1V, 2A	Yes
1B.3	00:00:02:15	01:45:14:10	01:45:16:24	01:44:16:25	01:45:33:00	1V, 2A	Yes

Figure 1.10 Edit log in TextEdit from the Final Cut Pro batch list with spacing reset and unwanted data removed

The batch list can also be opened in Microsoft Excel, as in Figure 1.11. Use the Delimited file type. This puts all of the batch list information into columns that are easy to work with and edit. Excel makes a great cutting log, and management of the information is efficient and simple. You can also make a cutting log by exporting an Avid exchange list from Final Cut Pro and opening in Excel. This brings even more information into the cutting log.

Opening the telecine log in Cinema Tools is a fast way to get a batch list, a cutting log, and, you now have a database that you can use if you ever want to retelecine to a better format. Or, for color correction, cut the negative or even scan the negative and make a digital intermediate for a 35 mm theatrical release.

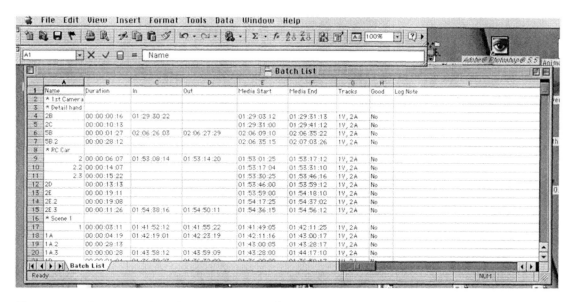

Figure 1.11 Edit log in Excel from the Final Cut Pro batch list

Retelecine

On some projects the workflow may include retelecine. In this case, the first telecine would include little if any color correction and the "real" color correction would be done in a second and, often, even a third telecine. The database can guide the colorist back to the footage, but to expedite the process, in telecine, a hole is punched at the head of each camera roll and this is used as the zero "A" frame. Now the colorist can wind quickly into the proper footage on the retelecine. If you intend this workflow, inform the telecine facility so they can use a hole punch on the zero frame.

Reverse Telecine for Film and 24P Finish

If the project is going to be finished in a digital video format at 29.97, then there is no need to reverse telecine. If, however, the project is to be finished on film or in a 24P digital format, or if you are planning to copy the video onto film (film out), the added fields from the telecine process need to be removed. Because the pull-down pattern was recorded into the database and because we know how the A, B, C, and D frames line up with the time code, it is simple to remove the added fields. And, it is easy to merge the odd and even fields into progressive frames. This must be done to the actual shots before editing. While it can be done to the original shots after editing, this will cause the edits to shift by one frame in some places. Once the edit is printed back to tape, each shot has a different 0-A frame reference, making reverse telecine impossible. However, if the project is edited at 23.98 with reversed footage, even if the project is printed to tape at 29.97, the entire tape has the same 0-A frame reference and can be reversed back to 23.98 at any time for printing to film, 23.98 DVD, or 23.98 or 24 FPS HD video.

You can see in Figure 1.12 that with a bit of shuffling, and throwing out one complete video frame, we end up with four pure frames A, B, C, D on time codes 0, 1, 3, 4 and again on 5, 6, 8, 9. The 2 s

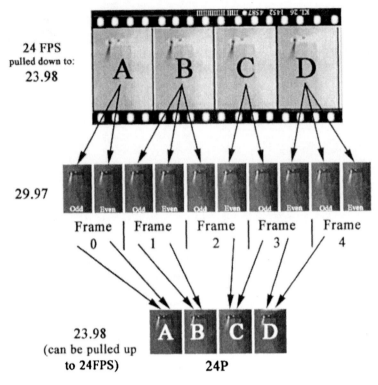

Figure 1.12 Removal of 3:2 pull down by reverse telecine

and 7s are removed. The new clip will play at 23.98 at video speed and 24 FPS at film speed. The resulting 24P digital "video" is an exact digital copy of the original 24 FPS film. The added frame is removed, as is the interlacing of odd and even fields.

Choosing a Frame Rate, 24 or 23.976 (23.98)

You can reverse to 23.98 FPS or 24 FPS and, as 24 may be the final frame rate, many people choose to put their project in 24, now avoiding pull-up and pull-down issues. But, 23.98 makes more sense for most projects. Remember that the only difference between 24 and 23.98 is how fast it plays. The number of frames stays the same. So it shouldn't make any real difference, and it wouldn't if it weren't for the audio. As we speed up and slow down, the sample rate and speed also changes up and down. And when importing audio into a project, if the sample rates don't match, the imported audio plays at a new speed. We want to keep our audio sample rate at 48 K or 96 K. Generally, 23.98 works better for the postproduction process. If the final product is digital, it can be projected at 23.98 and, if it is projected at 24, it will look fine. And if the final product is film print from negative, the audio can be pulled up to 24 FPS in the transfer to optical. This way the entire postproduction process can be done at video speed, 29.97 and 23.98. However, if your finish is film and film only, and you want to avoid pulling down and pulling up the audio, use 24. And if you are reversing to 24, DO

NOT sync in telecine. This pulls the audio down. Do not reverse to 24 and edit at 23.98, or reverse to 23.98 and edit at 24. This speed change should be made after the fact with the proper hardware.

In fact, the world would be a better place if 24 FPS retired. When film is shot at 24 FPS it is almost always immediately telecined at 23.98, so the resulting video plays at 29.97. This slows down the picture, so now the audio also must be slowed down. After all the postproduction work is finished, the audio must be sped back up to match the original 24 FPS. But if the film was shot at 23.98 in the first place, it would never be sped up or slowed down. The film is shot at 23.98, edited at 23.98, and projected at 23.98. This is why the new "24P" cameras really shoot at 23.98 and why most HD projects and some film projects are being shot at 23.98.

Again, if you are not going back to the film to finish on film, or finishing at 23.98 FPS on a format such as HD Cam, or planning to do a "film out" (shooting the video onto film) there is no reason to reverse telecine.

Reversing Telecine in Cinema Tools

After linking your media in Cinema Tools, select: File > Batch Reverse Telecine. Chose your frame rate, 23.98 or 24. If your telecine or down convert from High Definition was done to the 3:2 system covered here, then accept the defaults for the rest of the settings and click "OK." Then fix lunch; this will take a while.

You can also reverse one clip at a time with the Reverse Telecine button. Use this to fix problems or add in new shots. As this function forces a reverse starting on the frame where the play head is parked, make sure you are parked on a 0 or 5 frame. If the time code does not match the window burn, believe the window burn.

Check the Files

After the reverse process is finished, verify the accuracy by clicking on Open Clip just as you did after linking. Click on the Identify button. Now as you scroll up and down the key code numbers should advance with each frame and match the window burn, and the time code should also advance with each frame; however, the 2 and 7 frames should be missing.

You will now find that all of your original clips that were batched have been moved into a folder called Originals. The new, reversed clips are in a new folder called Reversed. There is also a reverse telecine log and there is a new folder called Skipped that holds any clips skipped because they were audio only, graphics, or had some problem. Check the folder for shots that were skipped because of problems and try to fix them. You may need to recapture them from tape. Or you can often fix these by opening them and parking on a frame where the A can be clearly seen in the key code burn window. If you click the reverse button, this will reverse only this clip and it will perform the operation from the point where the play head is parked. The batch process usually finds the A frames by matching time code; however, if the numbers don't jive for some reason, this will force the issue and repair the clip. Make sure to move the original and reversed files into the proper folders and out of the skipped folder. Notice that the reversed clips have the same name as the original with a .rev extension added. This will allow relinking because the file names match and the .rev will help you manage your files knowing which were reversed and which are original. Unless you have some specific reason, never change the names of the clips.

Sequence Settings

Once the reverse is finished, on returning to Final Cut you will see that all the clips are off-line. This is because they have been moved to the new folder called Originals. Go to Relink and direct the chooser to the matching reversed video file. This should bring all the clips back online as 23.98 or 24 FPS video. If you open a clip in the viewer and drag the size of the viewer out to 100 percent, both fields are displayed. (The canvas and viewer only display the first field until the window size is 100 percent, then it shows both fields.) There should be clear A, B, C, and Ds in the key code window. If there are two letters on top of each other, there is a problem with the clip.

Now you need to set the sequence settings to your frame rate. Go to Final Cut Pro > Audio Video Settings > Sequence settings. Check for the proper settings to already be here, and if they are not: Duplicate > Edit and make a copy of the video settings so you don't overwrite the DV NTSC 48 KHz settings. Name the copy DV NTSC 23.98 or 24 if you are using that, and then set the editing time base to your frame rate. Don't change any other settings. Even though you just made this preset, it is not set until you check the checkbox next to the preset and close the window. The next time you open Final Cut it will still be set up this way, so if you want to cut 29.97, you will need to return and reset by checking the checkbox next to your original DV 29.97. These settings are applied every time you create a new sequence in the project, and you can reset them whenever you wish. You can have a mix of different sequences in the project each with its own settings.

The sequence that was created by default when you opened Final Cut has whatever settings that were last used before the computer was shut down. It is likely a 29.97 sequence. Select New Sequence and this will create a new sequence with your defined sequence settings. You can then delete the original one.

If the settings are correct, you can edit your reversed clips into the timeline and they will not require any rendering or real-time playback. In other words, there will be no green, yellow, or red lines in the sequence and the sequence will play normally. The video will play on the video monitor normally as Final Cut is 3:2 converting on the fly to the firewire. You can record or print to video and the tape will be 29.97.

Workflow Overview

Historically, the workflow with film was to shoot on negative film, process this, and have a "work print" made. The sound was then transferred to film. Before 1960, this was optical sound but later "magnetic film" or "mag stock"—which was simply film base with magnetic oxide on one side—was used. The sound of the slate sticks being clapped was lined up with the image of the slate sticks and the film was projected in sync with the sound. The film was then edited by cutting and splicing the work print and the interlocked sound film. After editing the work print, the negative was edited (conformed) to match the work print, the sound tracks were mixed to a single track on optical film, and the film was color corrected. Next, it was printed with the sound track to an answer print that could be projected on a standard projector. If video was needed from this finished film, it was transferred with a film chain, a simple projector and video camera linked together.

This workflow has evolved over the last two decades and today, few, if any, films are edited using that workflow. Many films still conform the negative, but this is done to a computer printout of the edits called a cut list. Some films still make a work print and conform the work print to the cut list before conforming the negative to ensure the cut list is 100 percent accurate before cutting into the camera original.

Some films never edit the negative at all, but digitally scan the negative based on the cut list to a very high-definition digital intermediate, and then "shoot" this back to negative film and make prints. Still other films never make a film print at all, but finish the film totally on digital video. This digital video can also be "shot" back to negative and prints made for projection. While these prints do not look as good as prints made from a cut negative or digital intermediate, this process, known as virtual digital intermediate, is becoming more commonplace and the look is improving.

Basic Film Workflow

The most basic film workflow uses any DV video format. Perform the best possible telecine with color correction to any DV format including DVC Pro 50 and DVC Pro HD at 29.97 FPS. As you can capture from any DV format to a portable firewire drive, it is possible to capture and edit it natively from your drive with no need for an online edit. Any DV format other than HDV can also be edited and finished at 24P (23.98 frames per second) with a telecine log.

The higher bandwidth formats like HD Cam, Digi Beta, and D5 require very specialized equipment and this requires a finishing step in the workflow.

Alternate Film Workflows

There are three ways to approach this finishing step.

- Perform a best-possible telecine with color correction to HD Cam, Digi Beta, or D5. Capture from these tapes at a lower resolution in Final Cut Pro and recapture at high resolution later in online.

- Capture from DVCam clones of the HD Cam, Digi Beta, or D5 tapes and recapture from the high-resolution tapes in online.

- Perform a basic "work copy" telecine to DVCam tape and retelecine the film negative later at a higher resolution with final color correction.

In the first alternate workflow, you need to telecine with the best possible color correction to a high-quality tape format, that being your finishing format. You need to capture this video to your drive in a facility that supports your finish format, and this can be expensive. As you read the section on batch lists, you will see you don't need to log the footage to create a batch list if you have a telecine log, so this can be an unsupervised batch capture. And though the hourly rate is somewhat high, it can be done quickly. At some facilities it is even possible to capture to your drive as you telecine. The low-resolution setting is "off-line real-time photo JPEG." This is available in all frame rates.

The second workflow also requires telecine with the best possible color correction to a high-quality tape format. However, here you capture from DVCam tapes made during or after telecine. You capture on your own system and on your own time, so this saves money. These tapes cannot be plain copies of the higher-resolution tapes, they need to be "clones." The time code on these tapes must match your higher-resolution tapes. This system works well and is the preferred system for most projects.

It is a simple process to recapture all of the video from the higher-resolution tapes. However, this must be done at a competent postproduction house that supports your tape format. Additional color correction can be performed at this "online edit" or even after the online edit.

The third system requires more organization and more telecine time because the footage used in the edit will be telecined twice. However, as the first telecine is only a work copy, there is little need to meticulously color correct so it can go quite fast. In the second telecine, every frame telecined is used in the final edit so the color correction must be the best possible. Unlike the first two systems, however, there is no time wasted color correcting footage that will never be used. If your edit ratio is high, this may be the cheapest system. Be sure to inform the telecine facility what your workflow plan is as they will need to perform some extra prep prior to telecine to help guide the second telecine. This workflow will require reverse telecine to ensure accurate key code information. You will want two "window burns," windows printed on screen showing time code and key code information. You will also want a telecine log, as noted earlier.

Film to Digital Workflows

If you are shooting on film and finishing on 23.98 frames per second (FPS) HD Cam or D5 digital video, you can follow any of these same three workflows with some modifications. You can also use 23.98 or 24 FPS HD Cam and D5 as a film finish format treating it as a "virtual digital intermediate" by shooting the digital video onto 35 mm film.

- Perform a best-possible 16 × 9 animorphic telecine (see section following for more on animorphic telecine) with color correction to HD Cam at 23.98 FPS. Capture at 23.98 FPS from these tapes at a lower resolution in Final Cut Pro and recapture at high definition later in online. Because of the large color space of HD Cam, especially HD Cam SR, additional color correction can be applied in online.

- Perform a best-possible 16 × 9 animorphic telecine with color correction to HD Cam at 23.98 FPS. Make 4 × 3 letterboxed "down converts" of the HD Cam tapes to 29.97 FPS DVCam with time code window burns. Capture from the 29.97 FPS DVCam down converts and recapture from the high-definition tapes in online. This workflow will require reverse telecine.

- Perform a basic 4 × 3 letterbox "work copy" telecine to DVCam tape and retelecine the film negative later to HD Cam at 23.98 with final color correction. Make sure to include key code information in the telecine log to use as a guide to retelecine. This workflow will require reverse telecine to ensure accurate key code information.

The first workflow has the advantage of being extremely simple and straightforward. While the capture is somewhat expensive, this cost may be totally offset by not needing down converts or extra telecine.

The second workflow sounds complicated, but it is the most common workflow for 23.98 HD video. It is the same workflow most often used when shooting HD video at 23.98. Because the frame rate of the DVCam tapes do not match the frame rate of the HD Cam masters, the DVCam tapes need to be "down converts"—the time code on the two tapes match except for the frames column. The HD Cam tapes will have 23.98 NDF and the DVCam tapes will have 29.97 NDF time code. The DVCam work copies need to be made with two "window burns"—windows printed on screen showing both time codes. The HD Cam tapes will be 16 × 9 anamorphic, the DVCam down converts will be 4 × 3 letterbox. The DV Cam tapes will be captured at 29.97 FPS and then reverse telecined back to 23.98 FPS.

As with the standard definition workflow, the third system requires more organization and more telecine time. However, as the first telecine is only a work copy, it can be a more affordable standard definition. And, there is no need to do more than basic color correction, so it can go quite fast. The second telecine is expensive high definition; however, only shots actually used in the edit are telecined, so there is no time wasted color correcting footage that will never be used. Be sure to inform the telecine facility what your workflow plan is as they will need to perform some extra prep prior to telecine to help guide the second telecine. Get window burns for time code and key code information and a telecine log. This workflow will require reverse telecine to ensure accurate key code information.

Finishing on Film

If you are planning to finish on film, the telecine and capture stages are unique to this finish. Make sure to read and understand Chapter 5 on film finishing. There are many steps along the way that are unique to the film finish workflow.

Three ways to prepare for a film finish are:

- Perform a basic "work copy" telecine of all of the camera negative to DVCam tapes. Then work-print all camera negative or only circled takes.

- Work-print all camera negative or only circled takes. Perform a basic "work copy" telecine of all of the negative to DVCam tapes.

- Perform a basic "work copy" telecine of all of the camera negative to DVCam tapes.

On projects where work print will be made and cut, there are several options. Because work print is expensive, you may not want to print everything. Most 35 mm projects will only print certain takes. This is called "circled takes" because the takes to be printed are circled on the camera and sound reports. When the director gets a take they like, they call "print it" and the take is circled. This is not available for 16 mm.

Usually, the lab cuts these takes out of the camera rolls and splices them into "selects rolls." This is why many projects telecine all of the negative first; the splices can throw off the telecine reading of the edge code (key code) numbers. Cutting up the lab rolls after the telecine will throw off the database showing which camera rolls are in which lab rolls, but this can be avoided if the selects are compiled into "selects rolls" that match the lab rolls. In other words, lab roll one becomes selects one and outtakes one. If the selects were pulled before the telecine, be sure to inform the telecine operator of this, it can through the key code information off.

You may also choose to print ink edge code numbers on the work print if you are planning to do final editing to the work print. Some editors prefer to do final tightening up of the edit after the work print is conformed to the digital cut list, and the ink numbers can make matching the changes to the negative cut list go faster. The cinema Tools database supports ink edge code numbers, but few projects use inked numbers anymore.

In the third case you are telecining all the camera negative without work-printing. In this workflow you will edit digitally and go directly to cutting the film negative.

Be sure to inform the telecine facility if you are planning a film finish. Get window burns for time code and key code. Do not recompose any footage in telecine by zooming or framing up or down. This would require optical printing when cutting the negative. If you want to recompose any shots, do this in Final Cut Pro later. There will be more on this in Chapter 5 when we look at Final Cut Pro cut lists and optical printing. You can telecine full frame or letterboxed (masked) to the final aspect ratio, usually 1.85:1.

It is likely the telecine operator will give you what you need as long as you tell them you are finishing on film. You will be reversing the telecine after capturing to Final Cut Pro. In order to perform this step later, in telecine you need a zero frame "A" frame transfer with field "1" dominance and NTSC nondrop-frame time code (NDF). Ask for window burns for time code, key code with pulldown cycle identifier (for example, "A" frame) following the key number, and audio time code if any. Start the first tape at one hour exactly on the time code and set different hour codes for each tape if there are fewer than twenty-four tapes. And get a telecine log.

Capturing and Preparing *Lost Hope and More*

Let's take a look at the telecine and capture stages on the Kodak 35 mm project, *Lost Hope and More*. Because there was no direct access to a 35 mm screening room, dailies were not screened during this production. Instead, the film was sent to the lab and the lab reports were checked every morning for

Figure 1.13 *Lost Hope and More* poster

problems. This alerts production of an obvious technical problem with the footage, but it does not help with problems with performance, sound, or a host of other issues. Screening dailies is a much better workflow, but it is not always an option.

In order to save on the cost of printing, only "selects" were printed. During production, when the directors felt they had a good take, they would call "print." The take was circled on the camera reports and on the sound reports. Only these takes were printed and screened. (This option is not available on 16mm film.)

The work print was not sunc before the work print screening; this screening would used to check for picture problems only. A 35mm work print screening will show every little problem. Performance and sound would be evaluated in telecine.

So the initial workflow looked like this:

- Foto Kem labs pulled circled takes from the camera negative and spliced them in into "selects" rolls.

- Work print was printed from the selects rolls.

- Silent work print was projected to look for problems.

- PD4 DAT audio was transferred to DA88 tape by Laser Pacific. Clappers were logged by time code.

- Footage was telecined by Laser Pacific to DVCam with zero "A" frame and with field "1" dominance. NTSC nondrop-frame time code (NDF) was used with burn windows for:
  ○ Time code (lower left)
  ○ Key code with pull-down cycle identifier (lower right)
  ○ Audio time code (directly above video time code)

- 23.98 FPS HD Cam was also recorded at the telecine for DVD authoring. 23.98 NDF time code was recorded to the HD Cam, which was a match with 29.97 NDF DVCam time code except for frame rate.

- Each tape was given a different hour code.

- A telecine log was made.

- DA88 audio was sunc in telecine to the clapper logs.

- The telecine logs were imported into a new Cinema Tools database and a batch list was exported.

- The batch list was imported into a new Final Cut Pro project at 29.97 FPS.

- A batch list was also opened in Excel to create a cutting log.

- The DVCam footage was captured.

- The shots were linked to the database in Cinema Tools.

- All shots were batch reversed to 23.98 FPS.

- The 23.98 FPS shots were linked to the Final Cut Pro project.

Several problems were found in checking the database. Several slates were mislabeled. These were noted in the cutting log and database. As the editing moved forward, a major problem was encountered. When the first film list was exported to check for double uses, several double uses were reported. Yet these were not double uses, they weren't even from the same camera rolls. At first it looked like the almost impossible had happened, that there were two camera rolls with the same key code numbers. This turned out to not be the case.

Because the camera rolls had been spliced into selects rolls consisting of the circled takes, when the selects rolls were telecined, a splice had passed through the telecine without the colorist noticing. The telecine machine cannot read every key code number; many are interpolated from known key code numbers. When a splice goes through the telecine, if the new number is not entered, it will continue with the numeric sequence from the previous roll, logging the wrong key code information into the telecine log.

Close examination of the database showed that four shots had key code numbers from a different camera roll. Several fixes were discussed; the consensus was that the shots should be retelecined. As it turned out the fix was simple. The negative editor rolled into the selects rolls and found the shots with the wrong key code numbers. She wrote down the key code numbers for sticks close on the slates of the four shots. These key code numbers were entered into the Cinema Tools database on the corresponding sticks close frames. The key code information for the entire shot came online and the double use reports were cleared up. The window burns remained erroneous, but the database and film lists were accurate.

Also, because the telecine session was going over the scheduled time, toward the end, some shots were telecined in groups, slatted as "ser" or series. These needed to be telecined silent as there is no way to match slates on several shots at the same time. So, some shots needed to be sunc in Final Cut Pro after the reverse telecine. We cover this workflow in Chapter 3 on initial audio workflow.

The initial steps in the workflow are critical. Small errors can cause major problems and result in time and money being lost. Plan the entire workflow in advance all the way to the finished format. Keep everyone informed of the plan and any changes to the plan. Planning and communication are the keys to a smother postproduction, saving money, and ensuring a quality product.

2 When Shooting Digital Video

Shooting Standard Definition Video at 29.97 FPS

The most basic workflow in Final Cut Pro involves shooting 29.97 FPS digital video on any DV format including DVC Pro 50, DVC Pro HD, and HDV(see Figure 2.1). Audio can be recorded directly to the camera tape. The video and audio can simply be captured to any drive, even a removable firewire drive. Generally, these projects are finished right on the editing computer; any color correction is preformed with Color, Final Cut Pro color-correcting plug-ins or third-party, color-correcting plug-ins. The project is simply printed back to DV tape in the shooting format and/or QuickTime movies are exported for compression and burning or copying to DVD.

This simple workflow can be improved upon with several additions to the workflow. Any or all can be used depending on the demands of the project.

- Audio can be recorded on a separate recorder and sunc in Final Cut Pro to a slate with clapper.

- Audio can be exported to Pro Tools after the picture is edited to a locked cut, and sound edited and mixed with much more control. It can even be mixed to 5.1 surround sound.

- Improved titles and effects can be realized outside of Final Cut Pro.

- Improved color correction can be realized by taking the final videotape to a post house and color correcting shot by shot going tape-to-tape.

In the first example, audio can be recorded with or without time code on any sync-capable recorder. The advantage is simplified production as the recorder and mixer are not tied to the camera in any way, making it possible to move more freely and perhaps recording improved audio as a result of this freedom. See Chapter 3 for information on recording and importing audio as well as syncing audio to the slate.

Figure 2.1   DP Johnny Bishop Shoots *Son* using the DVX 100 on Brooks Institute stage one

The second workflow addition can remarkably improve the control and therefore quality of the audio mix and finished sound track. See Chapter 5 for information on exporting audio and working in Pro Tools.

The third suggestion can improve the finished titles especially the end title crawls. See Chapter 8 on improving titles.

Depending on the shooting format, the fourth added step can remarkably improve the overall look of the project. The process is simple but rather expensive for many small DV projects. The final, noncolor-corrected project is simply printed to digital videotape and taken to any good postproduction house capable of doing tape-to-tape with your DV format. Several DV formats present problems and may need to be dubbed (copied) to another format for tape-to-tape color correction. HDV has a very compressed and under-sampled color space and offers less control in color correction. The transports are also difficult to control in tape-to-tape and, so, most HDV projects will need to be transferred to HD Cam. Standard DV formats have limited time code features and make tape-to-tape deck control impossible. However, these DV tapes can be dubbed to another format for color correction. The format of choice at most post houses is not a DV format at all, but Digi Beta. Digi Beta offers excellent control of the tape transport as well as the color through the color correction equipment. This is usually the same color correction equipment used for telecine. (See Chapter 1 on film workflow.) DVCam and DVC Pro 50 are also often dubbed to Digi Beta, however tape-to-tape is possible from these formats. One advantage here is that the final master tape is delivered on Digi Beta, which is perhaps the most supported of all standard definition formats. DVC Pro HD is unique and will not be dubbed but color corrected in DVC Pro HD.

Non-DV formats such as HD Cam and Digi Beta have a higher bandwidth and require very specialized equipment, and this requires a finishing step called an online edit in the workflow.

There are two ways to approach this:

- Capture from the HD Cam or Digi Beta shooting tapes at a lower resolution in Final Cut Pro and recapture at full resolution later in online.

- Capture from DVCam clones of the HD Cam or Digi Beta and recapture from the high-resolution tapes in online.

In the first workflow, you log and capture the shooting format tapes at low-resolution to your drive in a facility that supports your finished format. This can be expensive because you need to log the tapes at the postproduction facility, and the hourly rate can be rather high. Excellent shooting reports with time code can greatly reduce this cost. The low-resolution setting is "Off-line real time photo JPEG."

The second workflow requires making DV copies or "clones" of the shooting tapes. The time code on these tapes must match your higher resolution tapes. You capture on your own system and on your own time, so this saves money. Simply capture from your DV tapes and start editing. This system works well and is the preferred system for most projects.

Because with both of these options, you will recapture in online, it is essential to properly name and number your tapes in the capture settings, as shown in Figure 2.2. As with the film workflows, a cutting log can be created in Excel or a Word program but with these workflows you export a batch list and open it in Excel or any Word program. This batch list can also be imported into Cinema Tools for reverse telecine and/or management of media.

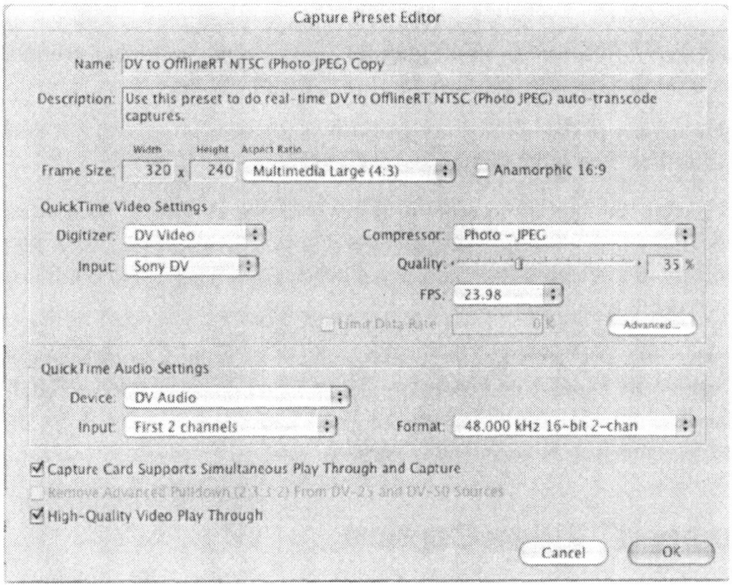

Figure 2.2   Off-line real-time photo JPEG setting

Shooting Standard Definition Digital Video at 24P (23.98)

The 24P format was created in an effort to make digital look more like film and be more compatible with film. The 24P workflows are also derived from film workflows, so it is necessary to understand the workflows from Chapter 1 before moving on to a 24P workflow. A 24P camera mimics a film camera and telecine. The 24P camera shoots approximately 24 (23.976) digital still pictures every second. Rather than record these pictures, the camera applies the same 3:2 cadence and interlacing that the telecine machine applies when transferring film to digital video. Unlike 24 FPS film, there is no need to pull down 24P because the actual frame rate is already video speed, 23.98. There are, therefore, no pull-up, pull-down issues with standard definition 24P.

This introduces the same step-frame look of film transferred to video. While many find this look distracting and less appealing than 29.97 interlaced video, 24P advocates feel it evokes a "film feel."

In postproduction workflow, the 24P video can be treated like any other 29.97 video. The 24P look is achieved entirely in the camera and no special workflow is required. However, just as film that has been telecined can be reversed back to the original frames, 24P can also be reverse telecined back to the original 23.98 digital still pictures. There are several reasons you may choose to reverse the footage and edit at 23.98:

- To "up rez" the standard-definition video to high-definition 23.98 or 24 FPS HD digital video: It is much more difficult to change this frame rate after the project has been edited.

- To copy the project to film for projection, also known as "film out": By reversing the video to the original digital still pictures captured in the camera, each digital frame can now be shot onto individual film frames, creating a high-quality film transfer.

- To make 23.98 FPS DVDs: All of the newer DVD players can play 23.98 video and add the 3:2 cadence sending 29.97 FPS to the video monitor. This allows for better compression and longer program material on the DVD.

If you are not planning any of these finishing workflows, there is no reason not to treat these formats as 29.97 video and follow that workflow.

Reverse telecine is achieved exactly as it is in film workflow. However, there are a few differences from the film workflow when working with 24P. As you don't have a negative, you don't need a cut list. And, you don't have a telecine log. You don't need a database either; however, the database is the easiest way to reverse telecine.

To create a database from 24P footage, begin the process in Final Cut Pro. Log and capture all of the shots. Then export the Final Cut Pro batch list, go to File > Export > Batch List. Now open Cinema Tools. Create a new database. Import the Final Cut Pro batch list. Link the media. You can now batch reverse telecine just as with a film project.

24PA "Advanced" Video Capture

Many of these cameras can also employ an "advanced" or "24PA" 2:3:3:2 cadence that makes reverse telecine real time and part of the capture. The advanced 2:3:3:2 cadence is set in the camera's menu. When the 2:3:3:2 cadence is used, the capture settings in Final Cut Pro must be set to 23.98 with advanced 2:3:3:2 removal (see Figure 2.3). The easiest way to achieve these settings is to do an "easy setup" to the appropriate video format, "DV NTSC Advanced 2:3:3:2 removal." If you are using DVC Pro 50 or DVC Pro HD, there may not be a "24PA Advanced 2:3:3:2 removal" for your format in easy setup. If it is not there you can make one by selecting your format in 24P (i.e., DVC Pro 50 24P) and making a copy of the setup. Open this and check the advanced 2:3:3:2 removal checkbox in the capture settings.

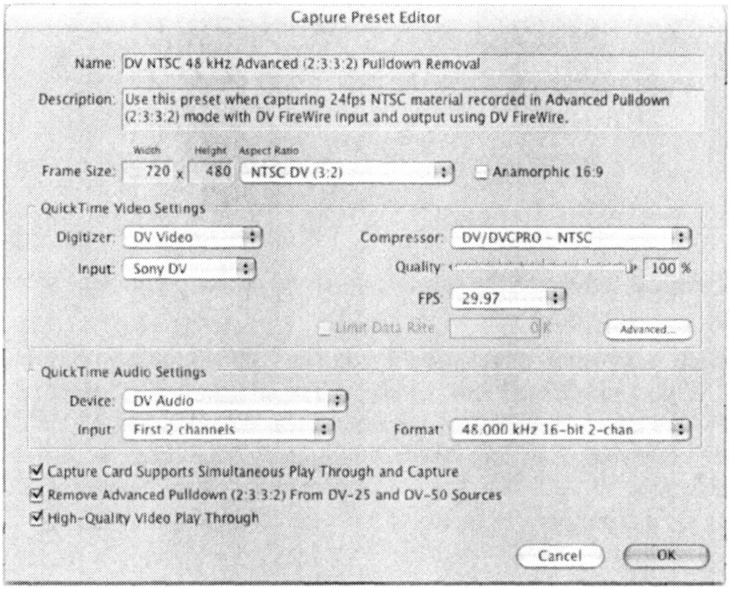

Figure 2.3 2:3:3:2 setting in capture settings

The video can now be captured as 23.98 video with no need for reverse telecine. This cadence produces an odd "stepped" motion on the 29.97 video and should only be captured at 23.98.

Because the data rates are much higher during capture with 2:3:3:2 removal, 23.98 PA should never be captured to a firewire drive, but directly to the fastest drive available, usually the internal hard drive. Once captured, it can be transferred to a removable firewire drive and edited.

The "advanced" pull-down pattern of 2:3:3:2 makes the reverse telecine process simpler and faster. As shown in Figure 2.4, by recording the A frame into both fields of the 0 frame, the B frame into both fields of the 1 frame, one field of B and one of C into the 2 frame, two fields of C into 3, and, finally, two fields of D into 4. Now all that is needed is to remove the 2 frame and you are reversed back to 23.98. So simple, it is done in capture in Final Cut Pro. The 24P cameras create this cadence in the camera and record to standard DV videotape. Compare this reverse telecine to Chapter 1 on film workflow.

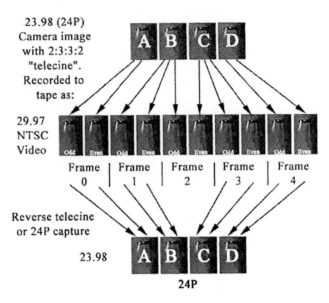

Figure 2.4 Advanced pull-down removal allowing the direct capture of 23.98pa video without reverse telecine

Once the 23.98 video is captured, or reversed if you are following that workflow, you are ready to edit at 23.98 FPS. When you print to video, Final Cut Pro adds in the 3:2 cadence, as seen in Figure 2.5, turning the 24P back into 29.97 video. Because it was edited at 23.98, this 29.97 master has 0 A frame reference throughout; it and any dubs with matching time code can be reversed back to 24P. It is also possible to print to tape with 2:3:3:2 cadence for direct capture in 24P for film out or up-rez to HD. Any QuickTime files exported will remain at 23.98 for authoring 23.98 DVDs.

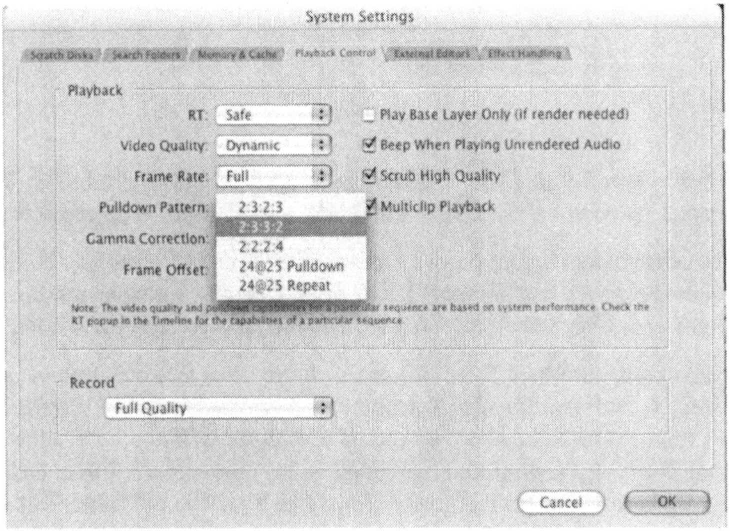

Figure 2.5 Output cadence settings in FCP

Mixing DV Formats

If you need to mix 24PA and 24P in a project, this is not a problem. Once reversed, all 24P (23.98) is the same. This is not the case when mixing DV formats. While DV, DVCam, and DVC Pro can be mixed in a project, these formats should not be mixed with DVC Pro 50 or DVC Pro HD. These formats can all be edited into the same timeline and rendered to the format of that timeline. However, the renders do not look nearly as good as proper transfers made tape-to-tape before capture. This is definitely true of HDV. This format is not compatible with any of the other DV formats; however, any video format can be dubbed to HDV tape-to-tape just as HDV can be dubbed to any other format. These dubs require very specialized equipment and should be done in a reputable postproduction facility.

Shooting HD Digital Video at 23.98 or 24 FPS

Figure 2.6 shows the shooting of HD for a video project. Some professional HD Cam and DVC Pro HD cameras shoot unusual frame rates, such as 23.98, 24, 25, 29.97, 30, 50, 59.94, and 60. Often, the higher frame rates are used to achieve slow motion, but these frame rates can be used for other purposes including special effects and conversion to European PAL format. As in standard definition, 23.98 is often used for its "film look" and ability to transfer to film. It can also be used on HD DVDs. While HDV can be shot at 23.98 FPS, unlike other DV formats, this requires special cameras and other equipment for both shooting and capture.

Figure 2.6 Director of Photography Gianny Trutmann shooting *All About the Music* on stage one at Brooks Institute using the Panavision version of the Sony F900

The workflow for HD DV is therefore very similar to standard definition DV. DVC Pro HD can be captured and reversed, or captured at 23.98 to the hard drive if advanced pull down was used in production. HDV can be shot directly to drive at 23.98 with the proper equipment. All of these formats can now be edited and color corrected with Final Cut Pro in their native format with no need for an online.

Workflow for 23.98 FPS and 24 FPS HD Cam is very similar to workflow for film telecined to 23.98 HD Cam. (See Chapter 1 on film to HD Cam workflow.) In this case, however, the HD Cam tapes are the original shooting media. There is no negative, telecine log, or Cinema Tools database to create a batch list with. So, in this regard, the workflow is also very similar to the 29.97 HD FPS workflow discussed earlier in this chapter.

There are two basic systems:

- Capture from the 23.98 FPS or 24 FPS HD Cam shooting tapes in their native frame rate at a lower resolution in Final Cut Pro and recapture at full resolution later in online.

- Capture from 29.97 FPS DVCam clones of the 23.98 FPS or 24 FPS HD Cam tapes, reverse telecine back to the original frame rate, and edit at that frame rate. In online, recapture from the high-resolution tapes at this same original frame rate.

As in 29.97 FPS workflow, in this first workflow, you log and capture the shooting format tapes at low-resolution to your drive in a facility that supports your finish format. They can capture at which-ever frame rate you shot at, off-line, real-time photo JPEG is available for all frame rates. Here, too, this can be expensive because you need to log the tapes at the postproduction facility.

The second workflow requires making DV copies or "down converts" of the shooting tapes. If the shooting frame rate is 24 FPS, then the original tapes will be "pulled down," in other words, played at 23.98 FPS in transfer to 29.97 FPS. This is the same process as film shot at 24 FPS being pulled down in telecine. Just as in 29.97 FPS workflow, the time code on these tapes must match your higher resolution tapes This is a problem because the frame rates no longer match. The 24 NDF time code now needs to become 29.97 NDF time code.

While the down converts are being dubbed, the time codes of both tapes will match except for the frames counter. The DV down converts will have 29.97 NDF and the original will have 23.98 NDF. This is even true of 24 FPS originals because they are being pulled in transfer to 23.98 FPS. Because of this dual time code problem, it is essential to have the down converts made with two window burns, a window showing the original time code and another window showing the new 29.97 NDF time code. When the down converts are captured at 29.97, the 29.97 NDF window will be accurate with the 23.98 NDF window showing overprinting of some numbers. After the video is reversed, the 29.97 NDF window will skip one number in 5, but the 23.98 NDF window will be accurate. If you shot at 24 FPS and wish to edit at 24 FPS, reverse to 24 instead of 23.98. Your 23.98 NDF window will now read in 24 NDF.

It's interesting to note that the reversing process not only changes the video frame rate, it also changes the time code frame rate of the captured video QuickTime files. The imbedded QuickTime time code will be 29.97 NDF on the original capture and therefore match the 29.97 window burn, but the reversed video files will have imbedded 23.98 NDF, which matches the 23.98 window burn. This is how Final Cut Pro and Cinema Tools are able to manage frame-accurate databases and edit lists in this new frame rate. Notice the two time code window burns in Figure 2.7.

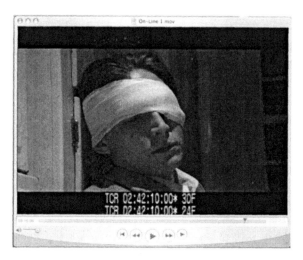

Figure 2.7 Actor Ethan Wilcox on the set of *Success.* Note the two window burns, one for 23.98 NDF and one for 29.97 NDF. When the SD 29.97 video is played, the upper window is frame-by-frame correct, when played at 23.98 FPS the lower window is correct.

The aspect ratio will also change—unless you tell the post house not to—the original 16 × 9 will be letterboxed on the 4 × 3 down converts. As with 29.97 workflow, you capture on your own system and on your own time, so this saves money. However this workflow is a bit more complicated than simply capturing from the original HD tape at lower resolution. In spite of the added complexity, this is the preferred system on most projects.

Because with both of these options you will recapture in online, it is essential to properly name and number your tapes in the capture settings. As with the film workflows, a cutting log can be created in Excel or a Word program.

If you did not record and capture audio on the camera tapes, you are ready to import audio and sync in Final Cut Pro. See Chapter 3 on audio capture.

Capturing in ProRes 422

ProRes 422 is the newest innovation from Apple available in Final Cut Pro 6. ProRes 422 is a 10-bit HD codec that looks almost like uncompressed HD while producing a file size smaller than DV50. ProRes 422 takes advantage of the multicore processor design in Mac Pro computers, the amount of real-time playback increases as the number of processors goes up. And this real-time playback works from firewire drives, not expensive RAID arrays. This also means that for facilities that share the same media via network from RAID, they can deliver even more streams of video to more editors. And because this codec is independent of the production format, it can be used with any format not supported in Final Cut Pro. There are two versions of the codec: standard and HQ. When the computer is equipped with an HD-SDI card, capture from any HD-SDI source is possible in real time. This makes it possible to capture to drive in ProRes 422 directly from camera or telecine.

One of the most valuable tools to use with ProRes 422 is the AJA ioHD (see Figure 2.8). This device encodes ProRes 422 in hardware and sends the data via firewire 800 to Final Cut Pro. The AJA ioHD

Figure 2.8 The AJA ioHD. This io device converts all HD and SD video formats into ProRes 422. Editing in ProRes 422 allows for mixing any and all formats together as well as allowing high bandwidth formats like HD Cam and DigiBeta to be edited from a single drive with no need to online edit

has almost any conceivable video and audio input and output connector and supports almost all video formats in NTSC, PAL, or HD. The device can be used to capture to ProRes 422 from any format, monitor during editing in ProRes 422, and output to any and all video formats from ProRes 422.

ProRes 422 can be used to edit any format other than 4 K. For workflows where SD video will be up converted to HD, ProRes 422 makes this simple by converting from SD to HD in hardware right in the ioHD during capture (see Figure 2.9).

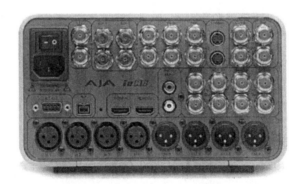

Figure 2.9 The back of the ioHD showing the myriad inputs and outputs for various video formats

Tapeless Capture

Many cameras now shoot to P2 card or directly to hard drive. In these cases, the video is not captured at all, but imported. There have been many horror stories about corrupted video when transferring from drive to drive or from chip to drive. For the most part, these are operator errors. Many people try to transfer from the P2 cards to drive blind, with no way to check the video and confirm that the transfer is good. Also, the media is particularly vulnerable when it is written to a drive or chip with no backup. Keep in mind, though, film is many times more vulnerable after it has been exposed, but this has not keep it from being used successfully for more than 100 years.

Ideally, the media should be downloaded to a redundant RAID and checked before the chips are cleared or the drive reformatted and reused on set. The chips and drives are expensive, and there is a tendency to dump the media to drive and clear and reuse the chip as soon as possible to avoid slowing down the production. But if you haven't checked the transfer, and a backup, don't be too quick to dump the media.

Red Camera Redcode

The Red One camera uses a unique codec called Redcode that is recorded directly to drive in camera. The removable drives can be taken to the postproduction facility and downloaded, or they can be downloaded on the set to a laptop or other Mac. The file size is very small, smaller than DV, so media management and playback is fast and simple.

Final Cut Pro 6 supports Redcode. Simply import the raw camera footage and start editing in native Redcode. While this sounds like voodoo, it requires no shaking of rattles or sacrificing of chickens. It doesn't even require any input/output devices or video monitors. The Redcode is viewed directly on the computer screen. The down side of this is that the image can only be viewed on the computer screen. This is not a bad thing, per se, but at this time the closest thing to a 4 K monitor is the Sony 4 k projector. And while this looks great, the $100,000 price tag is a bit high for most users. What's needed here is a 4 K version of the Apple Cinema Display or a 4 K projector that anyone can afford. In the meantime, we will all need to tough it out with the current HD Cinema Display.

Redcode is intended for projects headed for theatrical distribution. It projects as well as 35 mm or can be used to make 35 mm prints by simply treating the Redcode as a digital intermediate (DI). For projects headed to video, the Redcode can be down converted to HD video in any format. It down converts well to ProRes 422, and if there is no intent to use the Redcode, the camera footage can be converted to ProRes 422 after it is imported and before editing. This makes it possible to see the finished look of the HD video on your HD monitor. The ProRes 422 can be composted in Motion and graded in Color and output to any HD or SD video format.

Capturing and Preparing *Success* and *Son from the Ocean of Storms* by Glynn Beard

Success was shot on Sony HD Cam using the F900 Cine Alta. The production frame rate was 23.98 FPS. The capture phase of the workflow proceeded like this:

- The production tapes were down-converted to DV Cam at 29.97 FPS by Digital Film Tree in Los Angeles.

- These DV clones were logged and captured into Final Cut Pro.

- A batch list was exported from Final Cut and this batch list was imported into Cinema Tools. This became the Cinema Tools database, which was linked to the original 29.97 DV video media bringing all of the shots online in Cinema Tools.

Figure 2.10 *Success* poster. Image Courtesy of Glynn Beard and Teresa Steppe

- All of the shots were then batch-reverse telecined back to the original 23.98 FPS frame rate in Cinema Tools.

- All of the clips in the Final Cut Pro project were then relinked to the new 23.98 FPS footage, a 23.98 FPS timeline was created in Final Cut Pro, and the project was edited at DV 23.98.

Son was shot on the DVX 100 by Panasonic. The production frame rate was 23.98 FPS, which is to say, 24P. The cadence was 2:3:3:2 or "advanced" 24PA.

- The shots were logged and captured at 23.98 using the advanced pull down removal in Final Cut Pro.

- The project was edited at 23.98 FPS.

While there are many similarities between these steps used with digital video and the film workflows from Chapter 1, there are also many differences. Overall the digital workflows are more streamlined, especially true with the newest formats, ProRes 422 and Redcode. Many of the problems in digital video workflow come from lack of planning. While a film workflow demands pre-planning, digital video often lulls the editor into a false sense of simplicity, and thinking that anything can be done at any time. It's not enough to have a good idea where you are at and in what direction you are headed, you also need to know where you need to end up before you take even one step on the journey.

3 Initial Audio Workflow, Importing Production Audio, and Syncing

The Production Audio Recorder

There are several decisions made in production that determine workflow in postproduction. The use of time code recorders and slates, analog or digital recorders, optical disc recorders, and flash memory recorders dramatically alter the postproduction workflow. You may have little or no input on the choice of the recorder, but if you understand their operation, you will be better able to plan your workflow.

Audio recorders, used in motion picture production, must be able to play back at the exact speed they recorded. Nagra (and some other) analog recorders achieve this by recording a pilot signal in the audio and then comparing it to a known reference in playback. Several Nagra models, such as the one shown in Figure 3.1, can record time code, but most do not. For years, this was the standard for motion picture production and is still widely used by analog purists and low-budget, independent productions. It's an excellent system and outperforms many digital alternatives. Analog recorders usually record to one-quarter-inch reel-to-reel tape; however, some record to audio cassette tape.

Digital recorders are much more widely used. They achieve sync by sampling the sound at a very accurate rate and playing those samples back at the exact same rate. While 48 KHz and 96 KHz are most often used, several sample rates are used and new ones come along now and then. But the key to sync is accuracy: playing at the exact same sample rate as the recording.

In production, sync is achieved by locking each device to its own internal clock. In postproduction, all playback machines and recorders need to be locked to the same clock. While sync can be held

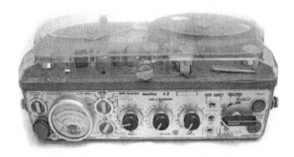

Figure 3.1 The classic analog Nagra recorder. First used in the early 1950s, this recorder is still preferred by some mixers and filmmakers.

for some time by locking everything to its internal clock, there are micro differences between clocks. And in postproduction it is necessary to maintain sync through the entire program. So, in postproduction it is best practice to lock all playback and record devices to a common "house" clock. In this way, even if there are micro errors in the clock rate that cause the playback to run too fast or slow, all video and audio devices will change speed together in sync.

Time code is also often used, as a database, as a sync reference, and to find sync in the first place. If you know what audio time code corresponds to what video time code, you can use this information to quickly pull the two elements into sync. Time code can also be compared to the "house" sync reference to ensure that the playback speed is 100 percent in sync. And time code can be used to make a database containing the location of each take on the original recording media as well as its usage in the final edit. This database can be used to make an audio edit decision list or "audio EDL," which can be used to recapture any production audio if the workflow requires it. While EDL workflows are quickly becoming a thing of the past, some facilities still prefer that workflow.

Many digital recorders do not record time code yet can still be used for sync sound recording. In this case, sync is held only through playback accuracy; as long as the playback sample rate matches the recording sample rate, the playback will stay in sync for several minutes.

Digital recorders record to many different media. Some record to Digital Audio Tape (DAT), other digital recorders record to flash memory, or even directly to drive. Flash memory chips can be removed and used as the recording media; however, it is much more common to download the audio files to a removable drive or burn them to a CD, either in the recorder if it is equipped with a CD burner, or on a laptop computer.

So, planning your initial audio workflow will require several choices. First, the production sound may be delivered on one-quarter-inch tape, DAT, CD, portable drive, or even flash memory. In some cases, you will transfer this audio to another format before syncing. If you are shooting film, you can sync in telecine or sync later in Final Cut Pro before editing. And you may need to "pull down." Let's take a closer look at these options.

Pull Down when Shooting Film

Pull down is an issue when shooting film at 24 FPS and finishing or editing on video. In telecine, the film will be slowed by .1 percent and, so, the audio recording must be matched to this new speed. Slowing the film to 23.98 FPS to produce 29.97 FPS video will cause the sound to slowly move out of sync. It will be one full frame out of sync after 33 seconds. When syncing up film either in telecine or after it has been telecined, it is necessary to also slow the audio by the same .1 percent. For more information, see Chapter 1 on telecine and pull-down.

Here again, film speed will refer to any film or digital video or audio that plays at 24 FPS or 30 FPS. Video speed will refer to film, video, or digital that plays at 29.97 FPS or 23.98 FPS. If you are changing from film speed to video speed, you are pulling down. If you are changing from video speed to film speed you are pulling up.

Some digital recorders have pull-up and sometimes pull-down sample rates. In this case, the recorder would be set for pull up (48,048 Hz or 96,096 Hz) while filming and normal (48 K or 96 K) for transferring to Pro Tools or tape. It would also be played at 48 K or 96 K if syncing in telecine.

Some recorders have this pull-up, pull-down feature but don't call it pull up or down. Often, this is expressed as 30 FPS and 29.97 FPS. Audio recorders don't actually record frames, but this is a convenient way to express the speed. Here, too, if the recording is done at 30 FPS and playback is set to 29.97 FPS, the audio has been pulled down.

Many of these recorders also lay time code from a free-running time code generator or a time-of-day time code generator. These can usually generate several different time code formats, both drop frame (DF) and nondrop frame (NDF) in 23.98, 24, 29.97 and 30 FPS. (For more information on time code, see Appendix 5 on understanding time code.) If the production time code is 24 or 30 FPS, the pulled down audio will be 23.98 and 29.97, respectively. This is why some production recorders offer 30 and 24 DF, which are not real or rational time code formats. These time codes become 29.97 DF and 23.98 DF, which are real time code formats.

Hard Lock Versus Soft Lock

There are many ways to lock sound and picture together for sync, but they can be divided into two types: soft lock and hard lock. There was a time when only hard lock was used in motion picture production and postproduction. But, thirty years ago, when new, more accurate technologies became available, soft lock systems came into common usage.

In a hard lock system the elements are locked together so that they must move at the same speed. Original systems often used mechanical systems, gears and chains with common motors. There were also electrical systems that used selsyn motors to lock separate machines together. Often the camera and audio recorder would be locked to a common speed reference.

Later, pilot tone systems came into usage. Figure 3.2 shows an early system. The camera sent a pilot signal to the audio recorder that could then record the speed of the camera with the audio. This was used to hard lock all audio recorders and players to the speed of the camera. All of these systems are examples of hard lock where the separate devices are either locked together or are locked to a common speed reference.

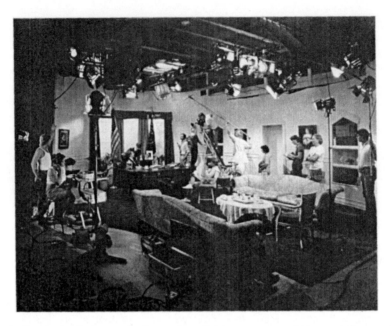

Figure 3.2 Early Brooks Institute production using pilot tone sync and Nagra 4.2 recorder.

In soft lock, the devices are locked to a sync reference, but each device has its own sync reference. An early example of this is "crystal sync." In crystal sync, the audio recorder has an internal crystal reference generator, which is very accurate. The camera also has an accurate crystal reference generator that is used to control the speed of the camera. If the two crystal clocks are running at the same speed, then the audio and picture will be in sync.

But if there are micro errors in one or both of the clocks, the sync will drift. This system will usually hold sync to within one frame in an hour, which is more than acceptable for production dailies, but certainly not for holding sync over an entire feature film.

The biggest problem with soft lock is cumulative errors. If every recording, transfer, or capture introduces an error of one-tenth of a frame, the shot may end up drifting in and out of sync.

Best-practice workflow, therefore, allows soft lock when necessary or sometimes even just for convenience, while understanding its limitations. And, hard lock whenever it is possible and always when it is necessary.

Smart Slate

Time code can be locked to a slate and the time code numbers photographed on film from the slate In most cases, the slate will have its own time code generator (smart slate), which can be synced to the generator in the recorder. Often, the time-of-day time code is used as a reference, or the generator can simply "free run" throughout the day. All recorders, video cameras, and slates to be used for the day are synchronized at the start of the day by connecting them with a cable and "jamming," which is to say setting one to match the other. Now, any and all video cameras, recorders, and slates will show the same time code. When the sticks on the slate are closed, the time code changes to a reference stamp, which is often the date. This makes it easy to find the frame where the sticks close and you can have a record of the time and date the shot was made.

Because every device is soft locked to its own reference clock, micro clock errors will cause the devices to drift apart over time. All devices should be rejammed several times through the day to ensure they are all in sync with each other.

Syncing is now much faster as the time code on the audio recorder can be matched to the number photographed onto the film from the slate. Syncing can now be done in telecine as the film is transferred. The audio time code is simply read from the slate and entered on a keypad in the telecine room. Some recorders do not record time code and can only be sunc to the clapper sticks after the telecine or transferred to time code DAT before telecine.

In spite of having this photographic reference filmed or videotaped, many people still prefer to sync to the sticks close. Even though it is possible to only film the time code on the slate, the sticks are still snapped shut. This serves several purposes even if you are planning to sync to the time code from the slate rather than the sticks. First, it's a great backup. If something goes wrong and the time codes don't match, or the slate is out of focus, then you can still sync to the sticks closing as long as it can be seen in the shot. Second, it confirms that this is a sync shot and was not shot MOS (without sound). When shooting MOS, it is best practice to keep the sticks open with a hand through the opening blocking the sticks from closing to announce visually, this shot has no sound. Third, verbally calling the slate and snapping the sticks closed helps announce to everyone on set that the camera is running and sound is being recorded.

The time code slate works well in a number of circumstances, especially when shooting live events with multicameras. Consider a five-film and one video camera shoot of a concert. One or even two time code DAT or other type of time code digital audio recorders can be fed from the stage audio mixer. One of the audio recorders can be jammed to the other and the video camera and five slates can also be jammed to the same time code as the audio recorders. All audio, video, and slates will now show the exact same time code. The video shots can now be pulled into sync with the DAT audio with a simple "merge clip to time code" command in Final Cut Pro. (More on this later in this chapter.) As the time code of the video, audio, and slates are all the same format, probably 29.97 DF or NDF, the slate numbers will advance in sync with the video.

The problem is not as straightforward with film to be edited on digital video. In this case, the camera is rolling at 24 FPS, but the transferred video will be 29.97 and may be reversed to 23.98. Choosing the time code for the audio and the slate therefore becomes a problem. Often, the audio time code will be 30 DF or NDF, when this audio is pulled down the rate will be 29.97 DF or NDF. The video time code used in telecine will probably be 29.97 NDF, so this sounds like a good match. But because the camera is running at 24 FPS, the numbers on the slate will be advancing faster than the film, and this will cause photographed numbers to be skipped and/or overprinted. Running the audio time code at 24 FPS is not much better; the 29.97 video will have repeated numbers and any reversed 23.98 digital video may be overprinted.

In Figure 3.3, the slate from *Lost Hope and More*, several problems can be seen. First, the slate time code numbers are overprinted. The frame number was 11 and advanced to 12 with the film shutter

Figure 3.3 Slating a scene from *Lost Hope and More* using a digital "smart slate"

open. In this case, we know what time is represented; however, what if the number is an 8? It could be a 7 overprinted with an 8, an 8 or even an 8 overprinted with a 9. So it's hard to say what time code this matches. Moreover, notice that the audio time code burn window, (lower left) shows 16:17:08:05 yet the slate shows 22:31:52:12. The reason for this huge difference is not a jamming problem or an error with the slate or recorder. In this case, the telecine session was running long and the decision was made to stop syncing in telecine and sync the remaining shots to the clapper later. On the video, the audio time code is not advancing but is parked on 16:17:08:05. The assistant editor should make note of this in the cutting log and, after the video is sunc, the actual time code should be entered into the Cinema Tools database to preserve the accuracy of the audio database.

Such problems are so common as to be considered normal. They are the principal reason for keeping detailed notes and a cutting log, and for always having a backup system like the clapper sticks.

Partly because of these problems, most telecine facilities use a hybrid workflow for syncing in telecine. First the production audio is transferred to a time code DAT format, often DA88 format. If the production audio has time code, the time code is cloned onto the DA88 tape keeping the same time code as the slate and production tapes. If the audio needs to be pulled down, this can be done in this transfer. For example, if the production audio was recorded with a sample rate of 48,048, it can be played at 48,000 in the transfer. If the production audio was recorded at 48,000, the DA88 can record at 30 FPS and be played at 29.97 FPS in telecine. All recorders and players will be locked with the same "house sync" reference during the transfer. Analog Nagra audio can also be locked to the house sync video reference during the transfer causing the Nagra to play .1 percent slower. If the production audio has no time code, time code will be added in this transfer and the audio database will now reference the DA88 transfer rather than the original production audio.

During the transfer, the time code locations of the clapper sticks are noted in the transfer logs. Syncing can now be done to these logs. The telecine colorist simply parks on the frame where the sticks can be seen fully closed, and then enters the audio time code location from the transfer log, which brings the DA88 into sync with the film. The telecine and the DA88 are both locked to the same house sync so there are no sync errors or drift.

Capturing Audio

Digital Capture

Audio can be imported directly into Final Cut Pro if it was recorded using a recorder that records directly to memory chips or disc and if the audio does not need to be pulled down.

A workflow that is often used, but is definitely not best practice, is to dub the DAT or Nagra tapes to DV videotape and capture the audio from the DV tapes. There are several problems with this system. First, while some workflows recapture the audio in sound design, most current workflows utilize the original audio in the final mix. So this transfer must be done well with proper levels. Many DV recorders do not have good metering; some don't have any at all and yet are sometimes used for this transfer. And the DV recorder may introduce noise from its analog input.

There are also sync issues. The DAT or Nagra is soft locked to its internal clock. The DV recorder is soft locked to its video input. The DV recorder will also be soft locked during capture of both video and audio. So, while the sync may be fair, it's not great and may be drifting in and out.

Tape Capture

If the audio needs to be captured from tape, or if it needs to be pulled down, this is best done in Pro Tools. For recording from tape, whether analog or DAT, the tape player will be patched into the Pro Tools inputs on the input-output interface (i.e., Pro Tools M box). A preferred system would be to use a Pro Tools HD or system that would allow the DAT or Nagra to be "hard locked" to the Pro Tools system by supplying the same sync reference to be sent to the Pro Tools Sync IO and the Nagra or DAT.

Or, in the case of DAT, the Pro Tools system can be locked to the DAT by using the SPDIF input and SPDIF sync reference on the Pro Tools HD IO interface. The SPDIF sync input locks the Pro Tools system to the clock in the DAT player insuring hard lock. SPDIF is also a digital-to-digital audio transfer that will insure proper levels and no addition of noise.

However, simply letting the DAT or Nagra "soft lock" to its internal clock and patching the audio outs into the Pro Tools audio inputs will hold frame-accurate sync for quite some time. And if the levels are properly matched, the audio quality of the transfer will be good with very little addition of noise. While this system would not be good enough to transfer an entire film, it will hold sync for all but the longest production takes.

The fastest and simplest way to capture from tape is to capture the entire tape or tapes, cut up the takes in the Pro Tools timeline and export the takes as files ready for import into Final Cut Pro. If necessary, the takes can be pulled down during this export. For audio recorded to chips or drive that needs to be pulled down, the audio takes can be imported into Pro Tools and then exported with pull down.

Track Management

First, create a new Pro Tools session (see Figure 3.6). The audio file type can be broadcast WAV (BWF) or AIFF. Both of these formats can be imported directly into Final Cut Pro with no need to render the audio. The bit depth can be 16 or 24 bit. Final Cut Pro supports both, but best practice would be to match the original bit depth from the production recording. The project can be expanded to 24 bit later in sound design if a 24-bit finish is planned.

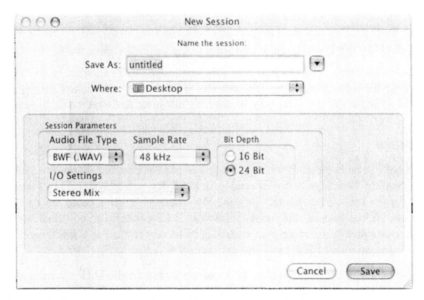

Figure 3.4 The Pro Tools new session window. From here the audio format, bit depth and sample rate is set

Audio capture is the first step in track management. It's very unlikely that the dialogue was recorded in stereo. Don't capture mono sound to a stereo track. If you are capturing two-channel DAT or two-, three-, or four-channel sound files, you need to know what is recorded in each channel. This information should be written in the production sound reports and/or the script notes. There are five common situations you may find.

- Mono sound from one microphone is recorded into one track.

- Mono sound from one microphone is recorded into both tracks at the same level.

- Mono sound from one microphone is recorded into both tracks with one track recorded 15 db lower as a safety backup.

- Two or more mono tracks are recorded from individual microphones.

- Stereo sound is recorded.

The first situation is simple. Capture the track with the recorded audio and ignore the other.

In the second situation, capture either track, but listen closely to both first. One may be cleaner than the other.

The third situation can be handled two different ways:

- Capture only the normal level takes knowing that the −15 db are on tape if needed later in post-production. If your sound edit workflow will include recapture from the audio EDL, this definitely makes the most sense, but it can be used in all workflows.

- Capture both tracks to separate mono tracks. Split up both into takes but only sync and edit the normal level takes. Place the −15 db takes in an audio folder for use if needed later in postproduction. This would probably be the best system for OMF-based workflows that will not include recapture. (For more information on recapture versus OMF, see Chapter 7 on sound edit workflows.)

The fourth situation is straightforward. Capture all tracks with sound to multiple mono tracks, sync and edit the footage with all tracks kept separate. Each take will likely have a different number or tracks. Read and follow the production sound reports closely. There may be −15 db safety tracks used in some takes where only one mic was used.

The fifth situation requires capturing the stereo tracks as stereo tracks. Do not capture multiple mono. Sync and edit the stereo tracks.

If you are capturing from tape, you will record to Pro Tools audio tracks in real time. Create the proper number and type of tracks based on your production audio. Set the inputs of these tracks to the appropriate input depending on how you have the tape player patched into the Pro Tools I/O device. Record-ready the track(s).

As the metering on the channels is rather basic, to get a better look at your levels add the plug-in "trim" to the channel(s), as seen in Figure 3.5. Compare the head tone on the tape to the level on the meter. If necessary, you can trim with the gain slider. Do this for each channel. Make sure you are setting to the proper reference. Check the sound reports to see what was recorded.

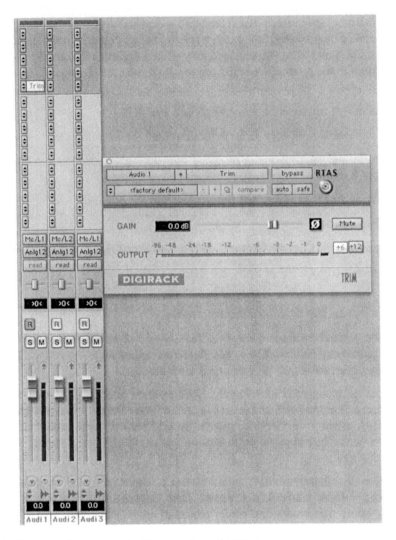

Figure 3.5 Pro Tools record track with trim plug-in and meter

Record-arm the transport and start the transfer. Record the entire tape to drive. Once you have captured the entire tape you are ready to break up the individual takes in the timeline.

As you break up the takes in the timeline, each new region will appear in the region list as a subclip. Name the regions as you go; likely, you will use the scene and take numbers. These subclips do not represent actual media, but rather reference the original capture of the entire tape. Before they can be used they must be exported as media files.

Highlight all of the new regions in the window that you want to export. Make sure to not select the original capture of the tape, as this would make an unnecessary copy of this media. From the Audio Regions pop-up menu, which is opened by clicking on the gray bar at the top of the region list, select Export Regions as Files (see Figure 3.6).

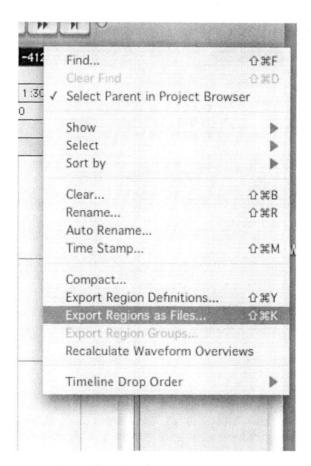

Figure 3.6 Pro Tools export region as files. This function creates new media from sub-clips in the region bin

This will open the Export Selected window. From here, you can export the regions in their original format, change them to a new sample rate or format and even pull up or pull down, as can be seen in Figure 3.9. You will likely want to keep your audio in its original format, but you may need to pull down. In the sample rate menu, you will find several sample rates as well as sample rates for pulling up and down. There are even sample rates here for changing 29.97 FPS NTSC to 25 FPS PAL. The sample rate you will use to pull down to match telecined film is 47,952. This will slow your audio by the needed .1 percent.

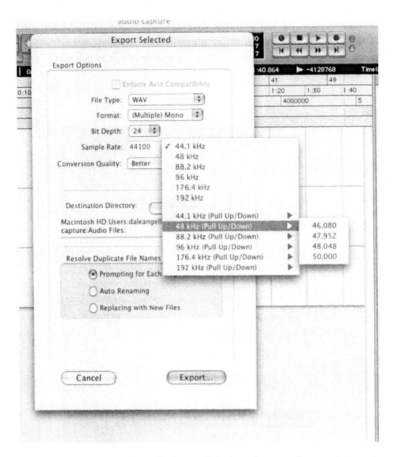

Figure 3.7   Export selected as files with pull down. This function can be used to make new media files that play at a new speed for pull up/down or convert to 25 FPS PAL

Be careful not to pull down audio that has already been pulled down. If the sample rate in production was 48,048, simply capturing into a session at 48,000 has already pulled it down.

The same is true of audio imported directly from drive or optical disc. If it was recorded at 48,048, it is pulled down when it is imported into Final Cut Pro with the audio sample rate at 48 K. If the imported audio was recorded at 48 K, and needs to be pulled down, this can be done the same way as the tape captured in Pro Tools. In this case, the audio is imported into Pro Tools with the Import Audio menu item. Depending on which version of Pro Tools you are using, you will find this in the Audio Region pop-up menu (the gray bar at the top of the regions list in version six) or in the File menu (import Audio to Region List in version seven). Make sure that the Pro Tools session settings match the audio format of the production audio otherwise it will be transcoded into the current settings.

With all of the regions selected in the Region List, open > Export Regions as Files from the Audio Region pop-up menu.

Just as with captured tape, you will want to set the sample rate to 47,952 in the 48 K pull up/down settings of the sample rate setting. This will slow your exported audio by the needed .1 percent. Be careful to export your new audio to a new folder, as shown in Figure 3.8, rather than the folder containing the original audio, otherwise the new files will overwrite the original files.

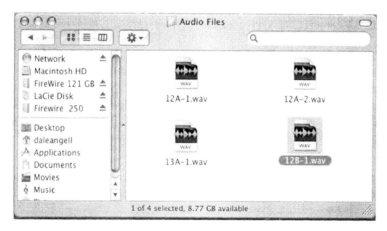

Figure 3.8 Audio files

Syncing in Final Cut Pro

If syncing was done in telecine, then there is no need to sync in editing. Some projects are sunc after the telecine. Either workflow works well. Many people like syncing their own dailies to save telecine time and cost and to make sure it's done well. As we saw in the telecine section in Chapter 1, problems often come up. Moreover, when syncing in telecine, the process may be rushed. Careful attention to detail by syncing after telecine may prevent problems later.

You will sync to the clapper. With all the audio imported and video captured in the browser, open each clip in the viewer one at a time by double clicking on it. On picture takes, look for the first frame where the slate sticks are fully closed. If there is motion blur, this is fine, as long as you see the sticks closed. If this is a slate at the head of the shot (head sticks) set an in point. If it is at the tail (tail sticks) set an out point. Move on to the next clip and continue with the rest of the clips. On audio takes, listen for the sound of the sticks and set an in point for head sticks or out point for tail sticks.

Now, pair the audio and video takes. Select the video take by clicking on it and then add the audio take by clicking on it while holding down the command key. With both clips selected, and only the two clips, go to Modify > Merge clip. Select the appropriate box, in point for head sticks, out point for tail sticks, and click "OK." This creates a merged clip in the browser window with a (dot) merged name. You will edit these clips. The original audio and video can be placed in a bin for future reference. However, it's likely you will not need them again.

If you need to manage an audio EDL, you can open the Cinema Tools database and enter the audio time code into the audio time code area of the database. (For information on audio EDLs, see Chapter 7 on sound edit workflows.) You will also want to reexport a batch list into Excel or a Word program to include the audio time code into the cut list.

If the time code matches between the audio and video, for example if you shot digital video with the time code generator in sync with the audio recorder, then you can proceed to the merge clip function and merge via time code. It is not possible to set a time code offset in the merge clip function, so the time code would need to match exactly.

Initial Audio Workflow on *Lost Hope and More*, *Success*, and *Son*

Much of the initial audio workflow on *Lost Hope and More* had been handled in telecine. All of the production DAT tapes were transferred to DA88 tape. Because the film was shot at 24 FPS, telecined to 29.97, and the edit was planned for 23.98, the audio needed to be pulled down. However, because the production DAT was recorded at 48,048 sample rate, the 48,000 Hz transfer to DA88 pulled the audio down. The production audio could have also been recorded at 48,000 sample rate and the pull down preformed on the DA88.

The "ser" or series shots that were telecined without sound needed to be sunc. Other production audio could be useful in the sound edit so all DAT tapes were recorded into Pro Tools. Then, the needed shots were exported as audio clips. The workflow steps were:

Figure 3.9 *Lost Hope and More* poster

- All DAT production audio was recorded tape-by-tape into Pro Tools.

- Shots that were not sunc in telecine were split off from the Pro Tools master clips of the DAT tapes.

- Because the DAT tapes were recorded at 48,048 Hz, no pull down was necessary. Subclips were exported from Pro Tools at 48,000 Hz.

- These audio clips were imported into the Final Cut Pro project.

- The audio clips had their clapper sound marked with an in point.

- The corresponding video shots were marked with an in point on sticks close.

- The shots were paired and merged with the merge clip function.

On *Success* and *Son*, audio was recorded on a Nagra 4.2. This analog audio was captured into Final Cut Pro by transferring all of the one-quarter-inch tape to DV Cam tape. This allowed for direct capture and provided a time code reference for the audio. The transfer to DV Cam was critical as this would be the final audio; however, the one-quarter inch was still available for recapture when necessary. The audio was sunc to the clapper sticks using the merge clip function.

All three projects used a form of soft lock, yet there were no sync issues with any of the three. Even the transfers for *Son* and *Success* were soft locked, which is defiantly not best practice, yet here too there were no sync problems. Many practices that are routinely used in production and syncing are unique to production and syncing and should not be used for final output. Understanding the type of recorder and sync system will help maintain a smooth cost-effective workflow in postproduction.

4 Editing Picture to Lock

Beginning the Edit

On larger projects, the edit can and should begin as soon as there are dailies sunc and organized into bins. New footage can be integrated into the edit as it becomes available. Different editors have different ways of working, but for the most part, editors like to "string out" the footage, bringing all of the best takes into the edit more or less in order. This very long edit is tightened over and over, bringing the scene and the entire project into a shorter and better-developed edit with each tightening.

It's entirely possible to have a very basic edit ready by the end of production. This is one reason why most large projects employ several assistant editors. It is usually their job to sync, log, manage the database and edit log, and even string out scenes.

Because this is such a common workflow, the Final Cut and Cinema Tools are designed to import new footage as it becomes available without scrambling the database. New logs and data when imported are added in seamlessly.

Adding Film Dailies to the Picture Edit

The picture edit can and should start the minute there are sunc dailies. New footage will be arriving daily and must be integrated into the project without disrupting the editing process.

When working from telecined film, the process is straightforward. Open the Cinema Tools database for the project and import the new telecine log(s). Export a new Final Cut Pro batch list. Open the Final Cut Pro project and import the new batch list. You may need to set the sequence settings in audio/video settings to your format at the standard 29.97 FPS so that the batch list will import at 29.97. The new shots will be sorted into the project off-line without affecting the original footage. Batch capture all off-line clips. Return to Cinema Tools and connect the new clips with the Connect Clips command in the Database menu.

If you are editing at 23.98 or 24 FPS, you can batch reverse telecine just as you did with the original footage. Return to Final Cut Pro. Just as with the original footage, the new reversed clips are now off-line. Connect all off-line clips to the new reversed clips.

Just as before, the Batch List can also be opened in a text editor or Excel spreadsheet. The new shots can be copied and pasted into the original text or Excel editing log without disturbing the original editing log and editing notes.

Adding Digital Dailies to the Picture Edit

In many cases, new digital shots can be simply logged and captured in the Final Cut Pro project. This would be true of projects edited at 29.97 FPS and 24P projects shot in 24 PA with 2:3:3:2 removal set in capture. It will also work for projects capturing and editing at 23.98 or 24 FPS using photo JPEG. An alternate workflow should be followed for:

- 24 FPS and 23.98 FPS HD Cam and D5 projects that are capturing from 29.97 FPS "clones" or "down converts"

- 24P projects being edited in 23.98 or 24 FPS needing reversal in Cinema Tools

- Projects maintaining an editing log in a text program or Excel

- Projects maintaining a Cinema Tools database

While these projects need to follow this alternate workflow, any project can follow this workflow if it is more convenient.

In this case, a new 29.97 FPS project is started for each set of dailies. The shots are logged in this project, but not captured. A Final Cut Pro batch list is exported.

Projects not maintaining a database or batch reversing in Cinema Tools can import the batch list directly into the editing project. The batch list is imported into the actual editing Final Cut Pro project. If you are editing at 23.98 or 24 FPS, you may need to set the sequence settings to your video format at 29.97 FPS (i.e., DV NTSC 48 KHz). This will allow the batch list to be imported at 29.97. You will need to set the sequence settings back before creating any new sequences at 23.98 or 24 FPS. You can now capture all off-line clips with batch capture.

For projects using Cinema Tools for reversing telecine and maintaining a database, the batch list is imported into the Cinema Tools database. A new Final Cut Pro batch list is exported from Cinema Tools and imported into the Final Cut Pro editing project at 29.97 FPS.

Just as with the original footage, the off-line clips can now be batch captured. The clips are now connected to the off-line clips in cinema tools and batch reversed. Back in Final Cut Pro, the new 23.98 or 24 FPS are linked to the now off-line clips in the editing project. (For more detail, see Chapter 2 on shooting 24P.)

Problems in Timeline Editing

Many editors like to use an editing technique known as vertical timeline editing. Several video tracks are used to place shots one on top of the other. Only the highest video clip in the timeline plays on the monitor. In this way, the shots can be easily moved around and arranged making changes simple and fast. This editing technique is quite problematic when exporting cut lists, EDLs, XMLs, and projects for online finishing. The multiple, overlaid video tracks are seen as superimpositions or, in some cases, not seen at all.

Cinema Tools looks only to the lowest two video tracks, V1 and V2. It sees anything in V1 as the actual edit and anything in V2 as an overlay or superimposition. All other video tracks are simply ignored. Some editors even use V3 for keeping notes with the title generator, knowing they will not end up in the Cinema Tools cut list. Online editing will reproduce the multiple video tracks, a waste of time, and a source of problems in the online.

The timeline therefore needs to be collapsed down to only one video track for the actual edit and one track for superimpositions or overlays on finishes involving cutting the camera negative. And the timeline needs to be collapsed down one video track containing the actual edit and the minimum number of video tracks to create any actual overlays and superimpositions on projects for online video editing.

On all but one type of workflow, this collapse can be done near the end of the edit as the picture is nearing picture lock or even after picture lock. The one exception is projects where the camera negative will be cut and printed. In this case, care must be taken not to use any footage more than once in the edit unless absolutely necessary. On these projects, the editor should check periodically for double uses, and this will require editing the project in V1 and V2.

The double-use report is created by exporting it from Final Cut Pro. In the edit menu export a Cinema Tools cut list. In "include the following," it is not necessary to select anything, but make sure that Duplicates is set to "warn." Also, save a Cinema Tools program file whenever exporting a film list. It can be used to make a change list. Final Cut Pro will ask for the Cinema Tools database, and then the report will open in text edit. Any double uses will be seen at the head of the report as a warning of double use. The warning also gives the time code and edge code location of the double uses. (For more information, see Chapter 5 on finishing on film.)

Changes After the Edit Is Locked

Once the edit is locked, many other processes and edits start. Depending on the project, the sound edit begins, the score may be written, work print or negative may be cut, or the online edit goes forward. It is assumed that the edit will not be changed, that it is locked. Yet it may be necessary to make some changes. This should never be the plan; changes after the edit is locked create a major problem for everyone working on the project.

When changes are made after the edit is locked, everyone on the project needs to be informed of the exact changes. This is done with a "change memo" or "change list." This contains the exact location and nature of the change. This way, sound elements can be moved up or down or even extended. Often the changes are very small, even one of two frames. They may be caused by errors in the negative edit or other problems found when the negative is examined. They may be larger changes to improve the edit or remove some unwanted footage. The change may even add a new shot into the edit. New QuickTime movies or videotape copies of the edit also need to be distributed to everyone working on the project.

Cinema Tools can export a change report referenced to the edge code information. This way, any work print conformed to the cut list can be recut to match the changes. Changing the negative cut is also possible, but may result in even more changes due to lost frames.

To create a Cinema Tools change report:

- In Final Cut Pro, select the new version of the edit.

- From the file menu, select export, Cinema Tools Change List.

- When the dialogue box opens, select the Cinema Tools program (pgm.) file that you saved with the cut list for the previous version.

- In the change list window, configure any settings and select any or all of the four options for change lists.

- The list can also include any of the standard Cinema Tools lists normally exported with an "export film list" command.

Change lists are only supported in 4 perf 35 mm referenced to the exact same Cinema Tools database. If you add any dailies, this will throw the change list off. If you are adding any new footage, reexport the original film list referenced to the new database containing the new footage before opening the changed version and exporting the change list. This change list can be used in Pro Tools to automatically change the sound edit to match the changed picture. (For more on this, see Chapter 7 on sound edit workflows.)

Editing *Lost Hope and More* to a Locked Cut

All of the shots were arranged into various bins and several sequences were created at 23.98 in the Final Cut Pro project. Different scenes were assembled in these sequences and slowly tightened toward a first edit. Early in this process, various pieces of temp music were imported from audio CD and used to help find the pace and feel of the scenes.

From the earliest edits, there were strong disagreements between the editor, the directors, and the producers. Often, the creative process is one of disagreement. At times, this disagreement becomes a matter of ego, and this can be totally destructive to the process and the end result. Often the disagreement is one of opinion on the best interest of the project. In the case of *Lost Hope and More*, there was a bit of both. But, in the end, everyone truly wanted to see the best film on the screen, no matter how that came into being.

This raises an important workflow issue: Who will be directing the edit and what will be his or her needs at different points as the edit goes forward? There may be a director's cut, then the project may be turned over the producer, the distributor, the network, and any of these people may be in the decision loop along the way. They may want test screenings, changes, new titles, new sound mixes, or even new footage.

While the outright wars among these people are part of Hollywood legend, and many films have been said to be ruined by the process, most of the time, the process works fine. Everyone stays amicable and focused on making the best possible film.

Figure 4.1 *Lost Hope and More* poster

Several screenings with mentors, faculty, and students gave everyone a chance to voice their opinions and come to agreement. The project received several major changes after the edit was locked, but everyone was in agreement that the changes were a significant improvement. Fortunately, the "problem" was great coverage. There were so many ways to edit the film that several good edits were always available.

Lost Hope and More was edited in several video tracks and needed to be shuffled into V1 only so that film cut lists could be exported. Several double uses turned up the first time this was done, but these were easily reedited to solve the problem.

Much of what is done in the initial phases of the workflow are intended to make the actual edit as smooth and trouble free as possible to insure the best possible, creative edit. It is also increases speed and accuracy, important when large amounts of money are being spent. Start the edit workflow as soon as the dailies are sunc, and try to end additions and changes once the edit is locked.

5 Finishing on Film

Film Editing Basics

Historically, films were edited on, you guessed it, film. The workflow went like this: The original negative was printed to a "work print." Sound was transferred to magnetic sound film (or pre-1950, optical sound film). This is simply clear film with an oxide coating allowing magnetic sound to be recorded, also known as "full coat" or "mag stripe." It is still available, although not used all that much. The sound film was cut, spliced, and matched to the clapper on the work print, putting the sound into sync with the picture. The work print reels were then projected interlocked to the sound reels at the "dailies" screening.

The work print and sound were then splice edited on a machine that looked like a green sewing machine, the ubiquitous Movieola upright. Later, these were replaced by "flatbed" editing machines that ran the film and sound horizontally on a tabletop.

After the film edit was completed or "locked," sound effects and music were edited on sound film, interlocked to the work print or a "dirty dupe" of the work print. These sound tracks were all interlocked together and mixed down to a final sound track. This was shot onto optical film for printing with the picture.

The camera negative was edited to match the edited work print in a process called "conforming." This was accomplished by matching "key code" numbers located on the edge of the film. These numbers were flashed on the edge of the film by the manufacturer and became visible when the negative was processed. They printed through onto the work print and could be read from the edited work print and matched to the original negative.

The conformed negative was color timed and printed in combination with the sound mix to a "first answer print." More adjustments were made to the color and the film was finished. The entire process, however, was actually quite a bit more complicated than this; the demons were in the details.

Fundamentally, this is still the workflow used today only with different hardware. Movieolas, flatbeds, and full-coat sound film are pretty much museum pieces, but key code negative conforming, work prints, color timing, answer prints, optical sound, and interlocked projections are very much alive and well.

Brief Discussion of Film and Printing

Figure 5.1 shows how film consists of two major components: the clear plastic base and the emulsion. The base is made of very flat, very clear plastic, often of very durable polyester. Historically, the film base has been made of cellulose triacetate, which is made from wood fiber. This led to film being called "celluloid." Early film bases were made of cellulose nitrate, often called nitrocellulose. This is a very flammable and even explosive plastic used in blasting and as "smokeless" gunpowder. Before 1951, an accidental spark could reduce a theater's projection booth to charred ruin in minutes.

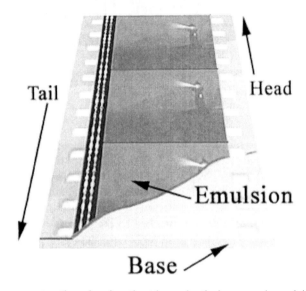

Figure 5.1   35 mm film cross section showing the clear plastic base and emulsion

The emulsion consists of light-sensitive, silver halides suspended in clear gelatin. This emulsion is spread evenly over one side of the base; color films have three such coatings, each sensitive to red, green, or blue. In the camera, the lens forms the image on the emulsion side of the film; if it were formed on the base side, the light would scatter through the base making the image soft. Because the camera lens inverts and flips the image, the developed image on the camera original is upside down and backwards when viewed from the emulsion side (through the emulsion). Film always travels down through the camera's gate, so the camera original, usually negative, will be right-side up and right reading when viewed through the base, the reel head up.

Figuring out which is the emulsion side of a piece of film is not always easy. On most negatives and prints, you can see the image "embossed" into the emulsion. After processing, some of the emulsion is stripped away in the lighter areas, giving a relief to the emulsion. The base is always smooth and shiny. Film with little or no image, like black or white leader, will be smooth and shiny on both sides. You can scrape away a small area; emulsion scrapes away easily whereas base is just tough clear plastic. Or, you can touch the film to your lower lip. The emulsion side will tend to stick whereas the base will not.

Prints, Film Wind, and Printers

Prints and Film Wind

There are several standard types of prints and with 16 mm, A- and B-wind prints. A and B wind is not the same as the A and B rolls, which are discussed later. They simply share a similar name. Wind prints are made off the reel from emulsion-up film (A) or emulsion-down film (B), as seen in Figure 5.2.

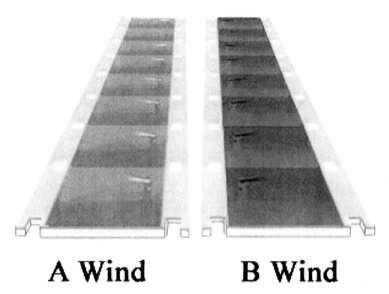

A Wind   B Wind

Figure 5.2   16 mm film negative and print. Because contact prints are made emulsion to emulsion, the image is reversed on each printing requiring the print to be flipped over placing the emulsion on the opposite side from the original. In this example the emulsion is up on both 16 mm strips of film. The B wind camera original negative on the right is wrong reading, the image is flipped. Because the contact print was made emulsion to emulsion, the A wind positive print on the left is right reading when viewed through the emulsion.

The common types of film and prints are:

- B-wind, camera-original negative: This is emulsion-down film as it spools off the reel. (There is also reversal direct projection camera film but it is rarely used anymore.)

- Work print: This is a noncolor-corrected positive print of the camera original used to screen dailies or for trial edits.

- Interpositive: This is a positive print of the camera negative used to reprint onto another film.

- Internegative: This is a print, usually of an interpositive, used to make release prints.

- Release print: This is a print for projection in a theater.

- Answer print: This is a print made directly off of the camera negative to check color correction.

Unless you are blowing up 16 mm to 35 mm or doing an optical effect, your negative will be contact printed. The contact printer holds the emulsion side of the negative tightly against the emulsion side of the print stock, and then passes light through the negative, exposing the print. Camera-original film is always B wind. Because all camera original is B wind, B-wind film will always be right-reading when viewed through the base, and backwards when viewed through the emulsion. Contact printing is always done emulsion-to-emulsion because if the film is printed though the base, the image will be soft. Therefore, the emulsion position of the print is always opposite the emulsion position of the film being printed. The "wind" of the film changes from B to A or A to B with each printing.

"A" and "B" terminology is not used in 35 mm; however, the emulsion position still changes with each printing. There are rigid standards for 35 mm printing. All negatives, both original and duplicate, are right-reading when viewed through the base. All 35 mm positives, including release prints, are right-reading when viewed through the emulsion.

Not so with 16 mm. A 16 mm projection print can be either A or B wind. It is necessary for all footage used in the print rolls to be B wind. If you contact printed any footage, often done with titles and effects, you need to make sure they are B wind and match your camera negative. This is usually not a problem as titles and effects are generally printed twice, once to an A-wind interpositive, and back again to a B-wind internegative.

Optical Printers

Film can also be optically printed. The optical printer, such as the one in Figure 5.3, is essentially a projector and a camera set up in such a way as to allow the camera to photograph the image in the

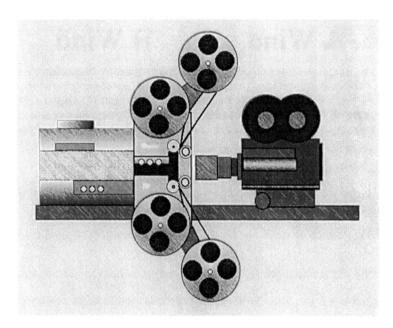

Figure 5.3 On the optical printer, film can be printed without reversing the position of the emulsion by printing through the clear plastic base. The optical printer can also re-compose the shot, blow-up 16 mm to 35 mm and make fades and dissolves. At one time the optical printer was also used to make complex visual effects, however digital effects have mostly replaced this use of the optical printer

gate of the projector. The projector is equipped with a three-color print head for making color adjustments. It also has twin feed reels and take-up reels, allowing two rolls of negative to be bi-packed at the gate, the film closest to the camera blocking areas of the rear film.

In optical printing, it is possible to print the picture in either A or B wind. By simply flipping the original in the gate of the printer's "projector," the emulsion position or the image can be flopped. When ordering 16 mm prints and effects to be made optically, you must specify the wind you want, either A or B.

More complex optical printers use "aerial" image, allowing the camera to be many feet from the projector. Second and even third projector heads can be added making it possible for many images to be composted together. As the goal is to produce a negative that can be cut in with the camera original, the film must be printed twice, once to an interpositive and then back to negative. So, while it's possible to print directly from the camera negative on the optical printer producing an interpositive, normally an interpositive (IP) is contact printed first and then printed back to negative on the optical printer. The two-step process is necessary anyway, and because the film is handled less, this helps protect the camera negative.

The optical printer can be used to create complicated, composted special effects as well as simple dissolves and fades. It can reposition the image, flip or flop the image, speed up or slow down the shot, soften the focus, blow up 16 mm to 35 mm, and reduce 35 mm to 16 mm. Many of the complex special-effects uses for the optical printer are now normally preformed digitally, but the optical printer is still widely used for simple effects, fades and dissolves, as well as titling and blowups.

Modern optical printers are computer controlled and cannot only create some great effects, they can be used to assemble and color correct an entire motion picture. This workflow, called "analog intermediate" or AI, can be used almost exactly like digital intermediate. The cut list is programmed into the optical printer and interpositive prints of the camera original are printed to a complete, color-corrected internegative ready to make release prints.

Some printers are equipped with a "liquid gate." The liquid gate printer is a contact or optical printer equipped with a system to coat the film to be printed with a coating of oil. The oil covers scratches and fills grain. It also gives the image a "soft" quality. It is often used when blowing up 16 mm to 35 mm. The grain of the 16 mm can be rather intense when blown up to 35 mm. While many people like the look of the liquid, or wet, gate print, others feel it overly softens the image. For some projects it may be the perfect look, for others it may be totally wrong.

Key Code on Film

During the telecine, bar codes imprinted on the film negative are read as a function of the telecine process. These bar codes are a machine-readable version of the key code numbers also on the edge of the negative. These numbers and bar codes are flashed onto the film during manufacture and become visible after the film is processed. They work in the exact same way as time code, and they contain other information as well, such as the manufacturer of the film and the type of stock.

The key code numbers, as shown in Figure 5.4, occur every foot on 35 mm film and every six inches on 16 mm film. A key code number may read something like this: KW80 7659 6497. In this case, the K designates a Kodak film, the W80 is the type of stock, and the rest of the number is simply a map to

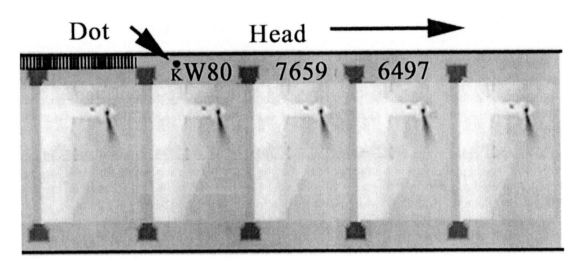

Figure 5.4   16 mm film negative with keycode number. The keycode number is also printed as a machine readable barcode. The small dot designates the actual frame represented by this keycode

find this frame. The numbers are printed onto the film sequentially starting at zeros and eventually repeat. The chances of getting two rolls with the same numbers are slim, but it can happen. There is also a small dot somewhere in the code. Because the number can be quite long, this is meant to mark the exact frame for this edge code. There is also a machine-readable bar code with this same information.

Every frame can be identified even if it does not have a corresponding key code by counting the number of frames back to the last key code number and adding this as a + number. Moreover, as the film is telecined, the pull down pattern discussed earlier is imprinted as a function of the edge code. This is called the pull-down cycle identifier. So, the key code in a telecine log may read like this: KL 25 8654 5438 +12C1. This code indicates that, if we rolled down into the film negative until we reached KL 25 8654 5438 and looked for the small dot, then counted twelve frames past that, this is the exact frame that was recorded on the videotape at that point, and it was the first field of a C-frame in the pull-down pattern. Assuming the telecine was done correctly, it was copied into the first field of a frame with time code ending in 3 or 8. If the negative has been work-printed, the numbers are visible on the print.

Reel Length

Depending on the length of your film, you will need to split it up into reels. If you show up at the lab with a 10,000-foot roll of negative and want it printed, there will be a problem. You need to cut the 35 mm film into sections not more than 2,000 feet long. As we are working with time code, that is not more than 22.2 minutes. The lab also needs to thread the printer, leaders, and whatnot, so keep your reels 21 minutes or fewer. If you are planning to cut 16 mm negative and blow up optically to 35 mm, the reel length is 850 feet of 16 mm, or still 21 minutes. Many people divide into 1,000 feet rolls, this was the standard before computer editing, either works.

It is best to end reels at scene changes. There may be color changes at the reel change and the sound will shift as well. Under no circumstances should a music cue cross the reel change. Even if the reel comes up short to avoid the reel change, this is better than a reel change in the middle of a scene.

Some people think that with platter projection systems and digital intermediate, this is no longer a problem. But, such is not the case. If you place a reel change in a scene, you will see it and hear it.

If you are finishing on 16mm, the reel length is 1,200 feet or 33 minutes with leaders or 31 minutes of program.

Exporting Cut Lists

To export a cut list in Final Cut Pro, go to File > export > Cinema Tools film List (see Figure 5.5). Click OK and Final Cut asks for the Cinema Tools database. Direct it to your database. Cinema Tools links only to V1 in the timeline. It sees V2 as a superimpose effect, and it ignores all other video tracks. So, keep your shots in V1 only. If you are doing opticals or A/B-roll conforming, you can place any superimpose or effects footage in V2. As they are totally ignored, you can make notes to yourself using the title generator in V3 or 4.

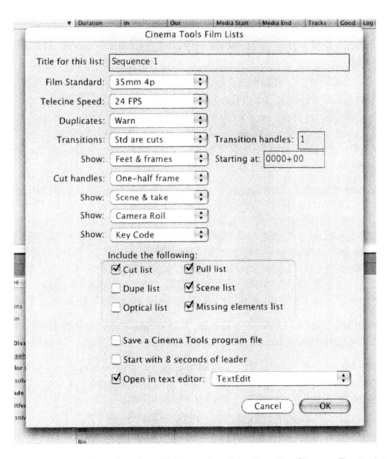

Figure 5.5 Export film lists in Final Cut Pro. This can be linked to the Cinema Tools database and film lists exported for conforming negative or workprint to the edit

Film standard and speed need to match the shooting format. Warn Duplicates warns of double use before exporting any lists. Transitions that should be All are cuts for conforming work print; Std are cuts for A/B negative rolls and All are opticals for single-roll negative assembly or digital intermediate. (For more information on A/B rolling, see Appendix 8 on editing film and conforming negative.) Cut handles will normally be one-half frame for 35 mm and one and one-half for 16 mm and longer lengths for zero cuts. Transition handles are normally two frames. However, check with your lab and negative editor on these settings. Different labs have different needs. (For more information on this, see Appendix 8 on editing film and conforming negative.)

If you are planning to cut the negative (rather than scanning for digital intermediate), you cannot use the same footage twice in the edit without duping that footage optically. And that is expensive. Better to not use the same footage twice unless you need to and can afford to. We often do this when editing video without even noticing it. But when cutting negative, not only can you only use the footage once, you need at least a frame between the shots for the splice.

Final Cut Pro can warn us when we reuse footage. Go to File > export > Cinema Tools film List. Select only Dupe List in the "Include the following" box and make sure the default Duplicates > Warn is selected. Make sure the rest matches your project. Click OK and Final Cut asks for the Cinema Tools database. Direct it to your database. A cut list now opens in TextEdit with a warning box showing any frames used in more than one place. Check often as you edit.

Titles can be laid into the edit as Final Cut titles, but because they are only digital elements in the project, they will come up on the missing elements list. The real titles need to be shot on film. Usually, these are shot at a title house. They are rarely telecined or printed. They are simply cut in where the titles go in the negative using the missing elements list as a guide. It's important that the Final Cut titles and the film titles are the same length. The title length becomes part of the Cut List in spite of having no footage to link. (See Chapter 8 on titling.)

All of the film lists are exported the same way as checking for dupes. Go to File > Export > Cinema Tools Film Lists. This time, include everything: the Cut List, the Dupe List, Optical List, Pull List, Scene List, and Missing Elements List. You will need a program file if you need to make a change list later, and as you have cut a digital countdown leader in, it will show in the missing elements list, so don't check 8-second countdown. Do check Open in TextEdit. If you are doing opticals, select All are opticals in Transitions. If you are AB rolling, select Std. are cuts. (For more information on AB rolling, see Appendix 8 on conforming film.) Talk to your negative cutter and make sure this works for him or her. If you get a dupe warning, you need to fix the problem. Then do this again.

The cut list opens in Rich Text Format. To change this to plain text, select Shift + Command + T or Format > Make plain text. Plain text works much better for these lists.

Check each shot on the edit to the cut list. The key code numbers should match at the burn window at the head and tail of every shot. If there is a problem, find it now not later. The numbers on the screen are correct, so if there is a problem, it is in the cut list.

Figure 5.6 shows a portion of the Cinema Tools films list.

- The first section of the list is information about the project.

- The second section is the double use list.

Figure 5.6 The information and double use list

There should nothing in the second section unless you are planning to dupe these. In Figure 5.6, there are no double uses. If you have double uses, you will need to find a way to recut the scene(s), removing the double use. This comes up often. Editors cutting on a digital system often reuse footage without ever being aware of it. In some cases, the footage will not be reused, but will be used into the cut handle. Remember, at least one frame is lost at each end of the shot even when using one-half frame cut handles, and so that frame cannot be used in either shot. It may happen that a double use is reported when there is not double use. This could be because two rolls of camera negative have the same key code numbers. The odds are more than a million to one, but it could happen. More likely, it is an erroneous key code number misread in telecine. This is an easy fix; check out the workflow for *Lost Hope and More* in Appendix 8.

The cut list, shown in Figure 5.7, is the next section of the Cinema Tools film list.

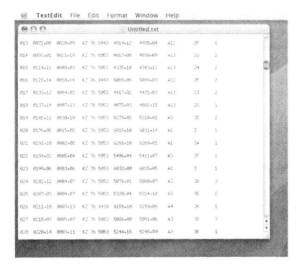

Figure 5.7 The cut list

- This next section, the cut list, is the show, in order, from starting key code to ending. It includes the duration, cam roll, scene, and take.

- The missing elements list includes the leaders, titles, anything not in the database but in the timeline. It shows the accurate length for the titles.

- The dupe list is the frames that have been double used and can be duped optically if you need to reuse them.

Figure 5.8 is the pull list portion of the Cinema Tools film list.

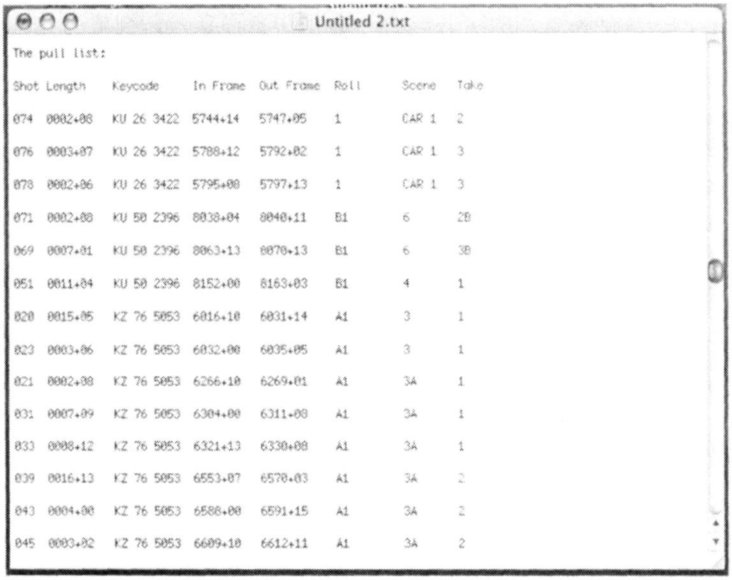

The pull list:

Shot	Length	Keycode	In Frame	Out Frame	Roll	Scene	Take
074	0002+08	KU 26 3422	5744+14	5747+05	1	CAR 1	2
076	0003+07	KU 26 3422	5788+12	5792+02	1	CAR 1	3
078	0002+06	KU 26 3422	5795+08	5797+13	1	CAR 1	3
071	0002+08	KU 50 2396	8038+04	8040+11	B1	6	29
069	0007+01	KU 50 2396	8063+13	8070+13	B1	6	38
051	0011+04	KU 50 2396	8152+00	8163+03	B1	4	1
020	0015+05	KZ 76 5053	6016+10	6031+14	A1	3	1
023	0003+06	KZ 76 5053	6032+00	6035+05	A1	3	1
021	0002+08	KZ 76 5053	6266+10	6269+01	A1	3A	1
031	0007+09	KZ 76 5053	6304+00	6311+08	A1	3A	1
033	0008+12	KZ 76 5053	6321+13	6330+08	A1	3A	1
039	0016+13	KZ 76 5053	6553+07	6570+03	A1	3A	2
043	0004+00	KZ 76 5053	6588+00	6591+15	A1	3A	2
045	0003+02	KZ 76 5053	6609+10	6612+11	A1	3A	2

Figure 5.8 The pull list

- The pull list is used to pull the shots from the camera rolls or lab rolls.

- The scene list is the same information listed by scene.

The optical list shows the key codes for the transitions and other opticals. It even shows some elaborate maps of how the opticals go together. The first optical in Figure 5.9 is a fade in. The second optical is a fade in and out. The optical scene list is a list of all the footage that will need to be pulled and sent to the optical house.

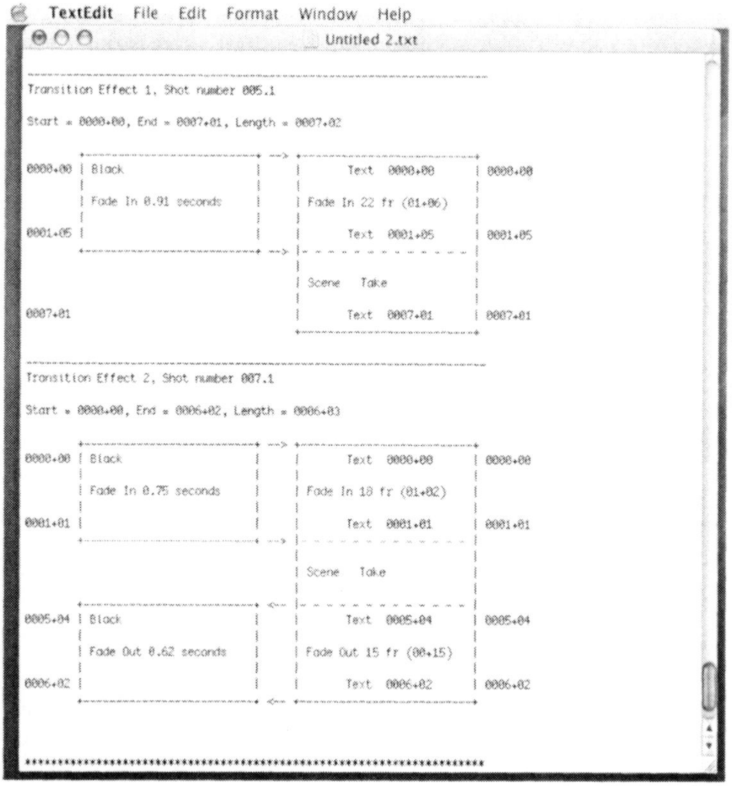

Figure 5.9 The optical list

If you have any superimpositions in V2, these will show up in a foreground cut list. These are easy in AB rolling and can be done optically, too.

Many other effects used often in Final Cut Pro can be optically printed and used in the film. But the database may not enter them into the cut list or understand them. They may come up as blank or missing. They can still be done, only you will need to communicate with the optical house and they can tell you how it's done and make the shot. Save and print the list. Don't be too intimidated by the optical list. Between your videotape, optical list, dupe, and cut list, the optical house will know how to handle the opticals.

Pulling and Conforming Work Print

Not all film finishes conform a work print; many don't even make a work print. It's entirely possible to simply deliver the film lists to the negative editor and have them conform the negative. Many editors don't feel comfortable doing this; if there is a problem in the cut list or if they don't like the edit once they see it projected on the big screen, it's difficult to make changes. The negative has been cut and spliced and can't simply be put back together.

Some of the problems that may be seen in a projected print that were not noticed in the digital edit can be small focus problems or scratches and hair on the negative. And some editors just don't like making final decisions from the digital edit; they want to see the actual film projected on a large screen. For this reason, some editors prefer to conform the work print before locking the cut. In this workflow, the work print is conformed, the sound edit is temp-mixed to magnetic film or DA88 and interlocked with the work print. Final editing decisions are made by editing the Final Cut Pro edit and then exporting a change list. The work print is recut to the change list and projected. This continues until the edit is locked. When following this workflow, having inked edge code numbers on the work print can speed the final changes.

Most projects will lock the edit before conforming the work print, making changes only if they are necessary.

Pulling and conforming the work print is fairly straightforward and usually performed by the assistant editor. The work print rolls may be assembled into lab rolls, selects rolls, or even camera rolls. These rolls should match the Cinema Tools database.

A special set of lists should be exported just for the work print edit. Work print needs no cut handles; however, there is no zero setting. Set this to one-half frame knowing that the list will show the number of the frame before the shot at the head and the frame after the last frame at the tail.

Set transitions to all are cuts with 0 handles. All overlapping effects such as wipes and dissolves will either be optically printed or printed by overlapping the negative on two rolls. The work print will not have any of these transitions; they will be represented with a simple splice in the center of the effect. Double check all of these transitions on the cut list to make sure you have not inadvertently cut all of the overlapping footage into the work print edit.

Work print also has no fades, only cuts. These effects are simply marked on the work print with a grease pencil. For a complete list of these marks and description of the negative cut and printing process, see Appendix 8 on conforming negatives.

The Cinema Tools pull list will guide you to the shots to pull. The shots are listed in the order they occur on the lab rolls. The pull list also shows what shot number they are in the program. The shots are marked with a grease pencil and cut out of the roll with a tape splicer. They are hung in a film bin on a numbered hook corresponding with their position in the edit. The lab roll is taped back together and the editor rolls down to the next shot.

When all the shots are pulled, they are assembled into the edit. This will match the cut list, and although all of the shots should simply be spliced together in the order they are hanging in the bin, double check against the cut list as you go.

If a mistake happens, it is a simple matter to either cut out the extra footage or wrong shot edited into the assembly, or pull the extra footage missing from the assembly. Because only tape splices are used, which are easy to take apart and put back together, and no footage is lost by cutting and splicing, changes are simple and fast.

If you need to "reel balance," which is to say, move scenes from one reel to another to achieve the proper length after the film is locked, this should be done after all other changes (if any) are done to the locked cut. Then, move the scene or scenes from one reel to the other and export a change list. Conform the work print to the change list by moving the scene on the work print.

You can also do an interlocked screening of the work print. You will need a temp dub of the sound edit. Transfer this to either magnetic film or DA88 digital tape. If you are editing at 23.98 FPS, you will need to pull up the temp mix to the 24 FPS film speed of the projection. (For more information on this, see Chapter 7 on the sound edit.) You can take the project to an interlock screening room and watch the movie. Look for sync problems. The final sound edit and sound dub will be made to a telecine of the work print.

While conforming the negative, the edited work print can be placed in the synchronizer with the negative ensuring that the negative cut is correct. There can still be problems working this way: a splice can break, a number be misread, any number of things. But, this is your best shot at avoiding mistakes. Conforming work print costs time and money and, if everything is correct, it is totally unnecessary. However it can prevent major problems if there is a mistake. Many projects go both ways; you choose.

Cutting the Negative

Normally, a professional cuts negative. Much is at risk; a mistake can ruin a shot. If you have made an expensive motion picture, it's not likely you will want to risk the negative to save a few thousand dollars. However, if you are working on a shoestring, you may have no choice. Or, you may want to involve yourself in every aspect of making your film. If you are conforming your own negative to save money or simply to learn the process, it's probable that you are using more affordable 16 mm film. Appendix 8 shows how to conform 16 mm film.

Before the final dub, the negative needs to be checked against the tracks to confirm that the negative is correct and in sync to the sound edit. This is a critical step if you are cutting the original negative. Errors do happen, and if the negative is off a frame or two, there is little chance it can be fixed. Hopefully the problem is small and doesn't create a problem that shows, like a flash frame or a "dead" character opening their eyes. If the problem can't be seen, all that is needed is to resync the sound edit to the erroneous negative.

There are two ways to assemble the conformed negative. The most basic system is to simply splice the shots together with glue splices. There are several problems with this basic system. First, the splices can show. The glue splice reaches well into the frame and, on full-frame projection, the splice will show at the bottom of the frame on every cut. However, most 35 mm prints are projected at 1.185:1 or 1.66:1, and in these aspect ratios, the splice will not show. In full-frame 1.33:1, Cinema-Scope, and 16 mm, the splice will show. When cutting the negative, hiding the splice requires A-B roll conforming.

Also many effects such as fades, dissolves, and superimpositions can be done when A-B rolling. In straight cuts conforming, all effects must be optical, so that they can be cut directly into the negative rolls. For more information on A-B rolling, see Appendix 8, on editing film and conforming negative.

To check the negative you need to make the first print, or "first answer print." This will also be the first try at color correction. The first answer print always has color problems; it is simply a first attempt to answer questions about the color timing. As there has not yet been a mix, the print is made silent. This print is interlocked with a temp dub of the sound and projected. The temp dub is transferred to magnetic film or DA88 digital tape for this screening. It also needs to be pulled up to match the 24 FPS speed of the film projection. You also need a quick-and-dirty telecine of the silent answer print to check sync. The telecine of the answer print is captured in Final Cut Pro from the Picture Start frame. Because this telecine is at 29.97 FPS, it should match the sound edit that was cut to the 23.98 QuickTime or the 29.97 videotape that was used in the sound edit. For more information of these sound issues, see Chapter 7 on the sound edit.

Finally, import this movie into the Pro Tools session and set the frame rate in the Session Setup Window to 29.97. The sync should match. Always look at sync on the NTSC or video monitor, never the computer screen.

Anamorphic Film Finish

Anamorphic processes may have little impact on film finishing workflow, or they may have a significant impact. Anamorphic process can be accomplished by shooting in CinemaScope or "scope." In scope, anamorphic lenses are used on the camera in production. These are tricky to use and expensive, making this format often shunned. When a film is shot in CinemaScope, postproduction is affected, but it's not that much different than working with full-frame 35 mm.

Because the image is squeezed on the negative, it must be unsqueezed in telecine. Telecine can be done to 16×9, but even so, the image will be squeezed on the video monitor. Normally, scope is telecined at $2.35 : 1$ unsqueezed, letterboxed on 4×3 video.

A-B rolls must be used in negative conforming because the squeezed image is full frame. The A-B rolls are used to hide the splices.

The CinemaScope workflow is not all that problematic. But there is another anamorphic process often used. Super 35 mm is usually finished as an anamorphic print. Shooting super 35 mm is not all that much different than shooting standard 35 mm. The super 35 mm frame is a little wider than standard 35 mm, but the production lenses are not anamorphic, and so, production cinematography is no different than standard 35 mm. The only difference is that a $2.35 : 1$ ground glass is used in the camera viewfinder so that the operator sees a $2.35 : 1$ image in the viewfinder.

The big difference with super 35 mm is finishing. The wider negative is squeezed to anamorphic 35 mm in printing. After the negative is conformed, it is printed to an interpositive on an optical printer through an anamorphic lens. Much of the original image is masked off and never seen, but the print is now full frame. The interpositive is printed to several print internegatives to make release prints.

There is another system for making this interpositive: T and T effects' Analogue Intermediate or AI. As of this writing, this process is not widely known or used. This system is closer to digital intermediate, but it's totally photochemical optical printing. In AI, the Cinema Tools cut list is loaded into a computer controller on an optical printer. Raw, interpositive stock is loaded into the camera of the optical printer and lab rolls of negative are loaded one by one on the projector side. The automated system then rolls back and forth building the show from the cut list directly from the camera or lab rolls to the interpositive. Color correction is added in this optical printing, as are optical effects such as slowing or speeding up the image, reframing, title superimpositions, and anything else that can be done on the optical printer, including anamorphic image. It can also be used to blow up 16 mm or super 16 mm to 35 mm, all with no negative conforming or splicing required.

Finishing on Film with Digital Intermediate

Digital intermediate (DI) is the cutting edge of film finish workflow and advancements are evolving almost daily. For years, the computer has been cutting a path straight through the middle of motion picture workflow. With the exception of digital, the project has always been shot on film and finished by cutting and splicing the film to match the digital edit for printing and release. Digital intermediate finally breaks the workflow in half (see equipment in Figure 5.10). The camera negative is never even in the same room with the print.

Figure 5.10   The Lasergraphics Director Scanner is used to scan the camera negative to 2 K or 4 K DI

The usual workflow is only slightly removed from a negative film finish. After the film is cut and locked, the pull list is used to pull negative on all the shots used in the film. They are pulled from flash to flash and spliced together. They are not spliced in the construction order from the cut list, but are left in the order they were pulled. They can in fact be in any order as they will be conformed into the construction order digitally. Often, an interpositive is printed from the assembled camera footage for safety. Then the camera negative is scanned to digital files, conformed to the cut list, color corrected and formatted, effects and titles added and then shot back onto film negative. A second pass is made on this negative adding the sound tracks and this negative is used to make release prints.

There is another workflow where the negative is conformed and spliced just as with standard negative cutting. Transitions are also handled by printing them optically just as with non-A-B roll negative conforming. This cuts the cost of DI because there is no conforming of the DI files. However, now there is the cost of negative conforming and opticals. Also, there is a problem when splices are scanned: they "bump." The thickness of the splice holds the emulsion on the top half of the frame, away from the scanner, causing it to go out of focus. Because this is digital, it can be repaired in color correction. There is a function of DI known as "restoration," where damage to the negative can be repaired by copying parts of one frame onto another. This process makes removing the "bump" fairly easy, but it takes time, and as noted, in DI, time is definitely money. The real advantage of this workflow is that the negative can be scanned to DI or printed to film. The film can be finished to a print and then if the decision is made to go to DI, it can still be done.

This system has been used since 1989 when it was used in *The Abyss* to composite digital effects. It is still used this way in films where the negative will be cut. In these cases, DI is only used to composite the effects shots. The footage shot to film to be used as the foreground action or background plates is scanned. The film elements are combined in software, computer-generated images (CGI) such as 3D animation; particle effects and painted mats are also composted into the shots.

It wasn't until the Coen brother's film *O Brother, Where Art Thou?* in 2000 that the entire film was scanned to DI. In this case, it was done not to composite effects or add CGI effects, but for color correction and stylistic reasons.

Titles in Digital Intermediate

Titles can be made digitally and added to the DI in conforming. This is especially handy on films with "intertitles" over picture throughout the film. The titles can be color, 3D, hidden "watermarks," and lots of other options. Yet many projects still shoot end title crawls on film and scan the film. Digital title crawls are often more expensive than film titles, and they have a "digital look," which some filmmakers don't like. Digital crawls tend to do odd things as the words step over the pixel lines. Either rendering them at higher resolution and down sampling and/or special rendering processes to blend the edges can deal with this. However digital title crawls are expensive because of the tremendous computer rendering needed to create smooth movement on 2 K or 4 K titles.

Scanning to Digital Intermediate

16 mm and 35 mm, as well as some exotic formats of film, can be scanned to DI. The cost has been extremely high. The cost to scan a 90-minute film, historically, has topped $100,000, and recording back to film once costs twice that. But, competition and new technologies are causing these prices to plunge. Unfortunately, some of this cost reduction has been accomplished by compromising quality. Some argue that the compromises can't be seen, that the finished quality of the digital intermediate release print is still better than a traditional release print pulled from a photochemical internegative. However many "analog purists" disagree.

The most obvious compromise is in resolution. Resolution is quantified by the number of horizontal pixels; the average negative scan for digital intermediate is 2 K; that is to say, approximately 2,000 pixels wide (2,048 × 1,556 for full-frame 35 mm). The actual resolution of the 35 mm negative is closer to 6 K. It is not possible to put the full 6 K on the screen, however. Even a first-generation print will only be around 4 K. Before digital intermediate, shots for digital effects scenes were scanned at 4 K (4,096 × 3,112) on pin-registered scanners. Pin-registered scanners lock the negative in place with several pins before scanning. This ensures that no unwanted movement or jitter will be added in scanning. The process is slow, on the older scanners taking three to fifteen seconds to scan each frame. Scanning a feature film this way takes more than a week. It also generates massive uncompressed image files of 52 megabytes per frame requiring 7–8 terabytes of storage. Newer scanners are much faster, produce smaller files, and are, therefore, much more affordable.

In an effort to reduce the cost by speeding the process, datacine machines have been developed. Something of a hybrid between a scanner and a telecine machine, the datacine can "scan" in real time at 2 K, or on some even 4 K. And the newest Spirit Datacine scans at up to 30 FPS. Unlike scanners, most do not have "pin registration" but still produce a very steady image, yet small problems may show up in composite effects. When two film elements are overlaid, if they are moving around in opposite directions, even by a tiny amount, the movement appears doubled and looks very bad. For this reason, pin-registered scanners have always been used for effects compositing. However, new compositing software can remove any movement introduced by the datacine by digitally tracking any unwanted movement and removing it.

In telecine, most color correction is performed as the image is "scanned." Because video formats have a limited "color space," there is more control over the image while the film is on the telecine as you can control the print light and color. While there is a lot of control over HD Cam SR or D5, once the film is recorded to any video format, there is less control over the final look.

When using a scanner or datacine to record to 2 K or 4 K, it is digitized in either the Cineon or DPX (Digital Moving Picture exchange) format. These are either 8 or 10 bit, although 10 bit is normally used, and can have a fixed color space or use a look-up table. (See Appendix 1 on digital video formats.) So in these formats, it is possible to scan the entire film onto the drives, with all color and contrast information intact, and color correct later. In fact, the digital scan becomes a virtual full-frame negative, allowing formatting and additional color correction for video release, high-def broadcast, or standard broadcast. Also, because in most workflows, the entire shot is scanned flash to flash, even recutting is possible. And, as a 2 K DI of a feature film is under 2 terabytes, the entire film can be archived on removable drives. A 4 K feature is four times bigger, or about 7–8 terabytes.

Many of the systems used in the DI workflow cannot play 4 K in real time. The amount of data is huge, and any processing of the data takes time. So some systems will only work with 2 K files. However, the footage can still be scanned at 4 K. The 4 K is resampled down to 2 K, creating what is called "enhanced 2 K." While not looking as sharp as 4 K, it is much sharper than standard scanned 2 K. Keep in mind it is even more expensive than 4 K. It still requires a 4 K scan, plus, this needs to be resampled, requiring hours or even days of computer time. But now color correction and conforming can be done in less time and on more affordable systems.

With DI, there is a small loss of quality. Some subtle details in the shadow and highlights, which can be pulled in when scanning and color correcting directly off of the negative, are lost, however, the loss is small and the control and convenience, huge.

Conforming Digital Intermediate

Once the negative is scanned, most workflows require that the shots now be conformed to the cut list. At one time, this was a real problem. The older scanners didn't record the key code numbers for the film, and, so, matching the DI to the cut list had to be done by foot and frame. At the head of every roll, before any useable picture, a hole is punched. This becomes the zero footage point for the reel. In the original telecine, the time code laid to tape was matched to this hole punch, so the video time code and an exported EDL can be used to find the frame in the roll. This will only work if the lab roll is not cut between telecine and scanning for the DI.

In workflows where the pull list is used to pull the shots from the lab rolls, the shots are now in a totally different order. But as the new scanners read the key code numbers, this data can be used to match the DI to the cut list. The cut list is used to create a timeline and the DI scans are linked to that. Once conformed, the DI is ready for color correction.

Color Correction in Digital Intermediate

The DPX or Cineon image looks very bland. There has been no color or contrast correction and the scanned image is flat and dull. But almost the entire image from the negative is here, ready for color correction. The amount of control you have over the digital intermediate image is incredible. There is certainly nothing like it in film-to-film printing. Individual colors can be controlled and even replaced. Color correction can be applied to selected areas of the screen with "power windows." Many filmmakers feel that even though the DI process is a compromise, the control makes it worth it. Add to that the ability to add effects seamlessly and the advantages soon outweigh the compromises.

Once the DI is color corrected, it is ready to shoot back to film. The best film recorders scan the image back onto film one pixel at a time, one frame at a time, with three color lasers. Other systems are nothing more than a device for recording a high-definition video image onto the film.

Film Recording

Very fine-grained film, usually internegative film, is used in recorders such as the one in Figure 5.11. It is also possible to shoot to interpositive and then make an internegative off that interpositive. Often, the internegative will be damaged while printing at high speed, making thousands of release prints. Also, to speed the process, often several internegatives are made so that many prints can be printed at the same time. So, having an interpositive makes it possible to make scores of internegatives. But the release prints are one generation down and don't look as good as prints pulled directly from the film recorder internegative. Current internegative film is made of very strong polyester and with the cost of film recording coming down, the usual workflow now is to shoot to internegative. Big films that need thousands of prints also have big budgets and can afford to make as many internegatives in the digital film recorder as will be needed.

Figure 5.11 The Lasergraphics P2 Film recorder, used to shoot 2 K or 4 K DI back to 35 mm film

But, they may not have the time to do that. The cameras are slow, some taking as long as eight seconds to shoot a frame but, on average, take closer to two seconds. This still means that a single camera will take eighteen to thirty-six hours to output one 2,000-foot internegative. And there are five or six such rolls in a typical feature. But, the process is mostly unsupervised, and many facilities now have many cameras shooting at the same time.

Logic would say that if the film recorder is only recording the digital image, then why not just project the digital image? The principal reason film is being used for projection is because that's what theaters use. Some theaters have installed high-definition digital projectors, but these are generally 1080 HD systems, not 4 K. Kodak has developed a 4 K projection system that some would say is indistinguishable from film recorded from 4 K. HD digital "prints" are now available to theaters, as well as are 35 mm on some movies, and soon this may be the norm.

Virtual Film

With prices coming down, it is likely that, on large budget films, the circled take "dailies" will be soon be scanned to virtual negative 2 K and the camera negative never cut or printed. In fact, some films are already doing this.

This is definitely not a common workflow, but someday it may be the primary workflow. After the negative is processed, all circled takes are scanned and the negative is vaulted. If all goes well, the negative will never be touched again.

The 2 K is put in sync with the sound and the 2 K dailies screened at full resolution. The 2 K is down-sampled to something editable, perhaps photo JPEG, JPEG 2000, or MPEG4, and this is distributed to everyone in the postproduction chain via network. The edit project can also be moved around and even linked back to the 2 K whenever the editor wants to screen in full resolution.

This workflow is expensive, and full of unknown problems, yet simple and straightforward, and also likely to be the future. Not long ago, workflow was predictable, well known, and, more or less, simple. Technology has opened creative doors and simplified much of the filmmaking process, but workflow has gotten more complicated—almost unfathomable at times. Perhaps its time for technology to simplify workflow, too.

Virtual Digital Intermediate

Virtual digital intermediate workflow is very similar to the virtual film workflow except it does not use a 2 K or 4 K scan. In this case, the DI is actually an HD telecine to D5, HD Cam, or HD Cam SR.

In this workflow, the circled takes are color corrected and telecined to HD tape at 23.98 FPS and down converts made to DV Cam at 29.97. This exact workflow is detailed in Chapter 6 in the section on finishing on 23.98 FPS or 24 FPS HD Video. While this is the exact same workflow through the HD online, the final film finish is the same as DI. In this case, the finished HD video is shot back to internegative or interpositive on a film recorder and the final sound mix is shot to optical sound and also printed to the interpositive.

While this is very similar to the virtual film workflow, because the film is telecined to HD rather than being scanned to 2 K or 4 K DPX or Cineon, much of the color correction is done in the telecine rather than in finishing, as it is in DI. The control is, therefore, less and the image quality compromised.

In terms of cost savings, this is definitely a savings over true DI. However, it is not likely to save anything over cutting the negative. And as the image is compromised when compared to DI or direct printing, it seems that no one would use this workflow. Yet, it has become the most popular workflow among low-budget, independent filmmakers who are making their film on spec with no distribution in place.

The advantage is not just in terms of what the costs are, but when the costs are encountered. With this workflow, the film can be finished to HD video and then shopped around for distribution and entered in festivals that accept HD. If a theatrical deal is made, the HD can be finished on film. These costs can be passed to the distributor or paid from any cash advance. If the film is sold in a direct video deal to cable and/or home video, there is no need for this expensive film finish and no money was wasted making 35 mm prints that will never be seen.

Requiem for the Negative Cutter

It's sad to note that in the virtual digital intermediate workflow, even after the HD online, if the film is finished to 35 mm, the negative could still be cut by simply exporting Cinema Tools film lists rather than shooting the HD back to film. It looks much better and doesn't really cost any more.

One of the problems is that many of these independent films are shot on HD and don't have a negative to cut. But many are shot back to film because it's easy and straightforward. Many are shot back because the workflow was not designed toward cutting the negative or editing systems were used that simply don't allow for this workflow. So, the image is compromised and really for no good reason.

As many big-budget films are now using DI and small-budget, independent films are using virtual DI, many independent negative cutters are going out of business. Most of the labs still offer this service, but fewer projects are cutting negative every year.

Lost Hope and More—The Negative Edit

Figure 5.12 *Lost Hope and More* poster

Once the edit was locked, the edit was printed to video with the window burns visible. This was transferred to VHS and used as a reality check. All key code numbers were checked against the video as the film was assembled.

- Film lists were exported including
  - Double use list
  - Dupe list
  - Pull list
  - Cut list
  - Optical list

Work print shots were pulled to the pull list and conformed to the cut list by the assistant editors working at the negative editor's facility in Burbank. An audio temp dub was made at the Brooks mix room in Ventura and transferred to DA88 tape with 29.97 NDF time code. This was interlocked at film speed to the work print and screened at the Foto Kem screening room. Everything looked fine and sync was good. Next,

- The negative editor, Chris Webber, pulled negative for the optical effects using the pull list and the optical list.

- The negative for the opticals was printed to IP.

- Titles and opticals were made at T and T effects using the IP. The title workflow is examined in Chapter 8 on titles for digital video and film. After the title negative was delivered to the negative editor, the negative cut was ready to go forward.

- Negative was pulled to the pull list from the selects rolls.

- Camera negative was conformed using the cut list. The edited work print was lined up in the film synchronizer and also served as a guide to conforming the negative.

- The conformed negative was spliced into A-B rolls.

- Color was timed and a silent, first answer print was made. The cinematographer and directors sat with the colorist at Foto Kem as the first color correction was recorded into the automated printing system.

The silent answer print was interlocked to the temp dub DA88 tape and screened several times, looking for color correction and sound problems. Adjustments were made in the color settings in preparation for the second answer print. The first answer print was telecined to DVCam and Beta SP for use as the dubbing picture. Everything was now ready for the final dub and Dolby encoding (see Chapter 7 on the sound edit and dub).

After the sound dub and Dolby encoding, the encoded DA88 tape was printed to optical sound at NT audio.

- By combining the optical sound and the A-B rolls, a second answer print was printed with sound. Again, everything was screened and examined for color or any other problems.

- Final color corrections were made and a third answer print was printed. Everything looked good.

- Three release prints were made. Because there wasn't a need for more than three prints, an inter-negative was not made.

While it was very satisfying to see the movie on the screen, as they say, it's not over 'til it's over. There was still the DVD to be authored and duplicated as well as assembling the press kits, posters, and other distributing needs. And then we had to get ready for the roller coaster of the festival circuit. We look at these projects in Chapter 6, covering the HD online, and in Chapter 9 on after the film is finished.

6 Finishing on Digital Video, the Online Edit

Finishing on Digital Video

The basic workflow for digital video finishing consists of several stages including a pre-editing phase where all the necessary elements are brought into the project as edit-ready digital files. In this phase, if there are film elements, they are transferred to digital video (telecine). Sound not already combined with picture is prepared and digitized as necessary and synchronized with the picture elements. In some workflows, color is corrected in this phase; in other workflows, it is corrected later. On some projects, frame rates will be adjusted to match shooting frame rates; on most, it will not.

Once the elements are all ready to edit, the off-line edit is performed. This is the actual editing of the project. It is referred to as "off-line" because there was a time when this video would never be used as a final project. Low-quality work copies of the high-quality videotapes were used. The quality was so poor that the project always needed to be reedited on higher definition equipment. No effects were possible in off-line, not even fades or dissolves. The off-line edit was used only as a guide to edit the original video for the final project. The goal of the off-line edit was the Edit Decision List (EDL), a file containing all the in and out points of all the shots used in the project with all transitions, audio, and even key effects. The purpose of the off-line edit was, and still is, cost savings by performing as much editing as possible on the lowest-cost equipment, cutting the time necessary on the most expensive equipment to a minimum.

When everyone was in agreement that the off-line edit was the best possible and there would be no changes, the edit was locked. The EDL was used to perform the online edit. The EDL was loaded into the online edit system and the original video matched to the off-line edit. Because the off-line acted as a frame-by-frame guide for the finished project including the sound track, any titles, or graphics that would be added later would be roughed in or simply "slugged," blank video used as a place holder in the edit. This was even true of the end titles.

The relationship of the off-line and online edits has changed dramatically. With software-based editing, it is possible to make edit decisions from very high-quality digital video without any expensive interfaces or equipment. Even a basic system with nothing more than a DV input and common hard drive can produce reasonable digital video. Any effects can be created and used in these edits, so the need for an online edit is greatly reduced. Many projects never go to online, the off-line being quite good enough. But for broadcast quality or some high definition, there is still a need to take many projects into online.

Before the online, titles and graphics must be created. If there will be no online, these graphic elements will be added into the off-line edit before the picture is locked. You also need to cut in a countdown leader if you have not done that yet. Cinema Tools comes with countdown leaders in all popular frame rates in PAL and NTSC. These are DV files, but can be used in other formats; however, this will require rendering. Do not use a different frame rate and render this. That will cause the frame count to be off, rendering the countdown leader useless.

Color correction and sound are preformed with the online or just after. With the newest workflows, color correction is sometimes performed in the pre-edit as a function of telecine or video capture. Sometimes, color correction is done in the off-line edit with good results. This is especially true if the project is finishing in off-line and not going to online. Color correction has historically been performed in online and, in many cases, it still is. Or, some editors now prefer to do color correction after the online, going tape to tape and correcting one shot at a time.

The final sound with music and effects is edited after the picture is locked in off-line and mixed before, during, or after the online. Or, if there is no online, the sound is mixed and laid back onto the off-line edit.

Finishing on Video without an Online Edit

Even though you are not recapturing at a higher resolution in an online edit, you still have a finishing phase containing many of the same processes historically reserved for the online. Color correcting, importing and syncing the final mix, final graphics, effects, and final output still need to be done. Because you are doing these steps on your own system and your own time, you can perform these steps in any order, revisit them as needed, change your mind, and be as creative as you want to be.

This is not to say you may not want to take a DV project to a postproduction facility for special treatment, color correction, or whatever. But part of the joy of these formats is the freedom to do whatever you want whenever you want. Figure 6.1 shows one of the Brooks Institute's setups for editing off-line. Among the software tools available for off-line, there are many third-party color correcting plug-ins for Final Cut Pro. However, don't underestimate the power of Apple's new color-correcting software, Color. Color provides high-quality output and excellent control in an easy-to-operate system.

Figure 6.1   One of Brook Institute's DVC Pro HD edit rooms. All DV formats and Pro Res 422 can be edited in their native format requiring no online edit

The Color application can be accessed at any time by sending the clip or entire project to Color from the Final Cut Pro file menu just as sound is sent to Sound Track Pro. Perhaps the only down side to having such a powerful color-correcting application in Final Cut Studio 2 is that the input from the skilled colorist is removed from the workflow. While many users never would have taken their project in for color correction, it's unlikely that high-end projects will be color corrected by the editor directly in the Final Cut Pro workflow. But, for the one-person shop or even smaller independent projects, Color allows for deep control of the look and feel, and provides many preset looks for the editor who knows little about color correction yet needs to be able to optimize the look without going out of house.

To import the Pro Tools mix, simply create a new sequence—make sure it's in the same DV format as your project—and drag the icon for your finished sequence into it. Now delete all of the audio tracks. Import the bounced audio track and drag it into the sequence. The two on the countdown leader should match the pop on the audio mix. (For more information on the audio mix, see Chapter 7 on sound edit workflows using Pro Tools.)

Finishing on Digital Video with an Online Edit

So far, we have been working in a lower resolution, either from DVCam, DVC Pro 50, or even DVC Pro HD, or in photo JPEG. If you are finishing in Digi Beta, D5, or HD Cam, you will need to online. Online is simple; however, it needs to be done in a facility that supports your finishing format. Some facilities still perform online from a CMX system going tape-to-tape. While this workflow is very outdated, a surprising number of postproduction houses still use it. In 1968, only months before NASA launched the first manned flight to the moon, narrow gauge steam locomotives were still used in daily freight service. Sometimes outdated technology hangs around well past its prime. Pardon the digression here, but this is the proper way to think of EDLs for CMX: a steam locomotive in a world of spaceships.

Using EDLs and XML

But, you may need to integrate Final Cut Pro into a CMX workflow. This is easily done. Once the edit is locked, export an EDL, Edit menu > Export > EDL (see Figure 6.3). You will need to know what CMX (or other) format the online system uses and enter this in the pull-down menu. Other information here will need to match the online system and edit structure. Find out from the post house what to use. The audio mapping is required as these systems can only support two or four audio tracks. All Final Cut Pro audio will need to be premixed to these tracks if audio will be handled in the online.

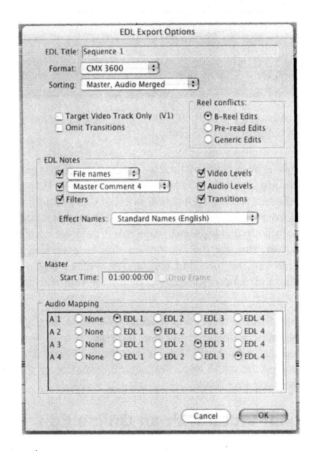

Figure 6.2 EDL export options

When you have an EDL, e-mail it to the post house and have them look it over. If there are mismatches with their system, they will be able to guide you to the problems.

The EDL is simply a plain language text file that can be read and edited if you know how. In fact, most of these were written by hand to window burn information when they were in common use.

There are many other uses for an EDL. As this is plain text, and it contains every aspect of the picture edit in plain language, it can be used in many situations where edit information is needed. You may even want to export one just to archive in the postproduction book with the cutting logs and other important information.

It is also possible to export the edit as a Final Cut Pro XML file. In some ways, this is similar to exporting an EDL. It, too, is plain language with some unusual formatting, but the format here is totally different. It's a "markup" language, similar to the HTML used on the Internet. Like an EDL, an editor who knows how to write in this format can actually edit with it (not that anyone would). But it can be used to batch certain changes like changing shot names.

Because it contains all of the information contained in the Final Cut Pro project file, it makes a great archive system. Even if Final Cut Pro 17 will not open your project file ten years from now, it will likely be able to import the old XML and update it. And like an EDL, it can be opened in a text editor or even a spreadsheet such as Excel, printed and placed in the postproduction book.

Some online editing systems can import this file and some can import a modified version. Here, too, it can function in the same way the EDL was historically used. Check with your online facility and see if they can use Apple's XML format. It comes in two types, XML1 and XML2. To export an XML, go to: Edit menu > Export > XML.

Other output formats are used in postproduction houses that are not supported directly in Final Cut Pro. Final Cut Pro plug-ins are available to export these formats. If your post house is using one of these formats, they will likely be able to get you a copy of the plug-in so that you can export in their format.

Using Media Manager

A faster way to online is to stay in Final Cut Pro. Many online facilities have a Final Cut Pro room. Some are exclusively Final Cut Pro. This makes online editing simple and straightforward.

As with all finishing, your edit in the timeline should be clean and not contain any overlaps or uses of video in extra video tracks unless they are a super or effect. Collapse everything else into V1.

The next step is to use media manager to make an off-line sequence. This may need to be performed at the post house. Most post houses use high-end video boards that require special codecs not supplied with Final Cut Pro. They may be able to give you a copy of their codec so you can install it on your system, but you can simply let them create the off-line sequence.

E-mail the post house a copy of your Final Cut project file. They can open it and look it over for problems. And they can run media manager, which is the next step. Or if you have the proper codec, you can do it on your system.

Figure 6.3 shows Media Manager. Use this to create a new off-line sequence. This refers to the new sequence being created with all media off-line. Go to the File menu, Media Manager. Choose Create Offline in the media section. You will need to set the sequences to the codec used by your finishing facility.

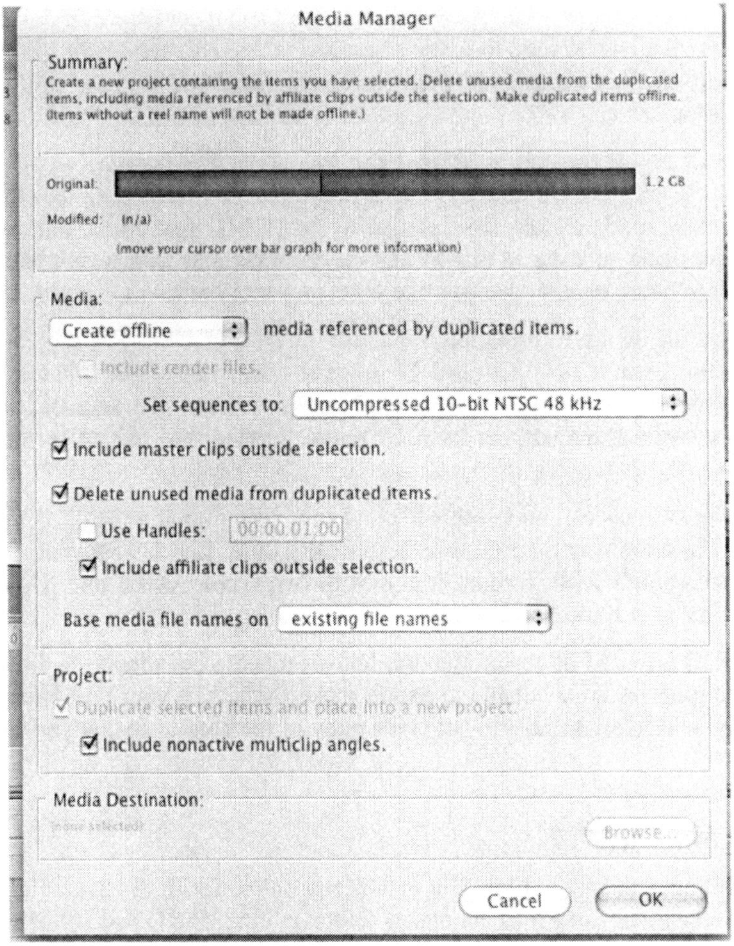

Figure 6.3 Using Media Manager to create an off-line edit in preparation for Final Cut Pro online editing

You can restrict your new sequence clips so that only the media used in the edit will be recaptured by selecting "delete unused media from duplicated items." Handles should be added to the clips, just in case you need to move an edit. Capturing one-second handles will add no measurable time to the capture. Needing handles and not having them can cost you half an hour.

Go to Log and Capture and, in the capture settings, set to the finishing format. Select video only. Click on Capture Scratch and set the capture scratch to the drive array that supports your format. Select Batch Capture and when Final Cut Pro asks for the first tape, load the corresponding higher-resolution videotape into the recorder. If you failed to give each tape a unique name, you will now run into major problems. Always name and label your tapes and set the tape name in the capture settings.

Everything in the sequence is now off-line. If the titles were made in Final Cut Pro, they will be brought up to full resolution when you render other titles not created in Final Cut Pro are off-line. You will need to arrive at the online with all of the original higher-resolution tapes and all titles and graphics in final resolution. (See Chapter 8 on titles and graphics.) The original countdown leader can be rendered into the new format; it will look fuzzy but it is only the countdown leader. Or, the post house can import one they have on hand. Don't leave anything to chance; more onlines are slowed by titles and graphics than anything else.

Interestingly, all of your video effects and color corrections are still in place. All that is needed is to render. While most projects will not color correct this way, you can. With the release of Color in Final Cut Studio 2, internal Final Cut Pro color correction is even more powerful. (See Chapter 9 on color grading with Color.)

Audio, Color, and Printing to Tape

You will want to have the audio mixed before the online; however, it can be added later if needed in the workflow. The mix can be delivered on DAT, DA88, or even BWF or AIF. Sync must be held through the entire program, so special care must be taken in output and delivery of the mix. (See Chapter 7 on sound edit workflows for more information.)

Color correction can be part of the online or done after the online, going tape-to-tape in a color-correcting suite. The postproduction house will give advice on this; proper workflow varies depending on their equipment and your budget.

The final color corrected online with sound is laid back to the master tape. You should also get a safety dub and any other submasters you will need. However, you can get these as needed.

After printing to tape, also export a QuickTime for importing into Compressor and DVD mastering. For 5.1 Dolby surround sound, the audio will be compressed, encoded, and brought into the DVD software separately. Again, for more information, see Chapter 7 on sound edit workflows and Chapter 9 on exporting media for compression and DVD authoring.

Matching Time Bases

This workflow only works when the original edit and the higher resolution or online video match time bases. You cannot change a 29.97 edit into a 23.98 final, or even a 23.98 to a 24. This is why the video must be reversed before editing. It is possible to reverse after editing but before online, however it's extra work, and the frame accuracy of your edits may be lost.

Converting this SD online to HD and converting 23.98 to 24 FPS is covered later in this chapter.

Finishing on 23.98 or 24 FPS High-Definition Video

The 23.98 online is only a bit different from the 29.97 online. As in the 29.97 online, you will be doing the online in a facility and they will be doing all the work.

If you shot on film, the telecine may have been done to HD at 23.98 and DVCam at 29.97, simultaneously, or the HD tapes may have been down-converted to DVCam. If you shot on HD, the same down converts should have been made. In either case, there should be a burn window on the DVCam tapes with the 29.97 time code (30 NDF) and a lower window with the 23.98 time code (24 NDF). The two windows should match exactly except for the frame numbers. The seconds should tick off in lock step. The lower window displays the time code from the HD tape. Before the reverse telecine, the 29.97 frame numbers in the upper window were perfect and the 23.98 lower frame numbers were blurred every few frames. After the reverse telecine the opposite is true.

If you captured from the HD tapes in photo JPEG, there are no window burns, and none are needed. Your photo JPEG matches in every way, including the frame rate to the HD tapes, except they are very low resolution and bandwidth.

As with the 29.97 online, use the media manager to create an off-line sequence, only in this case it will be an HD 23.98 off-line sequence.

Go to Log and Capture, and in the capture settings set to HD 23.98 format. Click on Capture Scratch and set the capture scratch to the high-speed hard disc array. Select Batch Capture and when Final Cut Pro asks for the first tape, load the corresponding HD tape into the recorder.

You will need to arrive at the online with all of the original HD tapes and all titles and graphics in final resolution. The best way to handle HD titles is to make them in 1,920 × 1,080 from the outset. When cut into a 720 × 486, if necessary, use the scale control in the motion tab to size them down. When imported into the HD online, they are the proper size.

Up-Rez: Converting Standard Definition Video into High-Definition Video

In some workflows, video shot in 24P SD is converted to 1080i, 1080p, or 720p HD video. Scaling is simple. All HD television sets have a scaler built in. These sets have inputs for NTSC SD video that they scale to 1080i and display. Some DVD players can also scale, playing SD DVDs to 1080i or even 720p.

The simplest system of scaling takes each pixel and makes exact copies of them; the old pixel is the same size, only now it is made up of several pixels. The problem with this system is that the resulting image looks exactly like the original making the scaling somewhat pointless. Ideally, we want the new image to look like it was shot in HD, not just "blown up" SD. The new pixels need to be created by averaging and interpreting all the original pixels around the new pixel. For interlaced pictures, the new pixels also need to take into account the color of the pixels in the frame before and the frame after the one being scaled to properly interpolate an interlaced frame.

The problems come from several places. Look at the SD image of the flag and pole in Figure 6.4. Where the lower flag meets the white, upper half of the flag, there are several rows of "blended" pixels. This is a necessary function of the DV codec. If the lower dark pixels met the white pixels directly, the edge would look jagged or "aliased." By creating blended pixels, the jagged edge is smoothed, a process known as "antialiasing." But in the HD image in Figure 6.5, the rows are now many pixels wide; the large blended pixels have been scaled with the rest of the image producing more blended pixels than needed to smooth the edge. The image now looks soft, the edges over-blended. Many of the scaling algorithms used in up scaling have edge-enhancing functions to try to restore the edges.

Figure 6.4 SD image blown up

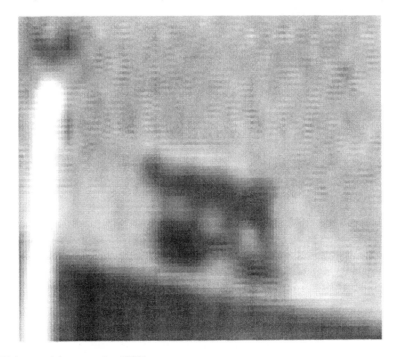

Figure 6.5 SD image blown up to 1080i

Another problem comes from the unwanted artifacts in the SD video. Any problems, even small problems may become exaggerated by the edge-enhancement function in the scaler. This can be seen in the noise in the right upper portion of the SD image where the white flag and blue sky meet. In the first HD image, banding and noise are exaggerated by the edge enhancement. The noise is still present in the second HD image in Figure 6.6, but it is blended, looking even better than the original SD image.

Figure 6.6 SD image blown up to 1080p by bicubic resampling

Another problem comes from converting one color space to another. This adds considerably to the rendering times and always creates color shifts. In worst cases, it can blow colors totally out or create banding in bright colors.

There are many scalers and some post houses have their own "top secret" system, "black box," or software. Some look better with graphics, others with softer images, some work best on sharper images. Some produce progressive video, some interlaced, and some produce images optimized for recording to film. Many produce unwanted artifacts, perhaps blowing out some colors, or bringing out the compression artifacts from the original DV video.

There are several ways to scale your Final Cut Pro SD project to HD. It is possible to print the 24P to videotape at 29.97, up-rez at a post house by rerecording tape-to-tape and reverse the HD 29.97 back to 24P. Because the edit was performed at 23.98, the entire edit has the same 0-A frame reference and can therefore be output to tape at 29.97 and reversed back to 24P. Note that projects that are shot at 24P but edited at 29.97 have a different 0-A frame reference for every shot and therefore cannot be reversed.

It is also possible to capture the project in ProRes 422 in the first place, making the up-rez unnecessary. It this case, the scaling is done in hardware. The SD video is converted in the I/O device, for example, the AJA ioHD. The advantage of this is not just that the full HD image is being edited, but also composted in Motion and graded in Color.

Some projects are converted in software. The simplest system involves taking the 23.98 SD sequence and dragging it into an empty 23.98 HD sequence in Final Cut Pro and rendering it to HD. Start by exporting your SD edit as a QuickTime. Import the QuickTime movie back into the project. If the SD video is 16×9, check its animorphic checkbox in the browser window. 16×9 video will up-rez full screen, 4×3 will be pillared.

In audio-video settings, set the sequence settings to your HD format. Final Cut Pro HD includes settings for 1080i, and 720p in several frame rates. Do not change the frame rate in this step; match the HD frame rate to the SD frame rate. Create a new sequence at the new settings.

Drag the SD QuickTime movie into the new sequence. The SD video will come in small in the HD sequence. Resize the image using the scale function in the motion tab of the viewer. Set the scale to 225 for 1080i.

You are now ready to render. Do several test renders to look for problems. The final render will be slow; the test renders will give you an idea of how much time you will need.

While this system works, transcoding any video this way produces some unwanted artifacts. While other rendering systems are also available at postproduction houses, most projects are transcoded from one format or resolution to another by recording tape-to-tape. This is the best way to convert 23.98 to 24 FPS as well. There are many syncing and stabilizing systems that can interlock two video decks and make the tape-to-tape dub. There are even systems that can record 29.97 to 23.98, but only if the entire 29.97 video has the same 0-A frame reference.

While the roll of the online edit is changing, there is still often a need to perform an online edit. This roll will continue to evolve, and the line between off-line and online will become even more blurred. Yet there will always be a need to have professionals oversee the final editing, ensuring quality controls and the best possible project.

7 Sound Edit Workflows

Final Cut Pro and Sound Track Pro

The question often comes up: Why do I need Pro Tools? The answer is that you don't. It is entirely possible to do the entire sound design in Final Cut Pro and Sound Track Pro, but the limitations soon create a real bottleneck in the workflow. The advantages of having at least a basic Pro Tools system are:

- A high-quality audio interface with mic and line inputs that even works as an audio interface with Final Cut Pro and Sound Track Pro

- Real-time playback without need to render 32 or more tracks

- Real-time preview of all plug-in effects before processing

- Pull-up and pull-down capabilities

- High-quality, sample rate conversion

- Portability to almost any professional audio facility

- MIDI interface

- A base starter price of about $350 for the M Box mini

Even though the advantages of using Pro Tools for the audio capture and sound design are huge, you may feel that Final Cut Pro and Sound Track Pro are sufficient for your needs. Let's look at audio workflow with only Final Cut Pro and Sound Track Pro.

When using a Final Cut Pro and Sound Track Pro workflow, the common workflow is to export any audio clip in need of special processing to Sound Track Pro from the export command in the File menu while working on the edit. This replaces the clip used in the timeline with new, processed media. The clip can easily be taken back to its original version or the amount of processing changed at any time.

The key here is not to do too much. You are working in a vacuum, only hearing the clip you are working on. Most audio decisions need to be made in context with all tracks playing. If the clip is in clear need of processing, say for broadband noise reduction or to add gain to a very low clip, this is fine. But don't try to fine-tune the clip's equalization or shape the reverb this way. Wait until all tracks are built and all sounds are edited in and then add these effects as part of the mixing process.

The final mix can be preformed right in Final Cut Pro; however, there are several serious limitations. Most Final Cut Pro systems lack serious audio monitoring. Even if you have professional-grade audio monitors, speaker placement and room acoustics are an issue. This is also true of a Pro Tools system. However, many Final Cut Pro edit systems lack good audio monitoring capabilities, yet are still used for final mixing.

Depending on the speed and memory size of your system, even a few audio tracks can reduce the real-time playback capabilities. Even with ten tracks, you will likely be rendering every sound you edit into a track. The slightest change also requires rendering.

The best workflow, therefore, looks like this. Edit the entire project in Final Cut Pro, export sound clips to Sound Track Pro only when processing is required, and keep the number of tracks within the capabilities of your system. Then, after the picture edit is locked, export the entire project to Sound Track Pro and finish the sound design there.

This is the best workflow no matter what sound edit software you are using. Many people prefer Cubase, Logic, or some other digital audio workstation. And, of course, with Pro Tools this is the proper workflow as well.

Sound Track Pro is a very capable system that can play many more tracks in real time than Final Cut Pro. This is because, as an audio-only system, its entire processing power is directed toward audio playback and processing. With Sound Track Pro 2 in Final Cut Studio 2, new features make this a great sound editing environment. One new feature is Apple's version of Virtual Katy for Pro Tools. When the edit is changed in Final Cut Pro, importing the new video into Sound Track Pro automatically conforms the sound edit to the new picture edit. While this is an expensive plug-in in Pro tools, it is simply part of Sound Track Pro 2. Apple has also added 5.1 mixing in Sound Track Pro 2, something available only in the HD Pro Tools systems.

In its basic software-only form, Sound Track Pro lacks an audio interface. While it can use your firewire AV device as an audio interface, this is probably your DV recorder and most of these are not intended as an audio interface. Most have only basic consumer −10 db audio inputs and outputs and naturally, no mic preamp or mic input. Sound Track Pro can also use the audio input and output on the computer, but this is even worse.

Sound Track Pro will interface with a wide variety of audio interfaces, including several of the Pro Tools LE interfaces. It also interfaces with a lot of other audio interfaces, including MIDI and many different control surfaces. There is more on control surfaces when we look at Pro Tools.

The entire sound edit can be finished and mixed in Sound Track Pro and then exported back to Final Cut Pro. The editing interface is simple and intuitive, and it has an automated real-time stereo mixer.

Sound Track Pro is probably best known for its loop editor and loop management-editing system. Many projects are brought into Sound Track Pro for no other purpose than to layout drum loops and even music beds. If interfaced with some type of audio interface and/or MIDI interface, other instruments can be recorded into additional sound tracks (see Figure 7.1).

Figure 7.1 Brooks MIDI room. MIDI keyboards and other devices are used to create MIDI tracks. The force of the keystroke is also recorded and this information is used to alter the sound sample being played. Photo by Benoit Doidic

The loop management system in Sound Track Pro makes looping samples simple and even fun. Thousands of loops are available and editing and making loops is also simple. And the capabilities of this software are expanding quickly. Apple would like to develop this into a true professional, digital audio workstation on the level of Pro Tools. While it is certainly not there yet, who can say what the next few years may bring.

Pro Tools

Sound is exported from the Final Cut Pro edit and imported into Pro Tools just as it is with Sound Track Pro. However, the output file, known as an OMF or OMFI, contains all of the audio media as well as the edited tracks. In a film finish, sometimes the original production audio is recaptured instead of converting from OMF. Depending on the production recorder, the audio in the Final Cut Pro project may have been transferred once or even twice, and rather than go looking for transfer problems, the original audio is simply recaptured directly into the Pro tools session.

When the production audio is recorded directly to drive in BWF, the Final Cut Pro project uses a bit-by-bit copy of this BWF audio. When an OMF is exported from Final Cut, the OMF also contains this BWF audio. When the OMF is opened in Pro Tools, you are still working with your original audio, so recapturing it would be redundant and a waste of time.

For those planning to recapture audio from the production DAT, an audio EDL is exported from Cinema Tools/Final Cut Pro and used to capture audio to Pro Tools. This assumes that there are audio time codes in the Cinema Tools database.

Several digital recorders and theater sound formats now support very high sample rates; 96 K at 24 bit is becoming common. The Mbox 2 Pro supports 96 K as do Pro Tools HD systems. Pro Tools HD is also capable of even higher sample rates. A 48 K 16 bit OMF can be converted into a 96 K 24 bit Pro Tools session using Digi Translator. Even though the dialogue from the OMF will be derived from 48 K 16 bit, the music and sound effects can still be recorded and mixed at 96 K 24 bit.

Sound Design

When the edit is finished, you have a locked cut. From this point on, any changes in the edit will result in major reworking to conform the audio to these changes. It's called a locked cut because that's what it's meant to be: locked. Changes can be made, and often need to be made, but the added work will be considerable. When changes are made, they are sent to everyone in the loop as a "change memo." Final Cut Pro can export change memos. See Chapter 2 on film conforming for information on how to make a change memo.

Some things to keep in mind as we prepare to export the project to Pro Tools: The Pro Tools session may require two drives. The files will not be very large, but they may require the speed of two drives. You need to cut a countdown leader into your timeline. The usual FCP countdown generated on "print to video" will not work; it needs to be edited into the timeline. Cinema Tools comes with several SMPTE countdown leaders in the Cinema Tools Extras folder in 24 FPS, 23.98 FPS, and 29.9 FPS.

If you don't have one and can't find one, you can make a 29.97 FPS one by opening a new sequence in Final Cut Pro and selecting print to video with nothing in the timeline. FPC will make its usual countdown that you can record on tape and then capture. Make sure in capture that there are exactly 60 frames from the 2 to the end, including the 2. This will only work for 29.97 FPS projects. Cut the countdown leader into your timeline.

Exporting the Project to Pro Tools

Make sure the Picture Start frame on the leader is the first frame of the project and that you are using a leader with the same frame rate as the edit. Export the video and audio as a QuickTime movie. Don't use QuickTime conversion. Pro Tools will be able to play your film in 29.97, 23.98 or 24 FPS. Export the movie onto a portable drive. Also, export the audio as an OMF.

You will need the Digi Translator plug-in, available from Digidesign. It can be purchased or even rented for three days on Digidesign's Web site. Launch Pro Tools and select: file > open session and find your OMF. This will create a new Pro Tools session. Set your session settings and name the session. If you are taking your mix back into Final Cut Pro, you may want to use 48 K 16- or 24-bit AIFF or BWF and a stereo I/O setting. Click OK and this will launch Digi Translator (see Figure 7.2). From here, you can convert your OMF into a Pro Tools session. Do not import any scratch or guide tracks you don't want imported into the Pro Tools session, but select import as new track or all wanted tracks.

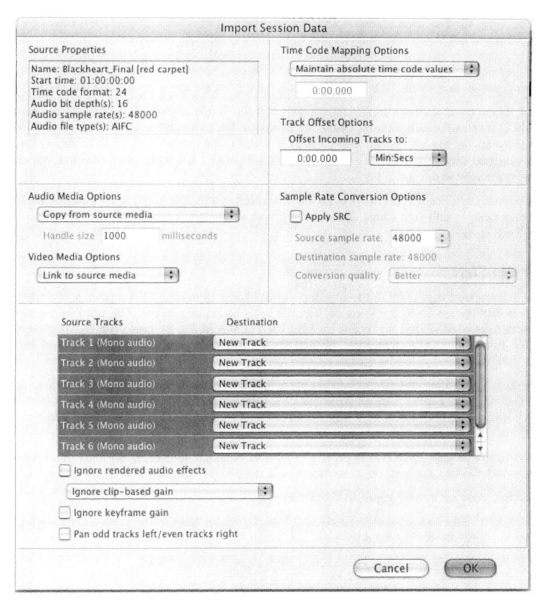

Figure 7.2 Digi Translator is used to convert OMF files exported from Final Cut Pro into Pro Tools sessions

Launch Pro Tools and select: open session and find your OMF. This will create a new Pro Tools session. Set your session settings and name the session. If you are taking your mix back into Final Cut Pro, you will want to use 48 K 16-bit or 24-bit AIFF or BWF and a stereo I/O setting. Click OK and this will launch Digi Translator.

From here you can convert your OMF into a Pro Tools session. Do not import any scratch or guide tracks you don't want imported into the Pro Tools session, but select import as new track or all wanted tracks. When the Pro Tools session opens, from the movie menu, select import movie and find the QuickTime movie. Also make sure that play to FireWire is selected. A movie window opens and the movie should play on the NTSC or HD monitor. You can close the movie window and the movie should still play on the video monitor. Check the 2 pop. As both the audio and video were the same length when exported, they should be in sync. If not, slip the sync of the movie to align the pop to the 2.

Also, import the audio from current movie. This will import the audio from the QuickTime movie, all the current tracks mixed down. Check the 2 pop for this audio and make sure it is in sync with the video and all the tracks. This will serve as a reality check, a way to check sync on any tracks you may inadvertently slip out of sync. Make the track inactive and make active any time you need to compare sync to this guide track.

Open the Session Setup Window from the Window menu. Set the frame rate to your frame rate. You are now ready to edit your sound design. All the tracks from the Final Cut Pro edit are now in the Pro Tools session.

Picture Start

The first frame of the Final Cut Pro timeline will be placed automatically at time code 01:00:00:00 This is the "Picture Start" frame on the Cinema Tools countdown leader. This can be reset in the session setup window. The zero frame has been used in film editing for years, although many sound editors have used 01 as picture start. This was never a time code number, but rather feet and frames (i.e., 00 ft 01 fr).

In video, the tradition has always been to place the first frame of the actual project at time code 01:00:00:00, with Picture Start on the countdown leader at 00:59:52:00. All color bars, slates, and black leader were before that. This way, the time code also functioned as a countdown leader to the program.

On multireel projects, each reel is given a successive hour setting (i.e., 02:00:00:00, 03:00:00:00, and so on). On PAL projects, the norm has been to use 10:00:00:00 for the first reel, and so on.

Therefore there are several standards for the Session Start:

- 00 ft 00 fr (time code equivalent 01:00:00:00) on the Picture Start frame of the countdown leader on film project's cutting negative

- 01:00:00:00 at the first frame of the actual program on NTSC programs

- 10:00:00:00 at the first frame of the actual program on PAL programs

When editing and mixing to videotape in Pro Tools, the tape will have a "standard" broadcast head leader:

Tape start at TC 00:58:50 followed by 10 seconds of black

00:59:00:00 30 seconds of color bars

00:59:30:00 5 seconds of black

00:59:35:00 15 seconds info slate (info about the program)

00:59:50:00 2 seconds of black

00:59:52:00 8 seconds of countdown leader (Picture Start frame)

01:00:00:00 Program Video (10:00:00:00 on PAL)

The head of the Pro Tools session will still be the Picture Start frame, but there will be more head leader on the tape.

When working from a QuickTime video in Pro Tools, the first frame of the QuickTime will be the Picture Start frame on the countdown leader. This will be set to 01:00:00:00 by Pro tools on import, but this can be reset to 00:59:52:00 in the session setup window. If you are cutting film and using the feet and frames counter, this can also be set to 00 ft, 00 fr in the session setup window.

It's also a good idea to time stamp all of the imported audio regions in the tracks. This is done in the region list pop-up menu at the top of the region list. Once time stamped, any audio inadvertently moved out of sync can be moved back with the spot mode.

Sound Design

The sound design will consist of three basic elements: dialogue, sound effects, and music. These three basic components have subcomponents, but the three basic elements must always be kept in their own area and eventually mixed into their own master tracks. These components, known as stems, are an asset of the project, and when a buyer makes a deal on the motion picture, they expect these assets to be included as separate components. A distributor will want to cut trailers and spots, and this is only possible if the stems are separate. Moreover, the film may be "dubbed" into other languages, in which case, only the effects and music (the M & E) will remain. It will require extra sound work to prepare the M & E for the foreign language dub. Sound effects from the production tracks that ended up in the dialogue stem will need to be replaced. A film may be sold to a foreign market even before it's shot, so, often a complete M & E is cut in the sound design. However, it may be mixed later after the comp dub is finished.

Dialogue—Splitting Off Production Tracks

Some editors like to do the basic production dialogue (dia) editing and track layout in Final Cut Pro before exporting the project for sound design in Pro Tools. The Pro Tools session will have the same layout and number of tracks as Final Cut Pro. The sound design will go much more smoothly if you start with well-organized tracks. You also have better sync reference here with the sync markers, showing how far out of sync any linked or merged tracks are.

The number of production tracks needed depends on the complexity of the project. A rule to keep in mind: Don't cut any sound clips up to each other unless they are derived from the same take. Although you can set a different level for each clip, in the final mix, you want total control of the level of the individual clips. This will be tricky if they are butted up together in the same track.

The simplest approach here looks like an A-B checkerboard layout with the fist clip in track one, the second in two, third back in one, and so on. However, this layout can be confusing in mixing. Characters move from track to track and the mixer really earns their keep riding the two production tracks.

It is more logical to put each character in a dedicated track. This is how Automatic Dialogue Replacement (ADR) is most often treated and it works when production recording is done with multitracks and multiple microphones (more on ADR in the following text). This is especially true with wireless mics as each person is already in their own track. However, production recording is different from ADR. ADR is all at the same basic level and it's okay to cut two takes together. Production tracks tend to be all over the place, so a cut in to a close-up or cut to the master butts two very different clips to each other in the same track. On a feature film, it is normal to have an A and B track for each character. This will create scores of production tracks making mixing and track management complex and tying up all your resources trying to put noise gates and filters on all of these tracks. But, this is how big projects are normally done. After all, they are big projects and should have big resources.

Every film and scene is different, and different sound editors and mixers have different ways of working. One common strategy on smaller projects is to create three or four production tracks and try to group things in the most logical manor. Try to put every main character in a scene in their own track even though they end up butt cut. And create a problem track. Put all the noisy wide shots in the problem track. (Wide shots are often a problem.) Put shots that you know need special treatment like filters in here.

Whether the production tracks were split off before bringing the project into Pro Tools or they will be split off in Pro Tools, it's a good idea to time stamp all dialogue (again, using the time stamp selected command in the audio regions pop-up menu). This way any sound moved out of sync can be moved back into sync in the spot edit mode.

Clean up any dialogue splitting and remove any sound effects by moving them to a sound effects track. You may want to place all effects moved from production in the same effects track so the mixer can deal with them more efficiently.

We are now ready to cue or "spot" the ADR. For years, this was done with a process called "looping" where the audio clips were cut into loops with cue pops and played in sync with a film recorder. The looped guide track served as a sync guide for the actor who rerecorded the lines in a sound booth or small stage.

In ADR, the entire film or reel is played as the cue pops are generated by the computer. Actors hear the three cue pops about one-half second apart just before the line, and the line to be replaced, and see the picture as they rerecord the line. Actors can get quite good at matching sync; however, some may like a different cueing system. Some don't like the pops and prefer to cue to their movement on screen. Others may want only two pops, faster pops, slower pops, and such. Many ADR systems let you customize to the actors' wishes, others don't.

Cueing or spotting the ADR is an art in itself. The person doing the cueing must decide which lines can be used and which ones need to be replaced. What problems can be fixed in the mix, what problems cannot? The performance is also an issue. Sometimes, the lines are replaced in an attempt to improve a weak performance. In this case the director and/or the producer need to be part of the process. Often, new off-camera lines are added.

Cueing should take place in a pseudo-mixing room or even right on a dub stage. The person doing the cueing needs to be able to hear what is on the track in a critical listening environment. It's also nice to have some basic mixing tools and noise reduction equipment like the tools that will be used in the mix to determine if a problem can be fixed. There is no attempt to actually fix any problems here, only decide what is fixable. Cueing ADR is a diagnostic process.

The lines to be replaced are listed by actor and time code. The exact line as used in the film, not just from the script, is transcribed. Depending on the type of ADR computer, the cues can be entered into the computer, or the cue pops laid into tracks. The cue sheets need to be copied and given to the effects editor who is also cueing as the ADR is being cued. The effects editor will need to know which production tracks are going to be removed so they can cue proper effects and Foley in these areas. Foley are very specific sound effects (discussed further in the Sound Effects section that follows).

In the ADR session, the ADR mixer, ADR editor, and actor are present. As performance is a big issue in ADR, the director should be there as well. It is important for the actors to put themselves into the scene. If they are screaming over a jet engine as fire burns all around, it may be harder for the actor in ADR to re-create the performance from the set. They are warm and comfortable in a studio, not panicking on an aircraft carrier. Sometimes actors need to run outside and race around the parking lot to get winded and into the scene. Whatever it takes.

The ADR mixer has a difficult job. He or she needs to record the line cleanly, match the sound of the nonreplaced lines, and keep the sound from sounding like it was recorded in the studio. Anyone can record clean audio; it takes an artist to record not-so-perfect, but nevertheless, just-right audio. Microphone selection and placement are the strongest tools of the ADR mixer. Some EQ can be used, but it's best left to the dub later on. Many ADR mixers use two mics, one of which is the same model used in production. One mic is placed somewhat close (the actor is never right on mic) and the "production" mic placed at a distance.

Usually two or three good takes are saved. This way, the ADR editor has some material to tweak. The ADR edit is all about using the right words from the right takes. Tweak until it fits. Everyone has noticed bad ADR in a movie. No one notices good ADR. The tracks are usually cut so that each character has his own track in the scene.

Recording ADR in ProTools

As we are not using an ADR computer, you will need cue pops. These can be cut from 1,000 Hz tone-generated with the tone Audio Suite plug-in. Edit three, one-frame pops about twenty frames apart and bounce these to disc. You will also need to set up a video monitor and headphones for the actor in the studio space if you do not already have that.

Create three new tracks, file > new track. Name them ADR 1, 2, and 3, as seen in Figure 7.3. Check the input assigns and set them for the input and microphone preamplifier that you are using for recording.

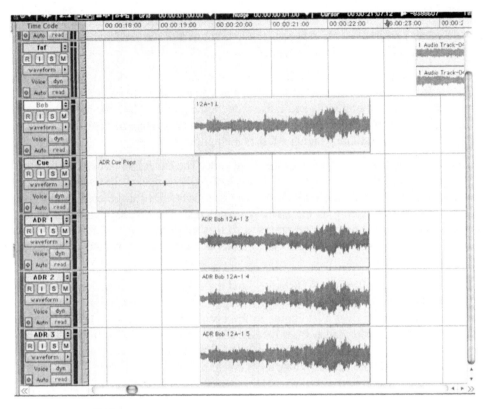

Figure 7.3 Pro Tools ADR setup

Create a new track and name it cue. Import and drop the three cue pops to a point just at the start of the line you want to replace. You can copy the cue pops and place a set before all the lines you need to replace.

Turn region linking off. Solo the cue track and the production track containing the original line. Set the in and out brackets in the timeline to a point just at the start of the cue pops and the end of the line to be replaced. Set options > loop playback. Record enable ADR 1.

Begin playback. The actor will hear the loop playing over and over in his headphones as he tries to match sync. When you feel the actor is ready, set the transport control to record and click play. This will record one take and stop. Check the line by soloing it on the Pro Tools mixer and unsoloing the cue and guide tracks. If you like the line, rename it in the region bin. If you want another, record enable ADR 2 and unenable ADR 1. If you don't want to keep the take, select it in the region bin and from the menu at the top of the region bin select delete. *Always rename or delete all takes.*

Cleaning Up the Production Dialogue

While the ADR is progressing, the dialogue editor still has some work to do on the production tracks. There are two strategies in editing production tracks. Both work in some instances. The trick is knowing which to use when.

The first technique is to carefully edit out any unwanted sounds like direction or a C stand falling over. Needless to say, if these things happen during dialogue, then the whole line is fixed with ADR and removed. And if there is no way to match the ADR, then the whole scene will need to be replaced, or at least this character's lines. Then, overlap the cuts from one clip to another slightly, filling any holes left from cutting things out with ambiance from other takes. Set up quick fades on the overlaps in an effort to make the ambient sound seamless.

The other technique requires that all lines be cut as close to the dialogue as possible. Remove anything that isn't dialogue. No ambience between lines, nothing between the lines. Then, find a good ambience quite similar to the original and lay it in on an effects track. Set up quick fades on the production lines so they don't pop on or off.

There is a great trick on the TDM and HD Pro Tools systems called virtual track switching. On these systems, you can assign a "voice" to a track (see Figure 7.4). Normally, each track has its own voice,

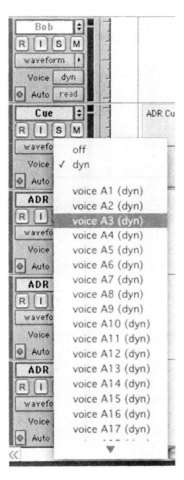

Figure 7.4 Pro Tools HD virtual track switching. With this function several tracks can be set to the same "voice" causing higher track numbers to "mute" when sound plays from a lower track

but you can assign a voice that is already used by another track. Only one track on a voice can play at the same time, that being the lower track number; in other words, the track nearer the top of the edit window. Therefore, if you lay an ambience in on track two and tight-cut dialogue in on track one, with both tracks assigned to the same voice, every time a line plays the ambience drops out. Neat trick in some cases. There is a preference in setup for the speed of the switch as well, so you can make the switch a very fast fade. Edit > strip silence can be used to remove all areas between dialogue lines when using this editing strategy, to ensure totally clean audio between lines.

In either case, the Audio Suite plug-ins can be used to clean up and match the dialogue on a clip-by-clip basis. Select the clip you want to work on in the timeline and open one of the Audio Suite plug-ins. Gain can be used to bring up low lines or lower hot lines. Only work on audio that clearly needs work, save tweaking for the mix.

You can use 7 band EQ to remove rumble and some hiss (see Figure 7.5). All of this is done to on the clip only, so final adjustments will always be made in the mix where all the tracks are heard at the same time. Don't overdo things here. Always do the least necessary to get close to where you need to be. The processing is not destructive, the originals are still in the region bin.

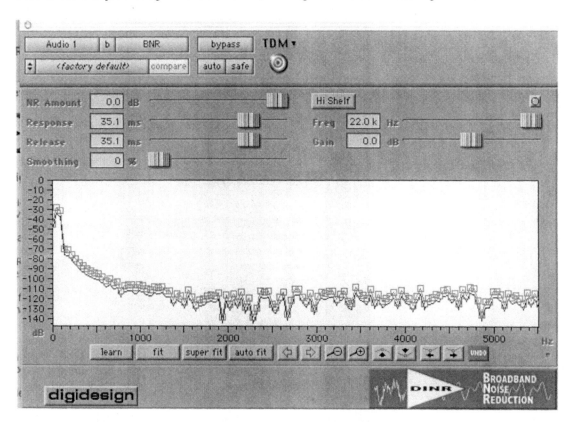

Figure 7.5 The Pro Tools plug-in DINR can be used to clean up some if not most of the background noise. Sample a small section of background sound only and let DINR use it as a guide to remove all similar sound

Sound Effects

Sound effects (FX) are cued differently than ADR. Critical listening is not required, critical thinking is. The FX editor needs to previsualize the mix, also called the dub. What is needed to make this scene play? Just because there is a production track doesn't mean the effects are there or clean enough. Moreover, the dialogue editor may have cut them out. In this case, you may want to cut the effects from the production track into your effects track. Or, the dialogue editor may have moved all of the effects into one effects track for you.

You may need to reinforce certain sounds, a doorknob, a match lighting, whatever. There will be sounds missing because they were never recorded. Subdivide into components. A massive chandelier crashing through a heavy table is not a sound you will find in a library. Nor do you want to attempt to record it! And the production sound, if any, is no doubt the sound of a plastic chandler smashing through a breakaway table. Look for a heavy wood crash, a heavy iron hit of some kind. What else can be seen? Chains rattling, wood splintering, glass breaking, plaster falling around the chandelier; you may need ten tracks, but you can build the sound from components.

Make a list of the sounds you need and their time codes. Try to remember the look and feel of the scene. Start listening to library effects. When you find something, don't just dump it to your drive, write down where it came from on your cue sheets. Get several of everything. Many sounds that sound perfect now may not fit with the picture when you try it. Go out and record the things you need. The real secret to effects editing is finding or recording the perfect sound. Don't think too much about the real sound; think about the scene and the film as a whole. The right sound may not be the most "real" sound, but the perfect sound.

In editing the effects tracks, use a logical track layout. Many editors like to put the more sync-specific, shorter effects, such as a door slam, in the higher (low number) tracks. Less specific sounds, like a car driving by or a tarp flapping in the wind, go in the middle tracks, and backgrounds in the lowest tracks (high number). This way, when you have fifty effects tracks and there is a gunshot that is giving the mixer a problem, he or she can go right to the area in the tracks, knowing where you would have placed it.

Every location should have a unique background (BG) sound. This may be several tracks: wind, birds, stream, traffic, and so on. The background helps define the look and feel of the scene. Sometimes the backgrounds are "submixed" in the final mix to make it simpler. The backgrounds are assigned to a group fader and the underlying BG tracks hidden. You have control of the BG through its fader, and if the submix is wrong, you still have access to, and control of, the individual tracks. Or, the backgrounds can be premixed inside the session to a "nested" track and the original tracks made inactive.

If the track count is becoming too high for a given system, many effects can be premixed in this manor. For example, the massive chandelier effect could be premixed into one effect. But always save the premix inactive tracks; in the final dub, you may want to hear more of the plaster falling effect, and the only way to do that is to go back to the premix and remix.

On stereo projects, all backgrounds should be stereo tracks. Close-up effects can be centered or even panned left or right, but backgrounds need to fill the stereo field. Use a stereo mic or two matched mics and record to a stereo recorder. For surround projects, the backgrounds need to be four tracks.

Rather than recording with a four-track recorder, this is most often done by recording two extremely similar stereo backgrounds and using one in the front channels and one in the rear.

Walla

One special type of background is walla, a group of human voices blending into a background. Editors, distributors, producers, and directors often disagree on whether walla is an effect or a dialogue. Should it be cut by the effects editor and/or end up in the effects stem? Walla is often recorded by the ADR editor who schedules a walla session with a group of walla actors (yes, there is such a thing). This walla is cut into an ADR track. Or, often the effects editors and friends put together their own walla session or pull walla from a library. In this case, the walla ends up in an effects track and possibly the effects stem. Whichever system you use, never premix the walla into the background; you may need to record it into the dialogue stem in the dub. Foreign language dubs may require foreign language walla. If not, it is a sound effect and should be edited into an effects track.

Foley

Foley is a special kind of sound effect recorded on a Foley stage in sync with the picture and guide track. The technique was originally used in radio to create sound effects live during the show, In the 1930s Jack Foley, after whom the process is named, started using the system to record movie sound effects in sync to a projected picture. Figure 7.6 shows a Foley room dedicated to recording specific sound needs. On large projects, there are often one or even two Foley editors. More often, Foley is handled by the effects editor. Foley is cued early in the sound design, often as ADR and effects are being cued. The usual things recorded on the Foley stage are footsteps, cloth movement, and any sync effects that are too sync-specific for wild recording or library effects. A glass of water being poured and drank, setting down a box of junk, a slap or punch, even something like a block of wood being sanded are recorded on a Foley stage. Often, Foley is used when the effect is hard to record outdoors because of background noise. The usual Foley crew consists of a Foley mixer and, because the chief product of the Foley is footsteps, two "steppers," often a man and a woman with lots of

Figure 7.6 Often a Foley stage looks more like a thrift store than a recording studio with the hundreds of props used to create Foley tracks stored on the stage or very near by. Photo courtesy of Richard Partlow's Complete Foley and Tom Ruff at Film Leaders

shoes. The Foley stage is similar to an ADR stage and often is used as an ADR stage at times, except a Foley stage has various floor surfaces and "pits," depressions in the floor that can be filled with sand, dirt, water, and such. There are also hundreds of props around a Foley stage that at times resembles a junkyard.

Foley is always cut into separate Foley-only tracks, never cut into an effects track. Mixing Foley is quite different from mixing effects because it is a studio recording and all at the same level.

Music

Music (MX) is composed to the locked cut. Figure 7.7 shows a typical scoring session. The composer usually is a contractor and the musicians, scoring stage, and even the music editor work for them. This can be a frustration for the producers, the dub mixers, and the sound designer as they often have no input on the music mix, which is often delivered as a stereo mix or at best a four-channel mix. This complicates a six-track surround dub as the music mixer may not have much control over the placement of the musical elements. The final mix is better if the music is not premixed to final tracks, but rather mixed in the final dub. Music may be delivered on 8, 16, or even 24 tracks or "stems" premixed by instrument types or whatever. Naturally, this adds a lot of tracks to an edit that already has lots of tracks. It's not uncommon for a large production to have more than a hundred tracks in the final dub.

Figure 7.7 Composer Randy Tico (left) records his score for *China, A Will to Rise* using traditional Chinese musical instruments. Photo by William Sallans

Along with audio tracks, the session may contain MIDI tracks. This is most often used to record and play music from a sampler, the sample being recorded into the sample player. Most often, the sample is a note from an instrument. The sample can be quite complex; many samples are recorded and edited together to form the beginning, middle, and end at several volumes. The sample is played from a MIDI keyboard, much like a piano keyboard. As the key is struck, the beginning of the sample is played at the proper volume for the strength of the keystroke, the middle is played until the key is lifted, and then the end is played. Only the keystroke is recorded as MIDI information into a Pro

Tools MIDI track. A MIDI track is not sound, but rather a set of instructions to send to a sample player. These tracks then need to be recorded as sound into a sound track before the mix is exported. However, as MIDI they are extremely editable. You can change the attack, even change the sample played. A piano becomes a saxophone. Figure 7.8 shows the Pro Tools MIDI tracks.

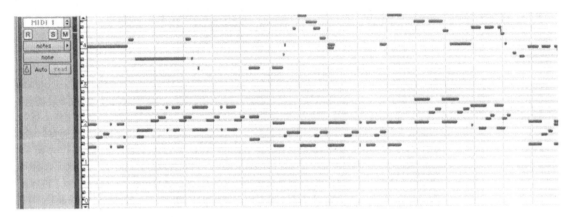

Figure 7.8 The dashes in MIDI tracks represent keystrokes on a keyboard or drum pad. The MIDI plays samples from a sample player. In this example a Pro Tools MIDI track had been created and contains music in MIDI form. The dark grey dashes represent keystrokes. The speed and pressure of the keystroke is also recorded and editable. The samples played by the keystroke can be any sampled sound, a musical instrument or a footstep

While MIDI is most often used for music, it can be used for some effects. Footsteps, for example, can be sampled and recorded in sync with the picture. Let your fingers do the walking. MIDI has been used for guns, hits of all kinds, and weird effects. Effects samples are available in many sound effects libraries.

Some sounds can be edited in a form of MIDI. Using MelodyneUno, music can be "converted" into a form of MIDI where the pitch and timing of the music can be edited. This can take an off-pitch vocalist, something that happens when actors are required to play singers, and put them right on pitch and rhythm. If there was a real-time version of this, Karaoke might be tolerable.

The Temp Dub

A temp dub is usually performed. This is a good attempt to mix the tracks without any real attention to detail, the goal here being to check that all the sounds are here and the show is mixable.

Historically, the temp dub or temp dubs were necessary because the scores of tracks could only be heard on a mixing stage. The sound editors had never heard more than two or three tracks at a time until the temp dub. Only then could decisions be made as to what really worked and what did not. This is why often several temp dubs would be made.

With modern digital audio workstations, it is possible to hear all of the tracks as they are being edited. Even if several people are working in several locations, everyone can be working on the same project files via Internet or changes can be FTP'd or even sneaker networked via portable drive.

This means that you know if a sound is going to work the way you want it to as you are editing it into the project. The need for a formal temp dub is diminished.

On a film finish workflow, there are critical points along the way where a temp dub is needed. If a work print is conformed, this should be interlocked with the sound track and projected. This requires a temp dub to be transferred to DA88 or magnetic film. So, in this case, the temp dub may be nothing more than a touchup of levels and a transfer for screening.

It is also necessary to interlock and screen the first answer print on workflows where a silent answer print is made. And this, too, requires a temp dub.

On all projects, there may be a need to screen a temp dub for producers, the director, network people, or whomever. In this case, the temp dub may be done in a Pro Tools mix room simply screening the Pro Tools session. More than likely, this will be a more formal screening from videotape in a screening room with a good audio system, such as the one shown in Figure 7.9. The temp dub will be exported or "bounced," sunc with video edit, and printed to tape. Pro Tools even offers a "bounce to QuickTime" for just this purpose.

Figure 7.9 Brooks Institute Pro Tools mix room. The mixing console is a "control surface" that controls Pro Tools and does not actually process any sound

On many projects, the temp dubs simply evolve into the final dub. On very large projects, this is common as they may have access to a mixing stage through the entire postproduction. This was the case on the *Lord of the Rings* trilogy. The mix stage was dedicated to the project for the entire time the films were being edited. The online session was mixed for months as the sounds including the score were being recorded. At the end, they gave the film a final set of adjustments and it was finished.

This is similar to how most small projects are mixed as well. As the no-budget gorilla filmmaker may be mixing on his own editing system, at some point he will give it one last set of tweaks and call it finished.

The "normal" workflow is much closer to the older conventional workflow. In this case, the sound is mixed as it is edited. At key points, a temp dub is preformed and screened until everyone in the decision loop is in agreement that the project is ready for the final dub.

The Final Dub

Figure 7.10 shows a mixing room. Most mixing facilities will want to start from scratch. As always, check with them as to their needs, but most likely they will want you to strip out all of your levels and filters so that they can hear just what they have to work with.

Figure 7.10 The main mix room at Juniper Post. A large system like this often uses several Pro Tools systems locked together. An advantage of using Pro Tools is being able to take the project to almost any professional facility. Photo by Jeff Merrit

Make a backup of the Pro Tools project so that if you need to get beck to your temp dub you can. Then, select the gain display for each track, select all, and press delete. Remove any pan or mute automation the same way. Then remove all mixing filters.

Few mixing facilities use QuickTime for video playback. They want to keep all of the computer resources available to Pro Tools. Normally, they use "machine control" where Pro Tools controls a videotape player and keeps it in sync with the Pro Tools session. If so, you will need to print your video to videotape in whatever format they use. Also, find out what time code format they prefer. They will want 01:00:00:00 on the videotape to correspond to the beginning of the Pro Tools session. You will probably need to have a professional videotape dub made to ensure proper format and time code placement.

If you are finishing on film, the absolute best workflow is to make the first answer print before the final dub. Then, telecine this answer print to the proper videotape format with the proper time code. This will ensure the video reference is an exact match of any future prints. If there is a sync problem, it could be because of an editing error, a conforming error, or any number of potential other problems. Rather than worry about how it happened, simply fix it here knowing that this is absolutely the accurate picture.

If you are finishing on video, you can also mix after the online for the same reason. However, it's much less important on a video finish because if there is a sync problem, it can be fixed by slipping the video shot rather than the audio. Because of this flexibility, in a video finish, the sound may be mixed before, during, or after the online edit.

It all comes down to this. Now, all the tracks are mixed as tightly as possible, every attention to every detail. Many of the decisions are subjective: how much background, how loud the music should be. Should we pan a sound as the character moves or not?

There are no rules, but there are guidelines:

- Never bury the dialogue. Keep the dialogue in the foreground over effects, music, everything. If you think the dialogue is forward enough, it's not. Go more.

- Keep the intent of the filmmaker. Don't get too big on effects and music unless it's a big film. Don't be afraid to go small with some effects. You don't need to always hear every footstep and shoe squeak. It's the filmmaker's film and it's his or her call. Everyone at the mix needs to do everything to achieve the filmmaker's goal and the filmmaker needs to express his or her desires.

- Much of what is going on is technical. Are the levels going too high? Do we need to save headroom for later when we need to get much louder? There are standards for everything. The monitor speakers should be set at a level so that truly loud sounds are being heard loudly.

- The acoustics of the room are also critical. Mix at a reputable facility.

Control Surfaces and Automation

A control surface looks very much like a mixing board, and it is used exactly like a mixing board. But, in fact, it is more like a computer keyboard/mouse. It only controls the software and has very little built-in function or active electronics. Some may have mic preamps or even a small monitoring mixer, but, for the most part, all of their function is provided by the software and audio I/O device.

You may ask, when one of the greatest advantages of the Pro Tools mixer is that it is virtual and therefore totally customizable, why tie yourself down to a huge hardware mixer? The advantage of such a controller is that many of the controls and sliders of the Pro Tools interface are now in the "real world" and can be quickly touched and manipulated. Moreover, several controls can be manipulated at the same time and with better control.

Another advantage of a control surface is that this allows the mixers to "live mix." That is to say, mix with the control surface while recording the output as a final mix. The advantage is that it's fast and, depending on the skill of the mixer, very creative.

Stems

As the mix is going forward the mixing board is often set up to simultaneously lay the music, effects, and dialogue stems off to another channel or channels. In many cases, they may be laid off later. With 5.1 and other multitrack finishing formats, there may be 5–6 music stems, 5–6 effects stems, and 3–5 dialogue stems.

DTS Dolby SR and 5.1 are encoded later from discrete channels. The encoding usually takes place in the optical transfer for film finish or in the DVD authoring. The simplest system, used often in digital video, is simply a stereo composite mix. Stems for a stereo mix are usually 1 or 2 dialogue, 2 (stereo) music, and 2 sound effects.

Exporting Stereo and Finishing

The stereo composite, stereo mix, and finishing in Final Cut Pro or on film can happen in the following workflow. When the mix is compiled in the Pro Tools session, the stereo mix is exported as a 48 K, 16 or 24 bit AIFF or BWF. Go to file > Bounce to disc, and direct it to your audio firewire. This will play the mix in real time with all MIDI tracks playing. The mix is recorded as an AIFF file. Import the AIFF into your Final Cut Pro project and line up the 2 pop with the picture.

If you are finishing on DVCam, you are done. If you are going to online editing, you are ready to online. If you are finishing on film, you are ready to pull up (if your frame rate was 23.98) and shoot the optical (see Chapter 5 on finishing on film).

Exporting the Mix and Finishing

The next steps are to export the surround composite mix and finish in DVD Studio Pro or on film. For DVD, 5.1 Dolby Pro Logic can be encoded in Apple's Compressor as a part of the authoring process. For 5.1 Dolby Pro Logic, the individual tracks are bounced as multimono and imported one at a time in Compressor. They are then compressed into a Dolby 5.1 AC3 audio file that is used in the DVD authoring.

For film finish, the Dolby encoding is done after the mix and before the optical transfer. There is a Dolby licensing fee. Dolby will send a technician to the mixing facility after the mix to encode the master tape.

Optical Sound and Pull Up

In a film finish, before the "married" answer print (answer print with sound) can be printed, the audio from the mix needs to be pulled up (only if you were editing at 23.98) and shot to optical sound. The optical sound can then be printed on the answer print. Don't confuse this with "pulling up" the optical track 26 frames before printing. Both processes are referred to as "pull up," but in this step we are speeding the sound back up to 24 FPS from 23.98 FPS.

Pulling up is more critical than pulling down. When we pulled the original sound down for syncing to 23.98 footage, we were slowing down by exactly .1 percent. Moreover, if we were off by some small fraction of this small percent, it rarely creates a problem as we only need to hold sync for the duration of the take, perhaps a few minutes on even a long take. The pull up, however, is done to the entire film. We need to hold exact sync, even a drift of .0001 percent will cause the picture to drift out of sync. It is not uncommon for pull downs to be done with the equipment locked to several sync clocks. Pro Tools may be locked to its internal clock, a Nagra may use its crystal and, as these are both very accurate clocks, we can hold sync through the take. But for truly accurate sync, every piece of equipment must be locked to the same clock reference. Typically, a video sync generator is fed through a distribution amplifier and sent to every piece of equipment in the facility. This is referred to as "house sync." Moreover, though the pull down was exactly .1 percent, the pull up is a difficult .1001001 percent.

There are many ways to do this and the lab or sound facility will use their favorite system. Pro Tools can perform the pull down and pull up, and the TDM and HD systems can be locked to house sync. The Pro Tools session can be bounced to disc with pull up set in the bounce dialogue window. The resulting AIFF or BWF can be delivered on hard drive. One very popular and accurate system is to record the comp mix (and any stems) on a DA 88 or compatible recorder with both the recorder and Pro Tools locked to house sync. Record at 29.97 FPS and have the lab shoot the optical with the DA88 set to 30 FPS, again with the DA88 and the optical recorder locked to the same reference. Because of the two speed settings on the DA88, it can be used as both a video and film master, and with 8 tracks it can handle even a 7.1 surround mix on a single tape.

Dolby LCRS is normally encoded on 35 mm prints as the optical track. LCRS provides four channels of high-quality audio. Encoding of any multitracks is usually performed before the optical transfer. Dolby encoding involves using phase angles to encode the various channels into the stereo optical track. Noise reduction and dynamic compression and expansion are also encoded, which dramatically improves the quality of the optical sound. A Dolby technician with encoding equipment is dispatched to the mixing facility after the mix is completed and the DA88 tape is encoded. The DA88 tape is then sent to the optical house to shoot the optical sound.

The optical track is a "picture" of the sound shot onto a narrow stripe just inside the sprocket holes of a black-and-white sound film. Figure 7.11 (left) shows 35 mm sound print and (right) negative. On 16 mm (Figure 7.11 center), the optical is laid in the area just outside the standard 4 × 3 picture area, extending all the way to the edge of the film. This area is used for picture in super 16 and sprocket holes on double perf film, so sound prints on 16 mm are always single perf and never super 16. Super 16 must be finished digitally or blown up to 35 mm.

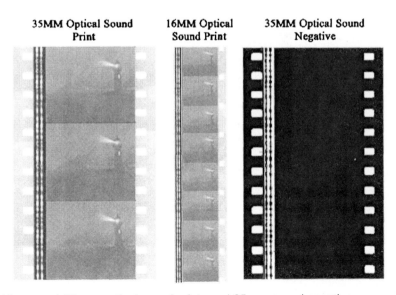

Figure 7.11   16 mm and 35 mm optical sound prints and 35 mm sound negative

There is no picture on the optical sound negative, it is only a black-and-white film negative containing the sound stripe image. It will be printed onto the answer print in one pass through the printer, the picture will be added in one or two more passes.

The Projection Print

There has always been a tremendous amount of unused space on the 35 mm film print; the sprocket holes are well in from the edges and there is a fair amount of space between them. Also, the area used for the optical sound is large by "modern" standards. With scores of new digital sound formats now being used, every square millimeter of nonpicture film is being used to store audio information. Figure 7.12 shows a variety of ways audio is stored on different films.

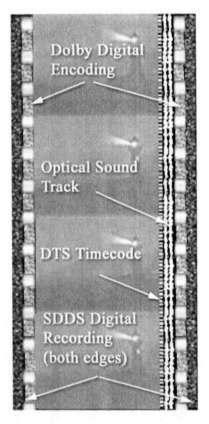

Figure 7.12   35 mm projection print with optical and digital soundtracks. Every part of the film is used for picture or sound, even the spaces between the sprocket holes

On Dolby Digital, all six channels of audio information are recorded between the sprocket holes. New formats now record up to eight channels of sound.

On DTS digital sound, the sound is recorded onto a compact optical disc (CD). A time code is added to the optical sound in the form of a continuous bar code between the picture and the optical stereo track. This time code pulls the digital sound into sync and constantly checks for sync. If there is a loss of sync or any problems detected by the system, it switches over to the optical sound until sync is restored. DTS is available for 16mm, however there are few 16mm DTS theaters.

On Sony SDDS, the sound track consists of an array of microscopic dots recorded onto both edges of the film just outside the sprocket holes.

Like the tiny pits on a CD, these are the actual digital sound. There is still an optical sound track recorded in case of system problems and for theaters that cannot play SDDS. While it is rare to find prints with all these formats, Dolby SR, Dolby Digital, DTS, and SDDS can all be encoded onto one print.

Lost Hope and More—Sound Design

Once the edit was locked:

Figure 7.13 *Lost Hope and More* poster

- The edit was exported as a QuickTime at 23.98 FPS.

- The audio was exported as an OMF.

- The OMF was opened in Pro Tools using Digi Translator.

The Pro Tools session was opened on a TDM system using Pro Tools version 6.4. Much of the editing was preformed on an LE system using Pro Tools version 7.0. While the older session will open on the 7.0 software, it is necessary to use "save as" version 6–6.9 when saving on the 7.0 software. Pro Tools has always been able to open sessions on any software or version of software. However, it may require a work-around similar to this.

As the sound design moved forward, Foley was recorded:

- Foley and effects were cued.

- The edit was recorded onto DVCam tape for Foley picture.

- Foley was recorded at Film Leaders.

Six tracks of Foley were recorded: three tracks of footsteps, two tracks of movement, and one track of props. After the Foley was recorded, several scenes received major recutting. Because of the complexity of these changes, an interesting workflow was used. The Foley was imported into the Final Cut Pro project and edited with the picture as the changes were made. This kept the Foley in sync and was the simplest way to make the changes to the Foley. The Foley was then exported from Final Cut Pro as an OMF. However, it could also have been exported as multiple AIF files. The OMF was opened using Digi Translator and this Pro Tools session was imported into the *Lost Hope* session by using the import session data function.

The new picture edit was loaded into Pro Tools and the remaining tracks were changed to the change lists. Because the changes had been made early in the sound edit, the effects and dialogue changes were relatively simple to make. The workflow continued as follows:

- ADR was cued and recorded in the Brooks ADR room. The score was written and recorded by two different composers. The "Apocalypse" scene was written and recorded by "Pease Frog," a Doors tribute band from Venice, California.

- Two DVDs were made with time code window burns. Each DVD had two QuickTimes, one with temp music in and one without temp music.

- The score was recorded at two studios using MIDI and live instruments.

- Music cues were placed online as they were recorded and these compressed MP3 files were converted and edited into the session. These were screened for approval.

- Once approved, the recordings were rerecorded as needed and delivered on CD as AIF files. The "Apocalypse" cue was delivered as a Pro Tools session so that the music could be remixed in the 5.1 mix. The score was delivered as premixed stereo.

- Sound effects were recorded and edited.

At this point, the portable drive containing the session crashed and was unrecoverable. Unfortunately, there was no resent backup of the session. The most current version was opened and the missing audio files were imported from original files or backups. One audio file was lost as there was no backup. Unfortunately, this was the electronic helicopter from the "Apocalypse" scene. This had taken four hours to create, and it needed to be re-created. The other repairs required only about two hours to make. This really drove home the importance of making backups. The next steps were:

- A temp dub was made and recorded to DA88 tape.
- The temp dub DA88 was interlocked with the work print and projected.

At this point, the new portable drive with the Pro Tools Session crashed. This time the session had been backed up in its entirety and so recovery only required going to the backup and confirming that everything was intact. The final stages of the workflow went smoothly.

- The answer print was telecined to DVCam and Beta SP for use as the dubbing picture.
- A copy of the original Pro Tools session was made to preserve the temp dub settings.
- All levels and EQ in the Pro Tools session used in the temp dub were removed.
- The final dub was preformed at Todd AO.
- Dolby LCRS was encoded to DA88 tape.
- Surround effects tracks were added to the session.
- The Pro Tools session with the mix levels intact was remixed to 5.1 at Sunset Screening Room.
- Dolby 5.1 was encoded to DA88 tape.
- Encoded audio from the DA88 was recorded to optical film at NT audio.
- A second answer print was printed with sound and screened.
- The six-channel mix was exported as six separate AIF files and sent to the DVD author for 5.1 encoding. Delivery was on CD.

The final release prints were made with two sound tracks, one in 5.1 Dolby and an optical LCRS Dolby track. All theaters can play the optical track; most can also play the 5.1 digital track.

Because audio is so fundamentally different than picture, many picture editors find it intimidating. And while the two are very different, and sound is normally handled by a "special team," in terms of postproduction workflow the two are inseparable and totally intertwined. When designing the workflow, they are both equally important.

8 Titles for Digital Video and Film

Managing Title Media

Entire books have been written on the subject of designing titles and titling software. As this is a book on workflow, we're not looking at graphic design or color theory, but at managing title media and title workflow in the digital world and on film.

Titles for Digital Video

The needs of each digital format are radically different and, therefore, the finishing format must be decided on and all graphics and titles created for that format. Working copies can be compressed and distorted, as long as the final version is the best possible. Because of improper workflow, often the reverse is true: the working copies are good, but on the final video the titles and graphics look terrible and are often unusable.

There are some basic problems when making titles and graphics for video. All video, be it interlaced or progressive, is made up of lines. (For more information on video formats, see Appendix 1 on understanding the NTSC video format and digital video.) All digital images are made up of pixels. As title media will eventually be digital video as well, it, too, will eventually be made up from pixels. It may be created directly from pixels from the outset, or it can be created with a vector system. A vector system creates titles and graphical elements as vectors, layers of position maps and objects. All title letters and fonts are vector-based graphical shapes. This is a resolution-independent system where nothing exists as pixels until it is rendered. For this reason, the image size in pixels can be changed at will to any size and rendered with no loss of quality.

The title generator in Final Cut Pro is a resolution-independent vector system. Titles made in Final Cut Pro can be simply kept in place in online and rerendered in any finishing format. But the title generator has some serious limitations. While it's great for simple titles, there are many things it simply can't do.

Adobe makes several great pieces of software that can be used to create graphics and titles. Photoshop, Illustrator, and After Effects work seamlessly with each other as well as Final Cut Pro. Each of these Adobe applications has functions necessary to creating, processing, and managing graphics and titles. There are many other graphic systems on the market, but these are the most popular.

Adobe's Illustrator is its vector-based system and is resolution independent. It can be used to create text and shapes in color, and because it is vector based, any text can be moved, resized, or edited in any way and rendered into any practical size or image format.

Illustrator files cannot be imported directly into Final Cut Pro; they must be rendered into a pixel-based image format first, as in Figure 8.1. The Illustrator files can be exported in any popular pixel-based image format and used directly in Final Cut Pro. It can also be exported as a PSD file and imported into Adobe's Photoshop, and "rasterized" or rendered, into a pixel-based image. The original Illustrator project remains intact and can be changed, resized, edited and reexported in the new size.

Figure 8.1   Adobe Illustrator titles

Photoshop is an incredibly powerful image processing and editing system. While it was originally created to edit photo images, it has become an indispensable image editor used in all graphic processes including motion picture special effects, animation, and graphic design (see Figure 8.2).

Figure 8.2 Photoshop title

While Photoshop is a pixel-based image processing system, on later versions, the shape and text tools are vector based. Fonts and shapes can be created and moved, resized, recolored, and rasterized into pixels at any image size.

The images must be rasterized into the proper size for import into Final Cut Pro. The images can be imported in a size larger than the editing format being used in Final Cut Pro and resized and rendered in Final Cut Pro. But, rerendering such titles in Final Cut Pro into a larger size or a different video format, especially taking SD to HD, it will degrade them severely. There are two workflow options to solve this problem:

- Render two versions, one in the finish format and one in the working format. Edit the working format into the off-line and take the finish version to the online for integration into the edit.

- Render only a final version of the title and edit it into the off-line. Scale it to fit the screen in the off-line format and render. It may not look good, but it will suffice for the off-line. Keep the original in a separate folder and replace the resized off-line version in the online.

There is an assumption that there is no point for images to have more rows of horizontal pixels than the number of lines used to display them. Two pixels being displayed on one line is, after all, still one line. As there are only 480 visible lines in DV, normally, there is no point in creating an image with more than 480 vertical pixels. This concept limits the number of horizontal pixels to 640 (480 × 1.33 = 638.4). To improve the horizontal resolution, a new standard was developed for the DV format, NTSC CCIR 601 where the pixel aspect ratio is not 1:1, but approximately .88:1, or, narrower than tall. This allows the number of horizontal pixels to be 720, or an image size of 720 × 480. DV uses this same 720 × 480 size in a 16 × 9 aspect ratio. In this aspect ratio, the pixel is now wider that tall. The difference is how the CCIR 601 format is displayed. A flag can be set in the "metadata," information recorded along with and embedded in the video, that this should be displayed at 16 × 9.

Computer monitors create issues when making pixel-based video titles. Computer monitors use a progressively scanned picture instead of interlaced, use RGB rather than YUV color space, and use square pixels. When making titles for the DV formats in CCIR 601 rectangular format, it is necessary to take this aspect ratio change into account.

Photoshop CS has a video output function that can send the image to a DV device for display in DV 4 × 3 or 16 × 9. On earlier versions of Photoshop, available plug-ins like Echo Fire can accomplish the same thing. While this can display the image with the proper colors and proportions, it requires that the image be exported to the firewire device, with no real-time feedback. So, while this is a great way to confirm that everything looks fine, it is no way to actually compose graphics.

The newest versions of Photoshop have a video preview mode that displays the image in the same aspect ratio as it will have when used in a video project. Older versions, as well other pixel-based graphic systems that do not have this preview mode, will need to use a workflow that involves rescaling the image.

In the Photoshop new project dialogue there are two preset pull-down menus. One is the Preset pull down, as seen in Figure 8.3. This menu contains various presets including all common video formats. And there is a second pull down, the Pixel Aspect Ratio menu. This, too, contains various video formats. In the Photoshop View menu, there is a setting for Pixel Aspect Ratio Correction. When this is set, the display changes into a real-time video, aspect ratio preview. This introduces a temporary artifact, but accurately predicts the final video proportions. Using 72 pixels per inch will open the title in a good working size on the computer screen.

Figure 8.3 New image dialogue in Photoshop

The rescaling workflow is easy and straightforward, and can be used on any pixel-based graphic system, and must be used with older versions of Photoshop.

This same technique can be used for DV at 16×9 aspect ratio as well. In this case, the pixel is wider than tall rather than taller than wide. The original 16×9 image is created at 852×480. This is also scaled to 720×480 in Photoshop. The computer image will now be taller than wide, but the displayed video image at 16×9 will be back to normal proportions (see Figures 8.4 and 8.5). This scaling should be done in Photoshop, not in Final Cut Pro.

Figure 8.4   Circle in ccir

Figure 8.5   Circle in sq pixels

The following chart shows several popular video formats and the sizes that should be used to create graphics in a pixel-based system like Photoshop. Several need to be scaled to a new size before importing into Final Cut Pro.

Video Format:	Design Graphics at:	Scale Image to:
4 × 3 Web Video	640 × 480	Scale to final output in FCP
DigiBeta MPEG IMX	720 × 486	No need to scale
DigiBeta at 16 × 9	853 × 486	720 × 486
SD DV formats at 4 × 3	1280 × 960	720 × 480
SD DV formats at 16 × 9	852 × 480	720 × 480
HD 720 P 16 × 9	1280 × 720	No need to scale
HD 1080 i or p 16 × 9	1920 × 1080	No need to scale
2 K Full Frame	2048 × 1556	Mask to final aspect ratio
4 K Full Frame	4096 × 3112	Mask to final aspect ratio

Table 8.1   Video Format Size Chart

To create a title or graphic in Photoshop, select New in the File menu. In the dialogue window, enter the horizontal and vertical size from the Video Format Size Chart in pixels. To scale the finished title, select Image Size in the Image menu. In the dialogue, enter the scaled size in the horizontal and vertical in pixels.

HD images use square pixels and so do not have these problems or require rescaling. They can be created in their native resolution and will have the proper proportions on the computer monitor. The HD image uses either 720 or 1,080 horizontal lines, and 1,280 × 720 or 1,920 × 1,080 pixels. It can be either progressive or interlaced and its standard aspect ratio is 16 × 9.

Alpha Channel

An alpha channel is a fourth channel in the image-defining areas of the image that are transparent. This is essential if you want to superimpose titles over picture. It is also a great way to reduce contrast to improve the look of the titles (more on this later in this chapter).

Some titling systems automatically create this alpha channel. The Final Cut Pro titler creates an alpha channel. Any title with an alpha channel can be simply placed in video 2 with the background video in video 1 and the title will automatically be superimposed over the video.

When creating titles in Photoshop you must set up your own alpha channel. When creating a new title, set the background to transparent as shown in Figure 8-3. Photoshop will now show as a gray checkerboard background. Lay out the title and save it as a Photoshop file. This will import directly into Final Cut Pro with an alpha channel that will allow the title to be superimposed over video, and you can control its opacity to control the contrast.

Colors are a problem as well. The computer uses RGB colors, NTSC uses a different "color space" called YUV. NTSC cannot reproduce many of the colors that can be displayed on the computer screen. Attempts to import and use many colors from a computer-generated image will drive the chrominance into "illegal" levels and cause distortion. Photoshop has an NTSC colors filter to limit the colors to NTSC "legal" limits. This helps, but the colors will still shift when imported into Final Cut Pro and are rendered into DV.

Different setups on the computer monitors also create problems; there is likely to be a color shift for no other reason than the computer monitor is using a different setup than the video monitor.

HD has its problems as well. HD Cam uses a compressed color space. HD Cam SR and D5 is much less compressed in its color space as is DVC Pro HD, however no video format displays the color space seen in 32-bit RGB color. And, as these are not firewire compatible, the firewire preview in Photoshop will not show the preview in the proper format.

The export to firewire devices can be a big help in determining what the final colors will look like in a DV format. In Photoshop CS2, the image can be exported to a firewire video device with the Export, send-image-to-video device in the File menu. Adjustments can be made to the color and a new preview exported, continuing until the colors look correct.

In spite of your best efforts, the colors will most likely be shifted when imported into the final edit. There are normally color adjustments made to the titles in the final video as part of the final color correction, a process called "sweetening" the titles.

Moving titles create a whole new set of problems. When rows of pixels move vertically over the lines of video, a "stair step" effect is created, as can be seen in Figure 8.6. Even the Final Cut Pro titler

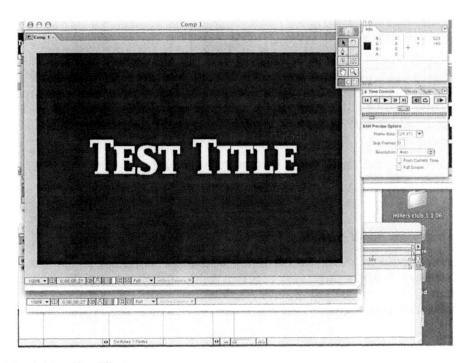

Figure 8.6 Adobe After Effects

produces this undesirable effect on scrolling titles. There are rendering systems that can drastically improve this problem; even Final Cut Pro has improved this problem over the six versions released.

Adobe's After Effects, as seen in Figure 8.6, can create great scrolling titles.

Titles can be imported from Illustrator and animated into scrolling titles. The rendering system produces great looking title crawls. Because only the vectors are moved, rather than moving already rendered pixels, there is no "stair step" effect. The software does much more than this, but After Effects is a great complement to the Adobe system when the project calls for moving the titles.

This problem with moving titles can even be seen in 3D titles created in 3D, animation software such as Lightwave or Maya. In this case the problem does not come from moving pixels, but moving crisp edges common in titles. The problem can be dramatically improved by rendering at double resolution and then resizing in Final Cut Pro. Some 3D software has a setting for 200 percent rendering, or the size can be set to double, for example 1,440 × 960. This requires four times the rendering time in the 3D rendering, but for something like hard-edged titles, it can look a lot better. These titles will be scaled to the proper size in Final Cut Pro.

Final Cut Pro comes bundled with LiveType. LiveType is not a resolution-independent system, but it produces great looking titles. Once a title is rendered, it becomes digital video in whatever format was set in the LiveType settings. It is a special effect titler used for highly stylized titles. While simple and elegant is not in its vocabulary, it does a remarkable job making wild titles. In terms of workflow, it's a straightforward system, just be sure to render the titles in the finish online format, not the working off-line format. Never scale or transcode DV titles into the finish format at online.

Considerations when Designing Titles

There are several things you can do in designing titles that will improve their look in any format. Generally titles are sharp-edged and very high in contrast. Most are white letters over black. This is an image that challenges even the best digital video formats. Digital video formats cover jagged pixel edges by blurring the edges. This is not very noticeable on moving video images, but on sharp-edged, high-contrast titles, this blurring can look horrible. Other digital compression artifacts also become very obvious on titles.

There are three things that can be done to help with this problem:

- Avoid sharp-edged titles.
- Reduce contrast.
- Use the best video format possible.

Avoiding sharp edges is an esthetic concern as well as a technical consideration. The look may simply call for sharp edges. But know there is a price to pay: these will show problems on highly compressed video such as DVD. Some fonts have softer edges or even softer curves that can help hide these problems. When choosing a font, do some test renders at DV settings and see what problems become obvious.

Reducing contrast is best accomplished by bringing the letters down from white. Even a light gray can still come off as white while looking much better. This can be done while creating the titles.

Another trick is keying the title over black and then bringing the opacity of the title down in the Final Cut Pro motion tab. This is a great system because you can change it later if you change your mind. It works with all titles with an alpha channel, including the Final Cut Pro titler. You can even tweak the black levels up to reduce contrast, and if you have used the opacity setting to reduce the white, it still looks great.

Interlaced video creates its own set of problems. If a fine horizontal line is only one pixel tall, it will only be displayed half of the time as it is only displayed in one field. This causes the line to flash on and off thirty times a second and look jittery. If the line is widened by one pixel, the problem gets worse. Now the line is in one place for 1/60 of a second and then just below that for 1/60 of a second. The line flashes up and down and looks even less stable. If the line is three pixels wide, it settles down a little; however, it is now alternating between a narrow line and a wider line. At four pixels, the line becomes as stable as it can be in an interlaced picture. To help this problem, the DV compressor blurs hard lines into soft lines. While this looks good when used with video, it makes graphics look soft.

The best solution is to use the heaviest font you can. Again, this is an esthetic concern. But, definitely avoid thin fonts or fonts with fine scrolls and ornaments. They will flicker, strobe, and show every digital compression artifact.

Naturally you want to use the best video format possible, and not just to make the titles look good. But tiles are unforgiving. They will show every little problem.

Titles for Film Finish
Photolithographs, or Liths

The photolithograph, or lith, is a high-contrast, black-and-white film negative. Liths are often 4 × 5 inches, as in Figure 8.7; however, some are shot larger than that, up to 8 × 10 inches. In most cases,

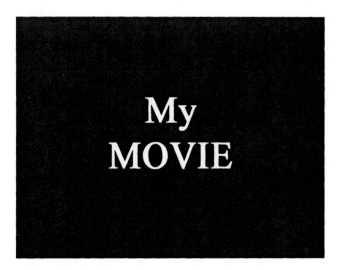

Figure 8.7 The photolithograph

it is a camera negative shot with a large-format copy camera. Most titles for film finish are still handled in a rather traditional way. It is possible to create titles digitally and then perform a "film out," that is to say, shoot the digital title onto negative film one frame at a time. The digital process does offer many advantages and makes many slow and difficult optical effects fast and easy, but it is expensive and the overall look is not the same as shooting titles the time-honored way. This is often true even on films that are not cutting the negative, but being scanned for a digital intermediate. It seems logical that if the entire film is going through a digital phase, it makes more sense to do the titles digitally. Yet many films going to digital intermediate will still make liths, shoot the liths to 35 mm film, and scan the film to digital. Film titles simply have a "film look."

The first step in making film titles, after deciding on the look, the font, and overall design, is shooting the liths. While the titles are shot on film and not made digitally, the liths are usually made digitally. The title art can be photographed directly onto graphic art film, often Kodalith from Kodak, but most graphic facilities laser print digitally produced files directly onto the lith film.

Most filmmakers have their titles made at a title house or lab. The super low-budget "gorillas" sometimes shoot them themselves. However, much of the process still requires working with a graphic art house or printing shop.

If you choose to shoot your own film titles, you still need to have a graphic house produce the lith with the title letters clear and the surrounding area a dense black. It is very important that the blacks be dense; a bright light should not be easily seen through the black film.

Many people save money by putting several titles on a large sheet; one large sheet is less expensive than several small ones. The titles can be cut apart or simply masked off with camera tape and black construction paper.

The liths are filmed on black-and-white reversal or black-and-white negative film. They are normally filmed on an animation stand where critical lineup can be achieved. The stand must be equipped with a light box for back lighting the lith. Exposure can be taken with a spot meter directly off the light box before mounting the lith. Depending on the meter, it may be necessary to open one stop over the reading. On meters set for 18 percent gray, open 1 to 1.5 stops. The lith is taped in place and the area around the lith is masked off with black paper tape and black construction paper so that the only sources of light in the room are the letters of the lith.

The low-budget "gorillas" often shoot the liths on a standard light box for viewing slides. A normal 16 mm or 35 mm camera is used on a tripod. Lineup is tricky, but if done correctly the finished title is indistinguishable from a professionally produced title.

If the titles are shot on negative black-and-white film and cut into the film negative, the final title will be exactly what you see on the lith: white letters on a black field. Or, the titles can be shot on reversal black and white, which produces black letters on a white field. A color can easily be added to the white letters or white field in color timing.

Superimposed Titles

Superimposing titles over picture is much more complicated. Even on films that are A and B rolled (see Appendix 8 on negative conforming), if the title is cut into one roll and picture into the other, the end result will be picture in letters. It will be black letters over picture if the title was shot on reversal film, or a black field with picture in the letters if the title was shot on negative film. While picture in letters can look good as an effect, it is not generally the goal of superimposed titles. Black letters over picture can work, but more often they tend to blend into the background image and are hard to read. White letters over picture often look better, but this requires more steps in the process. An example of each can be seen in Figure 8.8.

Figure 8.8 A and B rolled titles

Optical Printing

If you are not A and B rolling and doing fades and dissolves as opticals, a superimposed title can be made with the other opticals (see Chapter 5 on finishing on film and optical printing). In this case, you shoot negative black-and-white titles, the negative producing clear film with black letters. Now the title negative is "bi-packed" on the optical printer with the picture negative.

The title is placed in the optical printer in front of the image, the black letters keeping this area from exposing the print. The resulting positive print has white letters over picture (see Figure 8.9). As this is a positive (interpositive), it needs to be printed once more to produce a negative (internegative) that can be cut in with the camera original. This is a rather complicated system, and it involves working with the camera original on the optical printer, which is always avoided. There is a better and simpler way to go about this, but it's important to understand how this works.

Figure 8.9 Bi-pack optical titles

Contact Printing

There is a second and simpler way to produce white letters over picture. It can even be done on a contact printer. It is often less expensive, especially for projects that are A and B rolled, and it only involves working with the original while making the interpositive. The resulting internegative has negative image with black letters, which can be cut into the camera original producing a print with white letters (see Figure 8.10).

Figure 8.10   Contact printed title

The best titling system combines both techniques. In Figure 8.11, notice how the title can be shot on either black-and-white negative or reversal. However, they are usually shot on negative (lower left). The title film is printed to a positive that will be used as a mask (lower second from left). An interpositive is printed from the camera negative (upper left pair). The title negative is bi-packed with the interpositive and printed to an internegative. Then the positive title is used as a mask and a second pass is made to the internegative (center). Color can be added in this second pass and by altering the lineup; a drop shadow effect can be created as well. This is by far the most expensive system, as it requires multiple passes, bi-pack, and lineup on the optical printer, but it is the system most often used.

Figure 8.11   Titles in both techniques

While titles seem to be the simplest part of the postproduction process, more projects are delayed by title problems than any other reason. Perhaps this is because titles are often taken for granted. It is assumed that this is a simple process and something that can be done at the last minute. Like any part of the workflow, titles must be planned, created correctly, and be ready on time.

9 Color Timing and Color Grading

Color Timing Film

"Color timing" is the process of color correcting film in printing. "Color grading" is a term used to describe color adjustments made in digital imaging. Either way, the process involves multiple steps, starting in the camera with the exposure. Determining what aperture setting to use affects the light values and quality of the darks and lights as well as the amount of color in the lighter areas. Filters are also often used, especially on film cameras, to alter the color and give a baseline correction based on the quality and color of the light used on the set and the type of film stock.

The production designers among us might well argue that the real first step in color grading is choosing the colors of the design in the first place. This is a valid point to make. The production designer needs to be in sync with the director, colorist, and the cinematographer, or the end result may well be highly polished garbage. Case in point: When shooting *The Wizard of Oz*, the ruby slippers were originally supposed to be silver, but were changed to ruby red by the production designer (who worked for Technicolor) because they would look killer on Technicolor, and generally fit the look of the production design. Never mind that silver slippers walking on a road of gold bricks was meant to be a powerful metaphor for nineteenth century economical policies in America. Metaphor out; eye candy in, and one of the great American icons was born.

Varying Red, Green, and Blue

Film has historically been color corrected in film printing by varying the amount or red, green, and blue light being passed through the original film to the print stock. Normally, a "chip chart" is shot at the head of the camera roll and/or light setup as a reference. The printer light is split into its color components by dichotic mirrors, the same system used for splitting the color image in three-chip CCD cameras. The value of the colored-light intensity is controlled by shutters and is quantified on a scale of one to fifty, with twenty-five being "normal." The red, green, and blue values are listed in that order, RGB. So a print light of 25-25-25 would be a completely neutral print, in other words, no color added or exposure change.

When working with negative film, the color spectrum is flipped backwards. If the timer wants to remove red from the print, they add red in printing. So a value of 35-25-25 would have some red removed indicating that there may have been too much red in the original exposure or that the colorist wants a warm look.

Color and exposure are evaluated on Hazeltine systems. This is a special viewing system where the camera original is loaded on a film transport and the image is displayed on a video monitor. Different levels of RGB light are used to transfer the film image to the video screen allowing the colorist to try different RGB values and see the result on the video screen. The RGB value of each shot is recorded into the printing system, which controls the print lights during the printing process.

The first print, known as the first answer print, is processed and projected and reevaluated for further color correction. The RGB values are altered and a second answer print is struck. It usually takes three or even four attempts before everyone is comfortable with the color. It is critical to screen the print in a well maintained theater with the color and brightness of the lamp set to Society of Motion Picture and Television Engineers (SEMPTE) standards.

On films where the camera negative is conformed to the Final Cut Pro edit, this system and the camera exposure and filters will be the only color correction available.

While the control available in film printing is good, the control in digital grading is almost unlimited. Many films use a digital intermediate for no other reason than to gain more control over the look. This was the case with *O Brother Where Art Thou?*, the first film to use a digital intermediate just for color grading.

But even on films using the digital intermediate process, there are still color corrections made in film printing. While the systems to predict what the DI will look like once it is shot back to film work well, the process always produces some surprises. The first print from the film out will more than likely need some small adjustments as it is printed to release prints or to make an internegative.

Color Grading Film or Video when Finishing on Compressed Video

When shooting film to be finished on video, typically DV formats including HDV, color correction and image control in telecine is the next step in color grading. While there well never be as much control as there was in production, the amount of control in telecine is vast compared to the control over the compressed video.

For this reason, some projects return to telecine for final color correction. However if more of the image information from the camera negative is recorded in telecine by recording in an uncompressed format, then the amount of control over the digital image can be just as great as in telecine, making return to telecine redundant.

When finishing compressed digital video that was shot on video, the first step in color grading is still in the camera in production. On most formats, the amount of control of the compressed video image is very limited and extreme care must be used to get the color and image quality as close to a "clean" image as possible. The image may be stylized later, but if the necessary image information was not recorded in production it is not recoverable.

Because compressed digital images record much less contrast information than film does, digital cameras must offer more controls in camera than film cameras. White balance is used for a baseline correction of the light color, and other settings can be used to alter the gamma and contrast of the original image. On digital formats with large amounts of information recorded, the color can be controlled much better in postproduction. And, often these cameras and formats are shot as neutrally as possible so that the look can be better controlled in color grading at a later time.

While some larger projects will color grade at a professional facility, many smaller projects (and even some large projects) perform final color correction right in Final Cut Pro with the Color Corrector three way. While this is not the most advanced system, it has proven adequate for many projects. And because the filtration is part of the project, even if the video is relinked to higher resolution video in online, the filter settings stay intact and need only to be rerendered.

Working with Color

This color-correction workflow has been radically altered with the release of Final Cut Pro 6 and Final Cut Studio 2. Final Cut Studio now comes with Color, an advanced software-based color grading system that works brilliantly with Apple's new Pro Rez 422. Figure 9.1 shows the Color interface in use. Color was previously known as Final Touch from Silicon Color, with a suggested retail price of $25,000 for the 2 K version and $1,000 for the DV version. Color lets you see the color correction at any resolution in real time. When you have the look dialed in the way you want it, you can render it at full quality in record time. Color taps the power of the new generation of Macs to produce RGB output in resolutions up to 2 K at 4:4:4 color, using 32-bit float processing.

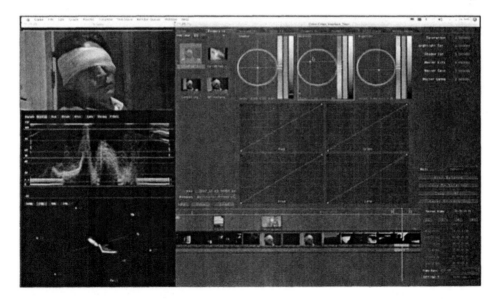

Figure 9.1 Apple's Color interface

Color is linked through the XML metadata in the project to the original media, so the project can move between Final Cut Pro and Color at any time and the color corrections stay intact in both projects. Color renders new versions of the original media, keeping it intact while linking both the Final Cut Pro and Color projects to the new corrected media. When changes are made, Color returns to the original media and rerenders it to the new grading replacing the older render. Each render is therefore a first-generation render of the original media, so there is no loss when layering color grading effects.

Color "Room"

Color uses eight screens or "rooms" to layer the grading in a step-by-step process. Remember, this is actually the second or third step in the color grading process, the first and most powerful step being in production with exposure, filtering, and camera settings. On film projects the next step is telecine, also a very powerful step in color correction. Once the image is captured into Final Cut Pro in a compressed format, Color can adjust and stylize the look, but the garbage rule is still in full effect: garbage in, garbage out.

The Color workflow starts with primary in. In this "room" the shots or even entire sequences are corrected to a consistent and "accurate" look. As the project is edited, the other steps or "rooms" can be visited in any order and returned to at any time. The following text details the other seven rooms.

Secondaries

From the secondary room, as shown in Figure 9.2, selected colors and areas can be manipulated individually. Called Power Windows by da Vinci Systems, these tools can be used to select an area

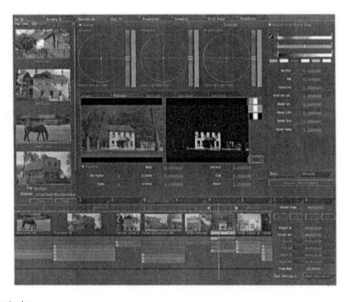

Figure 9.2 Secondaries

of the picture for correction while leaving the rest of the frame alone. The area can be tracked around the frame over time. Many shapes are available for the window area.

Color FX

Color FX creates color transitions and exotic looks. Preset looks are available in a nodal based drag-and-drop system, as shown in Figure 9.3. Many of these "canned" looks are great, even if used only as a jumping off point for further grading.

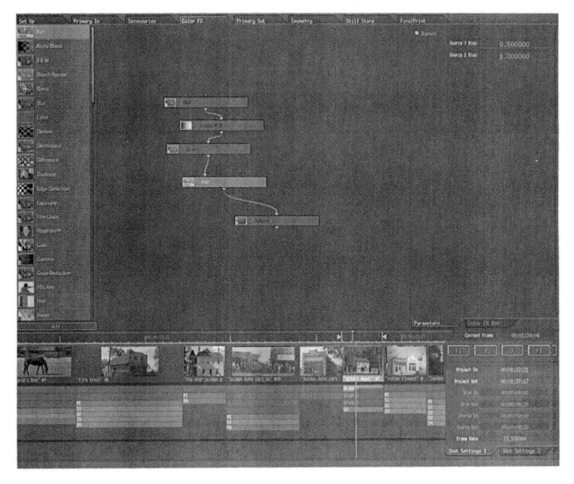

Figure 9.3 Color FX

Geometry/Pan and Scan

Figure 9.4 shows how, from this window, the image can be cropped and reframed, even to a new aspect ratio. The cropping can be changed and moved over time. The classic use here is to "pan and scan" a 16×9 frame to a 4×3. For more information, see Appendix 6 on aspect ratios and pan and scan.

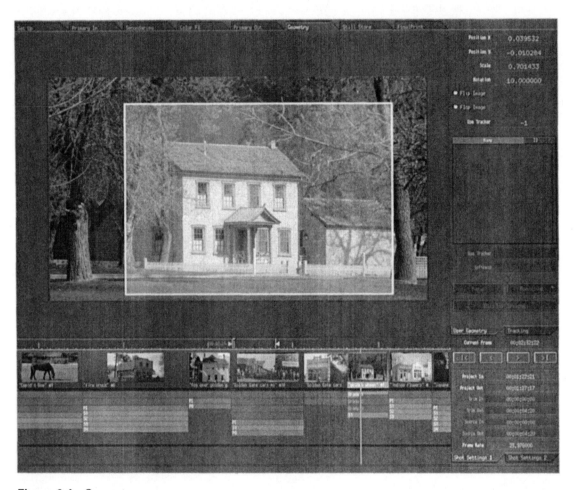

Figure 9.4 Geometry

Setup

The setup is automatic when you send a Final Cut Pro project to Color and, in normal use, there may be no reason to come here. However the "setup room," as seen in Figure 9.5, can be used to define special render settings; apply predefined, broadcast-safe settings, or manage the database of media origins.

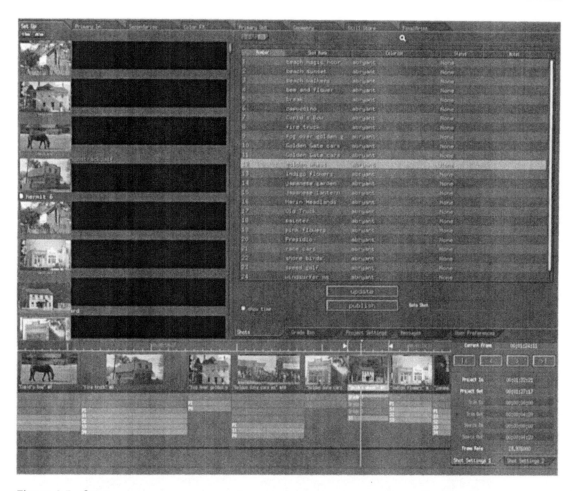

Figure 9.5 Setup

Primary Out

From this room, shown in Figure 9.6, you can set global adjustments to the entire project without changing the other settings.

Still Store

Figure 9.7 shows the still store "room," which is used to hold still frames from other shots to use as a grading guide. This helps match related scenes and shots by A-B comparison to stills from the still store room.

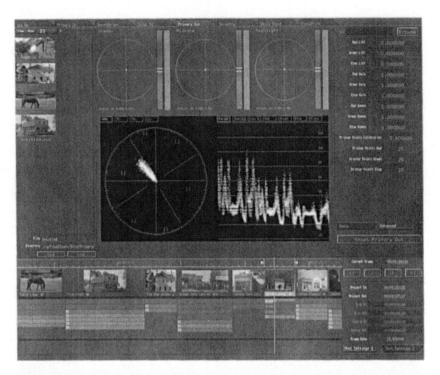

Figure 9.6   Primary out

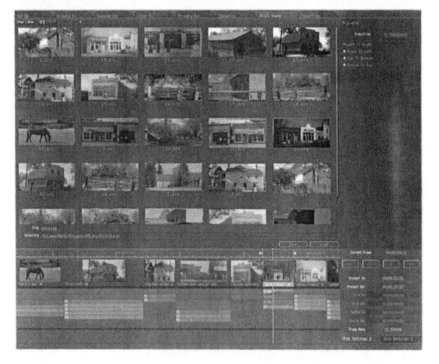

Figure 9.7   Still store

Render Queue

From the render queue, shown in Figure 9.8, you can set up and manage your final renders in various resolutions up to 4:4:4 2 K. As rendering is time consuming, this cue can be used to monitor background rendering or set up dedicated renders.

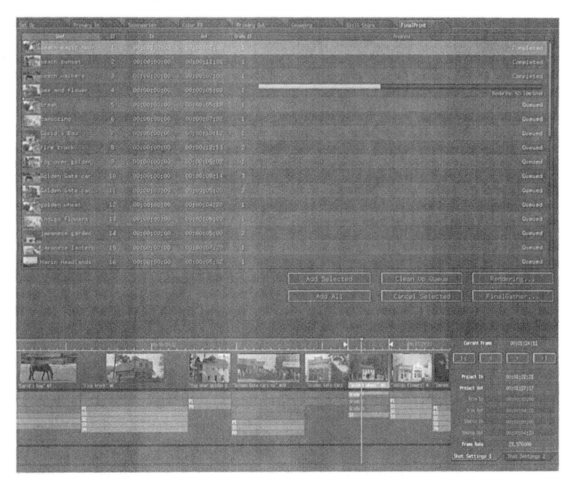

Figure 9.8 Render queue

Color Grading Film or Video when Finishing on Uncompressed Video or DI

Historically, the final color correction for uncompressed video has been in the online edit. The color correction equipment is there in the online room, and the adjustments can be made as the higher resolution video replaces the lower resolution video. However, with the costs of the best color grading equipment being very high, and with the online costs also being quite high, spending time color correcting while the rest of the online stands still makes no sense. So, many projects have been color correcting after the online by going tape-to-tape in a color-correction suite.

Because the color corrector three-way settings are automatically applied in the online, many projects have nothing more done to them than tweaking the three-way settings once the final image and color are seen. Now, with Color, it makes sense to follow the same basic workflow, but with Color as the grading software.

Also, with Apple's ProRes 422, there is no need to go to online unless you simply like that workflow. Which is a valid reason, the online is much more than equipment; it's people. Experts help put the chosen look on the screen. Experts give advice on technical issues and help in hundreds of ways, but at a cost.

So whether you are simply trying to save money, or you are a chronic do-it-yourselfer, which is also a valid reason, ProRes 422 and Color allow you to skip the online and color grade on your own system. It also seems very unlikely that someone would want to color grade their 2 K DI for 35 mm film out on their own system, but here, too, they can if they want to.

Many filmmakers are becoming "home movie rebels," taking the term *home movie* to a radical new level. Several A-list filmmakers have their own mixing theater and Final Cut Pro edit system, so no doubt they will also be grading their own color.

The power of the newer color grading systems have allowed filmmakers to create very unusual color manipulations, which have become common in films and video projects over the last ten years. These wild looks have become almost a signature for films made at the beginning of the new century, and may well be studied in film history classes twenty years from now. But the power of these systems have added a wonderful new tool to the filmmakers toolbox, and stylish trend or not, this genie is unlikely to ever go peacefully back into the bottle.

10 After the Film Is Finished: Distribution

Once a film is finished, there are still several steps in the workflow; the film must be distributed. This may be done on film, digital delivery to theaters, videotape, or DVD. Specialists will handle all of these possible delivery systems, but the film postproduction team will need to understand what the specialists need and be prepared to deliver to them what they need.

Distribution on Film

Distribution on film generally means distribution on 35 mm film. Figure 10.1 shows a typical theater film projection booth, which uses film. With the exception of IMAX, all other film projection formats are essentially dead. True, 70 mm and 16 mm are still used, however they are anachronisms; they have no commercial applications anymore.

Unless you need fewer than four or five release prints, you will need a print internegative. Several prints can be pulled directly from the camera negative, but every time the camera original is printed, it's at risk. Moreover, prints made off of the camera negative are more expensive. Although a print internegative is expensive, it pays for itself after about five prints.

As mentioned in earlier chapters, an internegative cannot be made directly from the camera negative, an interpositive must be made from the camera negative, and then the print internegative is made from the interpositive. The internegative is made from tough estar base film that can be printed at very high speed. On large films several print internegatives will be made allowing for thousands of prints to be made.

Prints are shipped on 2,000-foot reels, but are most often spliced together on the projection system that can typically hold about 15,000 feet of print. Most prints are self-contained; however, DTS prints are shipped with a separate sound track on CD.

Figure 10.1 Film projection booth. While film projectors are less complicated than digital projectors, the costs can be just as high. The disadvantages of film projection are large equipment, expensive and fragile film prints, building up prints, rewinding/cueing and expensive print shipping costs

Digital Theatrical Distribution

Digital projection and media server systems are becoming much more commonplace in theaters, such as the Sony SXRD 4 K digital projector. At this time, there is no standardized format. However, the advantages and cost savings are so huge the pressure is on to further develop this technology.

The motion picture can be delivered digitally to the theater in several ways:

- It can be shipped on portable drive. Even a two-terabyte portable drive is now less expensive than a 35 mm print, and it is reusable immediately. The theater simply downloads the movie and ships the drive back to the distributor.

- It can be downloaded via Internet or satellite. This is slow, as the media files are huge. However, it has been used successfully for years on a limited basis.

- It has even been suggested and tested to deliver on HDVD. While this is certainly not the best image available, at test screenings, the audiences have certainly found the image adequate, especially on a smaller screen. This may be an option for low-budget production and distribution.

At this time, 4 K Cineon or DPX are the gold standards for digital projection. While the latest generation of digital projectors can project directly in 4 K, they use a compressed version of 4 K. As Cineon and DPX are the same 4 K formats used in digital intermediate, the workflow from film is the same as the film finish on DI workflow discussed in Chapter 5. However, in this case the media will be compressed into a projection format.

The same facilities that are offering film DI also offer 2 K DI from digital finish. They can advise you on how to prepare your online for digital theatrical distribution.

While HDCam tape is often projected directly, it is very expensive and totally unnecessary. Tape will likely give way to projection only from server in 4 K or any media format compatible with the digital projection.

Distribution on Videotape

Distribution on videotape can mean delivery for broadcast or distribution on VHS. While VHS is, for the most part, another dead format, it is still used. Whether for VHS duplication or broadcast, the requirements for delivery are essentially the same. A broadcast master tape is delivered to the broadcaster or duplication house. These are usually made by the same facility that did the online edit. However, it is also common for producers to take the online edit master to a post house later for making submasters including broadcast masters. On delivery, the tape will be examined by the broadcaster or duplication house to look for problems. This inspection is called quality control or simply QC. Chrominance, luminance, and audio levels are checked. If there are any problems, the master tape is rejected. The examination is thorough; it is not uncommon for tapes to be rejected. Digi Beta and D-5 are often used for broadcast masters. VHS duplication masters are usually delivered on Digi Beta or sometimes even on Beta SP. HD broadcast masters are usually HD Cam or D-5.

The broadcast master should have a "standard" broadcast head leader:

Tape start at TC 00:58:50 followed by 10 seconds of black

00:59:00:00 30 seconds of color bars

00:59:30:00 5 seconds of black

00:59:35:00 15 seconds info slate (info about the program)

00:59:50:00 2 seconds of black

00:59:52:00 8 seconds of countdown leader (Picture Start frame)

01:00:00:00 Program Video (10:00:00:00 on PAL, 02:00:00:00, 03:00:00:00, and so on, on successive reels)

Distribution on DVD

DVD has become the most popular home video distribution format. DVD stands for Digital Versatile Disc, and it truly is that, although most people use Video instead of Versatile. The format is expanding constantly, with new features added every year. Most DVD consumers are totally unaware of the upgrades; they are usually compatible and automatic. People load a DVD into their player and simply expect it to play. And usually it does. Yet, there are many formats and options on DVD. They come in 4 × 3, 16 × 9, MPEG2, MPEG4, VC-1, H264/AVC (HDVD), and blue ray. Audio can be PCM, Dolby Digital, Dolby Digital Plus, STS, Dolby True HD, and DTS HD. They can also play PCM audio CDs, MP3 disc, Photo CD, Data CD, and 5.1 super discs. They are now also available in standard HDVD and Blue Ray. If all this sounds confusing and complicated, that's because it is. Yet, some of the authoring and burning systems are so simple that kids make thousands of DVDs every day.

Professional DVDs are authored by skilled people using much more complicated software than the average home enthusiast. Final Cut Pro Studio comes bundled with DVD Studio Pro, one of the best authoring systems in use. While it can be very simple to use, it can also "go deep," becoming a very complicated, robust system capable of authoring even the most elaborate DVDs.

DVD authoring software usually comes with some type of compression system that is often automatic. The user may be compressing without even knowing they are doing it. But for professional DVDs, compression must be controlled and optimized. There are many good compression applications available. Final Cut Pro Studio also comes bundled with Compressor, another great piece of software (see Figure 10.2). This, too, is often used professionally. While many Final Cut Pro Studio users may never use it, preferring to let DVD Studio Pro compress automatically, those who want to fine-tune their DVDs will find Compressor invaluable.

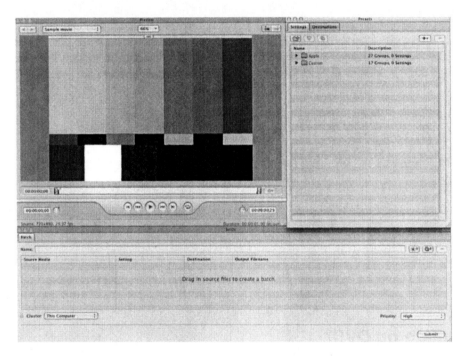

Figure 10.2 Compressor is used to compress the video and audio down to something compatible with DVD or Internet Streaming

As this is a book on workflow, we won't go into the use of DVD authoring and compression software. Instead, we focus on the steps necessary to deliver the project to the DVD author, and the various workflow steps he or she needs to go through in the process.

The film is delivered to the DVD author as a complete film exported as a media file. In Final Cut Pro, this will be a QuickTime movie. Although the film may have been edited in reels, it must be brought together in one timeline. Then, all that is needed is to Export QuickTime from the File menu.

For films that will not have an online, this will be part of the finishing. After the final mix is added to the timeline and all color correction is finished, simply export the movie as a Quicktime. This will export the movie in its native format with a stereo sound track. For 5.1 mixes, the Dolby AC3 audio will be encoded and compressed separately in Compressor, as seen in Figure 10.3, and added in DVD authoring.

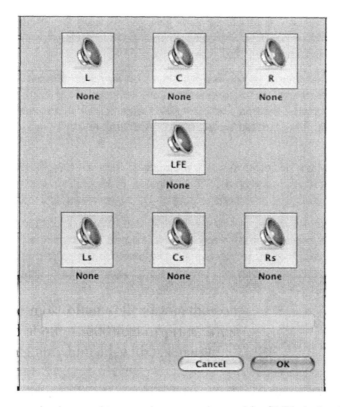

Figure 10.3 Compressor is also used to encode surround sound for DVD's in the AC3 format. Theatrical encoding must be done by a representative from Dolby, Sony or DTS using proprietary equipment and software

It may seem logical to "down convert" to a format like DV on export when using an HD or even DVC Pro 50 when you are planning a standard definition DVD. As the DVD is much more compressed than DV, down converting to DV seems like a logical workflow. However, this is disastrous. The compression software is designed to create the best possible compression from the data available; the more image information you give it the better it performs. Always compress the best available media and never double compress anything.

When a project is finished on film, there may not be any usable media to use in the DVD or as a broadcast master. The original telecine was probably a "best light" without very much color correction. It was most likely done to DVCam, and so this digital video is certainly not the best media available. As always there are several workflow options:

- After the negative is conformed and answer prints are made, telecine the conformed negative to a high-quality video format and capture this to drive and tape. This is problematic if the negative has been A-B rolled.

- If an interpositive is being made, it can be telecined rather than the camera negative. However, this does not look as good as telecining the negative.

- A low-contrast (or "lo con") print can be made just for telecining for broadcast and DVD. This is a very common workflow yet, here, too, this does not look as good as going back to the negative. The lo-con is telecined, captured, and exported.

- During the original telecine a HD or Digibeta tape can be made and used for onlining after the film is finished. This requires more meticulous color correction in the initial telecine and an online edit. It also requires that all opticals and titles added to the movie be telecined from the conformed negative. The results, however, can be excellent.

Stereo audio and broadcast surround sound will be added from the original comp mix media in the online and DVD surround audio added in DVD authorship. In all four of these workflows the captured video will need to have all markers added as part of the compression or DVD authoring.

The digital media contains metadata which, as mentioned in Chapter 8, is additional data "embedded" in the video. This data contains time codes, but also "markers." These can be chapter markers or compression markers. Many of these markers are embedded as the project is edited. The beginning of every shot has a compression marker, for example. Chapter markers can be added in the edit or they can be added in the DVD authoring.

For video only projects that are being onlined, the final film should be exported in its native format as part of the online. This may be too expensive or simply not possible depending on the online facilities capabilities. For example, they may not be able to export to a Mac-formatted drive. Also, if color correction is being preformed tape-to-tape, it is not possible to export the movie. In this case, the project can be recaptured later from the master tape or a submaster. This will likely strip all compression and chapter markers so your workflow should include placing all markers later either in Final Cut Pro or in compression.

Compression markers are necessary to achieve clean compression. While the author designing the compression will likely be adding new markers, they will also assume that there are markers present from the editing. Moreover, all markers can be added here in the edit before exporting the QuickTime, if that is the workflow you choose to follow. If the film is printed to video and recaptured, this will strip the markers and alter the metadata. While it is fine and even necessary to export the movie as a QuickTime, if the project is printed to tape, the markers may need to be replaced. It is also possible to strip all markers from the QuickTime on export if the workflow being followed is to add all markers manually in authoring.

Compression markers tell the compression to record a complete frame. This is called an "I frame." Oddly enough, most DVD-compliant video codices only record around two complete frames per second. The rest are interpolated. If an edit occurs inside this interpolated section, the edit will change from one shot to the other over time as each new frame is interpolated. This looks like a mess. The first frame of the new shot needs to be a new, complete frame. The person designing the compression will also want to place markers at any place where a complete frame will improve the look of the video. Any time the image changes abruptly—a snap pan, any sudden movement by characters or the camera—it should receive a compression marker at the beginning and end of the sudden change. Compression markers can be placed into the metadata from Final Cut Pro during the edit, or it can be added in DVD compression design. Chapter markers can also be added in the same way. Chapter markers can be used in the DVD menu for navigation.

To add compression and chapter markers in Final Cut Pro:

- While in the timeline, add a marker (M key or marker menu).

- In the marker menu, select Edit Marker.

- Select Compression or Chapter.

The compression can also be designed and performed right in Final Cut Pro. Once all the markers are in, export using compressor from the file menu. The compression is also designed by selecting what kind of compression will be used to create what codec and many other options.

The same graphic designer who is designing the posters and other art will likely create title media and graphics for menus and navigation. Photoshop files can be imported directly into DVD Studio Pro and converted to navigation menus. Many of the same guidelines discussed in Chapter 8 on digital titles will apply here, too.

There are two ways to deliver the finished DVD for DVD duplication:

- The finished files and DVD Studio Pro project can be delivered on a portable drive. They could also be sent via FTP over the Internet.

- A prototype DVD can be delivered. The labels should be delivered on separate media, perhaps a CD.

The duplicator will follow one of two workflows depending on his or her equipment and the number of duplicates requested:

- For smaller orders of fewer than 500, the copies will be "burned" to blank media. These are usually done on an automated system that burns the DVD and prints the label without any supervision. These are slow and more expensive per copy, but there is no prep or setup, and it is therefore less expensive on small orders.

- The project will be burned to a "glass master" and this will be used to make a stamping or casting mold. The copies can now be mass-produced at very high speed and very low cost. However, the glass mastering is rather expensive, making this system rarely used on small runs.

Glass-mastered DVDs also have the advantage of being much more stable and playable from all DVD players. The burned DVDs can only be played on more tolerant players. Burned DVDs will not play on about 15 percent of DVD players, including most portable players.

Distribution on the Web

Distribution on the Web is only slightly different than distribution on DVD. However, in Web distribution, there is no authoring, only compression. In this case, the entire project is prepared in Final Cut Pro and then compressed to one of many Web-compatible codices, frame sizes, and frame rates. It is possible to export directly from Final Cut Pro by using the Export QuickTime Converted; however, exporting to Compressor and optimizing the compression produces much better looking video and faster downloads.

All of the same rules for DVD compression apply here as well. However, the compliant formats and codices are totally different. Here, too, always compress the best possible media, never compress video that has already been compressed.

The Web supports many frame rates not used in any video format. A common rate is 15 FPS. Also, the Web supports both 16 × 9 and 4 × 3 aspect ratios. If the metadata contains a 16 × 9 flag, the QuickTime window will open in 16 × 9. Otherwise, it will open in 4 × 3. If a 16 × 9 sequence is exported, the flag is automatically set. It can also be set in Compressor or whatever compression software you choose.

A new "edict" has been handed down by some distribution people, saying that filmmakers should refrain from use of wide shots and tell the story in close-ups as much as possible because this works better when the film is viewed on a cell phone or ipod. And while this is a totally unwanted intrusion into the filmmaking process, it raises an interesting rhetorical question, do people really watch movies on their cell phone? I'll bet even Alexander Graham Bell never saw that one coming. And keep using wide shots, distributors never did have a clue.

Appendix 1
Understanding the NTSC Video Format and Digital Video

Analog Video

Before current workflows can be understood, it is necessary to fully understand video systems and the time code formats used with video. There are several video systems being used in the world; many are in a state of change with new high-definition systems replacing the older formats. In most of the world, the PAL and SECAM formats are standard. In the United States and Japan, the NTSC format has been standard, but is being replaced by HD. Even though the NTSC format is archaic, the newest digital formats follow some NTSC standards. Although it is often said that video plays at 30 FPS, more often than not, this is a misnomer. The speed is being rounded off to keep the math simple. While there are 30 FPS video formats, they are quite rare; virtually all standard definition video in the United States plays at 29.97 FPS.

The System

"The System" was invented by Philo T. Farnsworth, seen in Figure A1.1, from Beaver County, Utah. He claimed that the idea came to him one day while plowing a field. He envisioned how an image could be scanned from lines just as his field was plowed into lines. Being an avid electronics enthusiast, he came up with a way to electronically split up an image and rebuild it on a cathode ray tube. Later, he dashed out a pencil drawing of a camera image tube for one of his instructors at school, a drawing that was used years later to defend his patent for what was dubbed "Television." He was fourteen years old.

Figure A1.1 Philo T. Farnsworth and the farnovision

Philo's first system had 300 scan lines and was monochrome. Later systems, while still monochrome, operated at 30 FPS and had 525 lines. Years later, engineers came up with the NTSC format, a way to add color to the signal and maintain compatibility with the earlier monochrome system. They inserted some of the color information into a color subcarrier. This signal's frequency was a multiple of the frame rate and audio and caused undesirable color banding. Unfortunately, instead of detuning the color or audio subcarrier, they opted to detune the sync frequency by .1 percent, causing the frame rate to change to 29.97. We are still stuck with this frame rate even in most high-definition digital video displays.

Each frame of NTSC video is made up of two fields. The image is scanned onto the screen starting in the upper left of the picture. A "flying spot" of changing color and brightness speeds across the screen tracing in the picture as lines. The spot is moving quite fast; even on a small TV, it is traveling at more than 1,000 miles per hour.

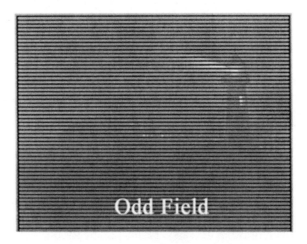

Figure A1.2 Odd video field. A total of 240 lines are scanned before the "spot" leaves the picture at the bottom. It continues scanning for 22.5 more lines drawing in unseen sync and blanking information before completing its journey. The first pass of the "spot" paints in the odd lines of the frame

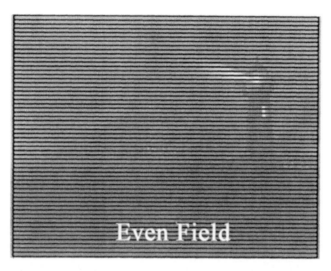

Figure A1.3 Even video field. The spot then traces in the even numbered lines, 240 more lines between the first set as well as 22.5 more lines of sync. On a properly set up TV, the odd and even lines are the exact right width so that they do not overlap or leave any spaces between the lines

Figure A1.4 Full frame video. The finished "interlaced" frame therefore consists of 480 lines of picture and 45 lines of sync for a total of 525 lines per frame. As the frame rate is 29.97 per second, the field rate is 59.94 fields per second

Does this mean that if we could freeze time, all that would be on the screen would be a tiny dot of color? To some extent, the answer is both yes and no. Different TV sets have different amounts of "lag," which is to say that once the "spot" area of the screen lights up, it takes a small fraction of a second for it to dim and go out. By then, the spot has moved on, and may even be several lines further down the screen. So if we could freeze time we would see a very narrow band of image across the screen, dimmer at the top than the bottom. The full image is created in the viewer's eyes and mind by the process of "persistence of vision," the phenomenon where bright images are held in the retina of the eye for a fraction of a second.

Modern Digital Formats

With the newer digital video formats, often the interlacing is removed or never used in the first place. These formats are referred to as "progressive" because the entire image is traced in one pass of the flying spot. This creates a much more stable image with much less jitter. However, if the frame rate stays at 29.97 or, even worse, 24, the image is now flashing on and off at such a slow speed that the image will appear to be flickering. To solve this problem, the image is traced in more than once. On most HD sets, all images are displayed interlaced at 59.94 fields per second. On some monitors, every frame is displayed twice, a process called line doubling.

This same system is used with motion picture film projection. In the theater, each frame is projected twice; the screen is flashing on and off 48 times per second. If the image were flashing at the frame rate of 24 per second, the image would be unwatchable.

New video formats contain an I or P in their names to indicate if they are interlaced or progressive. A format of 720p is therefore progressive, 1080i, interlaced. The number in the name of the newer HD video formats refers to the number of scan lines. The exception to this rule is 24P, an expression that refers to the frame rate. 24P is not a video format, but rather a collection of formats that run at a 24 or 23.976 FPS rate. The expression 60i also refers to the frame rate or, in this case, the field rate. The 60i simply refers to common 29.97 FPS interlaced video. This is called 60i instead of 30i to reinforce that in 60i interlaced video, each field is a unique slice of time. The image, and therefore the movement, were sampled and recorded almost 60 times every second and so is much smoother. Remember, 30 is a misnomer, the true frame rate is 29.97 and so the field rate is 59.94. 24P is also a misnomer; the real frame rate is usually 23.976, which also is usually rounded off as 23.98. It all means the same thing except there is a rarely used, true 24 FPS version of 24P.

While digital images are still displayed using Farnsworth's line scan system, digital video is recorded as frames of pixels, tiny picture elements of recorded color. Each pixel's color is recorded as a number value in binary code, and each number represents one specific color. The larger the number recorded, the more colors that can be reproduced. Most formats record this value as three separate binary numbers, one for the red component, one for the green, and one for the blue. Most formats record an 8-bit binary value, or 256 values of red, green, and blue for a total of 16,777,216 colors. Some high-end formats record a 10-bit number or 1,024 values of red, green, and blue for a total of 1,073,741,824 colors.

Some formats also use a "lookup table" of colors. Here is analogy for the way a lookup table works. In "standard" 8-bit color formats, every binary number represents a color, like a huge room with more than 16,000,000 crayons in it. Different formats have a different "color space." In other words, they use a different set of crayons. Each crayon has a code number on it and each pixel is colored in with the corresponding crayon. With a lookup table, there are an infinite number of crayons. At the beginning of the image, a code sets the lookup table; it picks 16 million of these crayons to put in the room and use in the image. If there are no reds in the image, there will be no red crayons placed in the room. Depending on the image, this dramatically increases the apparent "color space," but to truly increase this space, you need a bigger room. One that will hold more crayons, such as a 10-bit room with space for more than a billion crayons.

Logic would say that there is no reason to record more lines of pixels than lines displayed and, usually this is true. A frame of 1,080 displayed lines will usually consist of 1,080 rows of pixels.

Pixels in early digital formats were square, just as they are on a computer screen. In an effort to sharpen standard definition (SD) video, a rectangular pixel has become the norm. The 4 × 3 aspect DV formats use a pixel that is taller than wide, the CCIR 601 format. As there are only 480 lines displayed in SD NTSC video, there are only 480 lines of pixels used in the image. Formats that use a square pixel have 640 pixels on each line. The CCIR 601 format allows the number of horizontal pixels to be 720 or an image size of 720 × 480.

The frames seen in Figures A1.5 and A1.6 are extreme blowups of the frame from "No Fui Yo." Figure A1.5 is a frame displayed with a "normal" square pixel. Some digital video formats and all computers use this aspect ratio.

Figure A1.6 is a frame displayed in the CCIR 601 format used by DV and some other digital video formats. Notice that the pixel is no longer square, but slightly rectangular, taller than wide. This allows for an increase in the horizontal resolution.

The highlighted area in Figure A1.7 contains the same four pixels in each example. The highlight helps show the change in pixel aspect ratio.

This can be a problem when creating graphics and titles on a computer screen. As the pixels of the computer screen are square, the 720 × 480 image will be displayed wider than it will be when displayed on the video screen.

Figure A1.5 In this pixel close up of a frame from *No Fui Yo* by Roland De Middle Puch, it can be seen that the image is recorded as small pixels. In this case the image is displayed with a "normal" square pixel. In the video display each horizontal row of pixels will become one horizontal line of video. Image courtesy of Roland De Middle Puch

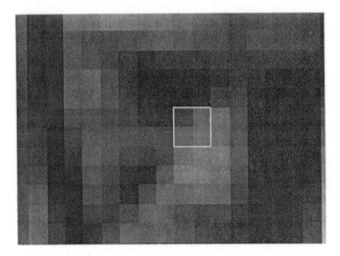

Figure A1.6   Pixel close up from *No Fui Yo* with square pixels

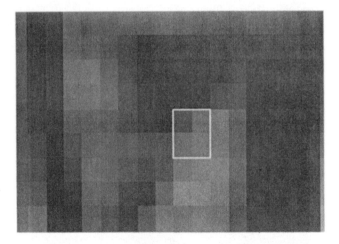

Figure A1.7   *No Fui Yo* pixel close up in CCIR 601 showing the taller-than-wide pixel aspect ratio

Videotape and Metadata

For the first twenty years of television, there was no videotape. Most of the programming was created live, even the commercials. Some shows were produced on film and the film broadcast from a "film chain" much like a telecine machine, but rather basic.

When videotape appeared, it was cumbersome and expensive. The tape needed to move at a high speed to gain enough bandwidth to record a video signal. Even a large roll of tape only held about four minutes of program. To solve this problem, a spinning head was developed. Now, instead of moving the tape at a high speed, the record and play heads moved at a high speed and the tape moved very slowly.

On the earliest systems, a spinning drum with the heads attached was placed perpendicular to the tape movement. The heads would spin across the width of the tape, which was two inches wide (see Figure A1.8). Because the tape was moving forward at a slow speed, each head crossed the tape at a slight angle creating slightly angled bands of signal across the tape. Thirty-two of these bands could hold one frame of analog video signal.

2 Inch Transverse Quad Videotape

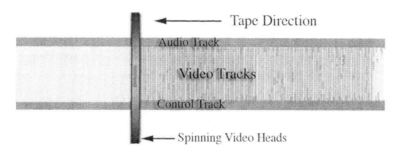

Figure A1.8 Two inch quad videotape track layout. Two inch quad was the "gold standard" for decades

On later systems, the tape was wound around the head drum in a helix, spiraling down from the top of the drum to the bottom. This made the signal bands much longer, several inches long even on a much narrower tape. Now, each field could be recorded on one band or two bands per frame.

While the video was recorded on the helical bands, audio was recorded on the edge of the tape with a fixed head. A "control track" was recorded on the opposite edge also with a fixed head. The control track is used to keep the speed of the moving tape interlocked with the video signal. Without it, the tape speeds up or slows down causing the video heads to loose alignment with the video tracks.

Time code can also be recorded by a fixed head on one of these "linear" or "longitudinal" tracks running along the edge of the tape.

On some machines, time code and even audio can be interleaved into the video on the helical tracks. Time code placed into the sync is called Vertical Interval Time Code (VITC). It is also possible to interleave copyright information and copy guard.

When digital recorders came on the scene, they used this same basic tape transport system. The helical heads could record the extremely high bandwidth needed when recording a digital data stream. One important difference between digital and analog recording is that an analog recording needs to be a constant stream of successive signal. However, digital data can be shuffled, compressed, and even mixed with other data. Digital recorders do not "waste" bandwidth recording sync information like an analog recorder does. The sync information is created in playback. A digital flag causes the sync video signal to be created by the playback machine at the proper time. Yet some digital recorders can still record and play VITC and copyright data by recording six lines of the sync signal just above the image. This requires capturing at 720 × 486. When capturing this video to drive, the VITC is stripped unless the capture settings are set to preserve these few lines of sync.

Where analog recorders interleaved some information into the sync signal, digital recorders can also interleave this information as well as a huge amount of information into the data stream. This information is called metadata, data about the video data. DV cameras record a wealth of information onto the DV tape along with the video. The tape track layout can be seen in Figure A1.9. This data contains four separate time codes including time of day, date, all camera settings including white balance, gain, menu settings, f-stop, shutter speed, and focal length. And there is space for "user-defined" data, data such as key code information from film transfer, user-defined time code, and will someday record information that hasn't even been thought of yet.

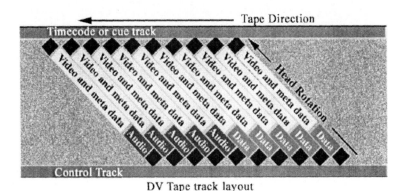

DV Tape track layout

Figure A1.9   DVC videotape track layout. Much of the information stored with each frame is "metadata", information about the image

When DV tape is captured to drive, most of this data is ignored, but not removed. Even after editing, this information can be extracted from any shot in the project. And the captured video can have even more data added as it is captured to drive, compressed, or printed to video.

Error Correction and Dropout

Logic would dictate that as the recording is digital—only ones and zeros—that the quality of tape and recording format would not effect the image quality. If the ones and zeros are recorded and playback intact, then the image will look fine; if the information is not playable, there will be no image. Not so. If a small amount of information is lost to dropout, the system rebuilds this lost data through a process of error correction.

Because the digital data can be shuffled and mixed with other data, several systems can be used to check for damaged data and repair or interpolate a repair. The first system is called "checksum error correction." It uses a fixed interval in the pixel information. All of the values of the pixels inside the interval are added together. This number is recorded at the end of the interval as the first checksum. Then, all of the pixel values are multiplied by their position in the interval; the second pixel value is multiplied by 2, the third by 3 and so on.

Let's look at a simplified example. Let's say we have 4 pixels in our interval. The values of the pixels are 2, 4, 7, and 5. So the first checksum is 18. Now the values are multiplied by their position. They become 2, 8, 21, and 20. The second checksum is therefore 51. Now let's say in playback we get values of 2, 6, 7, and 5. This checksum is 20, so we know something is over by 2. But which value is over? The second checksum is 55, or 4 over. Four is twice 2 so we know the second value is the errant pixel and it is repaired.

Another system uses interleaving and interpolation. In interleaving, the pixels are not recorded in order, but are recorded in a predictable pattern. The first pixel may be the fiftieth recorded, the second pixel may be the third recorded, the third may be the thirty-second value recorded. Now, if there is damage on the tape and twelve values in a row are dropped out, the missing information is scattered all over the image. If several values in the checksum interval have been lost, there is no hope of the checksum error correction fixing the problem. However, because the missing pixels are scattered all over the image, the pixels surrounding the missing pixel can be averaged and this value used in place of the missing pixel.

While good, this process cannot re-create the exact data. This creates undesirable artifacts and loss of image quality. All recordings have some dropout, DV recordings on poor tape have a lot more dropouts than DVCam or DVC Pro recordings on high-quality tape. Good tape and strong signal does make a difference.

In spite of the fact that videotape is the most common system for recording digital video, it is slowly becoming obsolete. At some point all video will likely be shot on hard drive, optical disc, or memory chips.

Compression

Any digital video signal that is being recorded or transmitted will be compressed. The amount of data needs to be brought down to a manageable bandwidth. Some formats claim to be "uncompressed," but this is not exactly true. They may be "lossless," in other words, all the compressed information is recovered intact in playback, but anyone would want to record as much data as possible. All formats use some compression, it would be foolish not to.

Here's an analog for lossless compression: Let's say you are a sheepherder and for some strange reason you want to count the sheep's feet. Look, it's just an analog, go with it for a minute. So rather than count the feet, it makes more sense to count the sheep and multiply by four. Unless one of the sheep has a really bad limp, you can assume this is 100 percent accurate, totally lossless compression of the data. But now let's say you don't want to count all those sheep every time. You need to know how many feet there are out there, so you dip one of every ten sheep in blue die. Now you can count the blue sheep, multiply by forty and that's how many feet they have. This is also more or less accurate, unless of course one of the sheep wanders off and gets eaten by a wolf. And if the herd can't be divided into tens, you will need to round the number off. So some of your data is now potentially lost using this "lossy" compression scheme.

We can do something similar with video compression. In this case, we need to know the color value of all of our pixels, but we don't want to record all of these values. The first thing we can do is look at all of the pixels around one pixel. If the first four pixels in a video line are all more or less the same value, like the sheep's feet, let's just record one and use it for all four. If the four pixels on the next line are more or less the same value, the first value can be used for all eight pixels in both lines.

This can also be used from one frame to the next. If the first pixel has the same value as that pixel in the first four frames, this value can be recorded once and used in all four frames. Compression within a single frame is called *spatial compression*. Compression over time from one frame to the next is called *temporal compression*.

There is also a system where the actual bit depth is reduced at times in certain parts of the picture. If your image is white titles over black, you don't need eight bits to record black. In can even be recorded with one.

The compression scheme of several popular video formats is based on the MPEG system, which is an offshoot of Apples QuickTime. There are many forms of MPEG, but all use these systems for compression.

In MPEG the screen is divided spatially and temporally. The block is 8 pixels wide, 8 pixels high and 8 frames deep. All of these values are compared and, if similar, one value is recorded and used in the entire block. If only some are similar, these are combined in smaller blocks until all pixels are being recorded individually. The amount of compression is controlled by the tolerance of the compared values. If the compression will only accept an exact match, the compression is lossless. If it rounds off values that are close but not a match, there is some loss but much more compression.

Most compression schemes constantly change the tolerance of the pixel matching up and down to keep the data stream within a specific bandwidth. At times, on a highly compressed image, the picture can look perfect; at times, it can break up into square chunks of image that extend over several frames. It depends on the amount of compression being used at that moment, which is controlled by the picture content and the limits of the bandwidth. A complicated image with many colors and lots of movement will cause a spike in the amount of compression and loss of quality. Conversely, a very static shot with broad fields of color will cause the compression to reduce and image quality to go up.

Color Compression

Often, the color information is compressed more than the black-and-white information. In the earliest color video, the color was added to an existing black-and-white signal. The color signal (chrominance) was always a much lower quality than the black-and-white signal (luminance). But as long as the luminance was sharp, the entire image looked, more or less, sharp.

RGB color can't use this trick because the three signals contain only color components. The luminance is the sum of all three. Compression of one or two of the colors while keeping the third color sharp would only add color shifts and look a mess. In order to selectively compress color while maintaining a sharp luminance requires a different type of component video.

The R−Y/B−Y/Y system was developed just for this purpose. In this case, the RGB is combined into a luminance signal called the Y. If the red information is subtracted from the Y, (R−Y) and the blue is subtracted from the Y, (B−Y) the remainder is the green information. If the R−Y and B−Y are compressed more than the Y, then the color information is uniformly effected but the Y, the black-and-white part of the information, is uncompressed and sharp.

This compression is now achieved by skipping R−Y and B−Y pixels. The grouping is done in groups of four pixels. A numbering system is used to express which pixels are being recorded and which are skipped. The Y is expressed first, followed by the compression cadence. So assuming that all of the Y pixels are recorded to keep the image sharp, the first number in the compression is four, all four pixels of Y recorded. Now let's say that only half of the color pixels are going to be recorded. So, we only record the odd-numbered R−Y pixels and the even-numbered B−Y pixels on each video line. Because the compression is line by line, the vertical resolution is unaffected, the horizontal luminance is equally unaffected, but the horizontal chrominance is down by half and the recorded data is down by 33 percent.

This is referred to as 4:2:2 color compression and it is used in many digital formats. Uncompressed color is referred to as 4:4:4. In 4:2:0 the compression is not line by line, but in pairs of lines. Again, all of the luminance is recorded, but the R−Y is recorded in odd-numbered pixels in the first two video lines and the B−Y is recorded into the even-numbered pixels on the next two lines. There is also 4:1:1, where the compression is line by line but the color information is only recorded for one pixel in the group of four.

True, this requires lots of math at the input and output of the video, but math is what computers do best. If this reduces bandwidth, it's well worth the math. After all, that's what compression is. The amazing thing is that this process is going on in real time while the digital video is being played or recorded; millions of calculations being performed every second.

Video has come a long way from Philo's potato field, and while digital imaging seems to have separated itself into a different category entirely, its video roots run deep. It's unlikely Philo ever imagined metadata being interleaved into the video data stream, yet alone recording video with a data stream in the first place. And there will be equally unimaginable developments in the future. Philo said that the proudest moment in his life was when live television was transmitted from the moon to the earth during the Apollo moon landings. Today almost all broadcast television is transmitted from satellites in space. And because of improved compression, soon that same transmitted digital video will be theatrical quality.

Appendix 2
Understanding the PAL Video Format

Jaime Estrada-Torres, London Film School

The Phase Alternate Line (PAL) color encoding system scans images into 625 horizontal lines to form a video frame every $\frac{1}{25}$ of a second. There are 2 fields per each video frame, which results in 50 fields for every 25 frames in each second. It is also possible to telecine with 2-2-2-2-2-2-2-2-2-2-2-3 cadence to produce video that plays without speed change, but at the cost of the one-to-one relationship between timecode and key code, as seen in Figure A2.1. This would, therefore, be inappropriate for a film edit, but may be used for video finish projects. The PAL system allows for a more defined color rendition than that of an NTSC image.

The burning, on the bottom left of frame in Figure A2.1, shows film key numbers, (new footage updates on the twentieth frame). The burning on the right shows 25 FPS time code (new, second updates on the twenty-fifth frame). A specific time code identifies a specific frame on the tape, in the same way that a particular key number relates to a particular film frame on the film negative/print.

Film shot at 24 FPS runs 4.1 percent faster during PAL telecine. This process creates a one-to-one correspondence between the film and video frames as illustrated in Figure A2.2. Each film frame makes up the two fields that constitute the standard PAL video frame.

Note that the recommended PAL route for film shot at 24 FPS is to telecine with the film running at 25 FPS. The Final Cut setting for the corresponding project must be set as follows: transfer at 25, and video time code at 25.

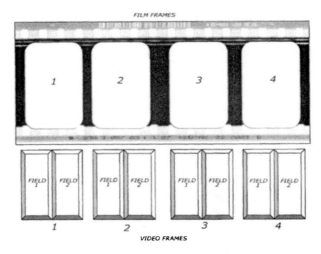

Figure A2.1 One-to-one PAL telecine

Figure A2.2 16mm film frames in PAL video

The data generated during the telecine session provides information relating to 25 FPS. This includes time code on the videotape, key code on the processed film, and, if required, information relating to the original sound time code.

Sound

The sound shot for picture at 24 FPS, and then synced to picture during 25 FPS PAL telecine, can only be used as guide during the nonlinear editing process. The edited sound must be reconformed from the original sources prior to track laying and final sound mix. This procedure is necessary to correct pitch alteration and sample loss during the 4.1 percent speed-up telecine process.

Unlike NTSC telecine, any sound undergoing PAL telecine has to be pitch-corrected to avoid loss of quality. This loss of quality is particularly noticeable on dialogues that will play back at a higher pitch than the original, and music that develops "wow" effects.

It is advisable to use continuous 25 FPS time code format (not time of day/discontinuous time code) for recording sync sound while shooting picture at 24 FPS. If Digislate is used to sync-jam 24 FPS time code for both film camera and sound recorder, it is necessary to make cloned DAT or DA 88 sound tapes with 25 FPS time code prior to editing.

The original 24 FPS time code is added to the data log generated during telecine. The resulting log is then imported into Final Cut Pro for digitizing and editing. Cloning original 24 FPS time-coded sound into new sources with 25 FPS time code does not affect the rate of play, but will generate the time code required for nonlinear PAL postproduction. The making of 25 FPS time code sound sources must follow the sync reference as outlined in Chapter 3, with the difference that sync will be generated from a PAL sync generator. New practices allow for sound to be recorded directly to hard disc. The resulting sound files can then be converted to import directly into Final Cut Pro.

SECAM

There is also the System Electronic Colour Avec Memore (SECAM). The SECAM system has, for the most part, merged with the PAL system as they were somewhat similar. SECAM has, more or less, vanished as a production format; any programming intended for SECAM can be produced in PAL and then converted to SECAM. PAL is often called the European format; however, PAL is a global system. While NTSC is used in North America and Japan, the rest of the world uses PAL.

Appendix 3
Current Video Formats

VHS, U-Matic ($^3/_4$-inch), Betacam, and Beta SP

VHS, U-Matic ($^3/_4$-inch), Betacam, and Beta SP are all obsolete analog standard definition (SD) video formats. All are available in PAL and NTSC formats. Although these are obsolete formats, all are still widely used. VHS, while always a nonprofessional, low-quality format, nevertheless has been, and still is, widely used in professional production as a "screener" format. This is a way to distribute rough temporary versions of a project to people in the production loop or to distributors. Other common home video formats (i.e., S-VHS, High 8, and a few other obscure formats) have never been widely used in professional production with the exception of S-VHS, which went through a brief period when it was used as a "semiprofessional" shooting format.

VHS is making a comeback as Digital S or D-9. This professional digital format uses VHS tape cassettes loaded with a very high-grade tape. The recorders are VHS and S VHS compatible. In terms of image quality, it is quite good, similar to DVC Pro 50 and Digital Beta (DVC stands for Digital Video Cassette). As yet, the format has not received wide acceptance. There is also a HD version for home use.

U-matic and Betacam (not to be confused with the obsolete home video format Betamax) were widely used for years as both scratch and production formats. Both are still used as "screener" or "work" formats simply because of the huge amount of equipment and archival tape left over from the time when these were common formats, but the equipment is no longer available or supported.

Beta SP (Betacam SP) was used until very recently as a broadcast production format. It has slid into use mostly as a "work" or reference format and is no longer considered a broadcast format. Beta SP machines can play Betacam tapes and are still manufactured. The image quality of Beta SP is similar to DV.

Figure A3.1   Sony HDWF 900 Cine Alta HD Cam Camera/Recorder

DV, DVCam, DVC Pro, DVC Pro 50, DVC Pro HD, and HDV

DV, DVCam, DVC Pro, DVC Pro 50, DVC Pro HD, and HDV are the DVC tape formats and all are widely used. HDV and DVC Pro HD (also known as DVC Pro 100, shown in Figure A3.2) are high definition, the rest are SD formats (CCIR 601 720 × 480). DV, DVCam, and DVC Pro are all basically the same format. Except for dropout rates, the image quality is virtually the same among these formats.

Figure A3.2   Panasonic HD 1700 DVC Pro HD Recorder

Some DV camcorders support 24P. These cameras produce only 23.98 FPS; however, they convert this and still record at 29.97. Using Final Cut Pro version 4.5 HD or newer, the extra fields can be removed while capturing, allowing editing of the original 23.98 or "24P." There is much more on this in Chapter 2 on digital video workflow.

Tape speeds are different between the formats as the track width on the tape is different. DV also supports an "LP" mode to fit two hours of program on a one-hour tape, with loss of quality due to dropouts. Other than this LP mode, all DV, DVCam, and DVC Pro tapes can be played in all recorders. However, most recorders can only record their specific format. DVC Pro HD can only be played on a DVC Pro HD machine; however, these recorders can play all DV formats, with the exception of HDV. DVC Pro 50 recorders can also play DV, DVCam, and DVC Pro but cannot play DVC Pro HD or HDV tapes.

DV was originally intended to be a consumer format and many manufacturers make DV recorders. Panasonic and Sony created DVC Pro and DVCam as professional DVC formats. Panasonic's DVC Pro runs at a faster tape speed than Sony's DVCam. These professional formats also have several other improvements over DV including improved time code support.

Tape Cassettes

There are a three sizes of DV cassettes: the large, medium, and mini. All recorders can play the mini cassettes; however, the DVC Pro, Pro 50, and Pro HD recorders require an adaptor to use mini cassettes for play only. Only these DVC Pro recorders use the medium cassette. DVCam and DVC Pro recorders all take the large cassette. DVCam recorders can record and play the mini cassette without an adaptor.

Figure A3.3 shows a variety of DV tape cassettes. Many tapes are labeled for use with a specific format; however, all tape stocks will work with all formats. Tapes labeled for use in the three DVC Pro formats are metal particle tape. Panasonic recommends the use of only metal particle tape when recording on DVC Pro machines. The difference between DVC Pro, DVC Pro 50, and DVC Pro HD tape is simply the quality of the tape. Any of these tapes work in all three formats. However, the quality and price vary widely.

Figure A3.3 DV tape cassettes

DV, HDV, and DVCam use a metal vapor tape. Here, also, the only difference between tapes labeled DV or DVCam is the quality of the tape and both work fine in both formats. Here, also, the price and quality vary widely.

Logic would dictate that as the recording is digital—only ones and zeros—that the quality of tape and recording format would not effect the image quality. If the ones and zeros are recorded and playback intact, then the image will look fine; if the information is not playable, there will be no image. Not so. As noted in Appendix 1, if a small amount of information is lost to dropout, the system rebuilds this lost data through a process of error correction. While good, this process cannot always re-create the data and must "guess" at the missing data. This creates undesirable artifacts and loss of image quality. All recordings have some dropout, DV recordings on poor tape have a lot more dropouts than DVCam or DVC Pro recordings on high-quality tape. Good tape does make a difference.

Format Selections

DVCam, shown in Figure A3.4, has become the "off-line" format of choice. While all these formats are often used on "industrial" and nonbroadcast projects, DVCam is the industry standard for "working copies" on broadcast projects that will be finished on a broadcast quality system in the final edit.

Figure A3.4 Sony DSR 1500a DVCam Recorder

DVC Pro 50 is a unique digital format that is much less compressed than the other DV formats, and the image is noticeably better. The image quality is virtually indistinguishable from the more expensive Digital Betacam and is used in broadcast. DVC Pro 50 recorders can play all DV formats and any size cassette (with the adaptor for mini DV).

DVC Pro HD is an HD format that can record in 720p or 1080i. DVC Pro HD is capable of recording various frame rates and can even achieve slow motion when recorded on the Panasonic® VariCam® (see Figure A3.5). With the HD versions of Final Cut Pro, it is now possible to digitize DVC Pro HD directly to a portable drive and edit natively in DVC Pro HD. DVC Pro HD recorders can play all digital videocassette formats from DVC Pro HD to DV with the exception of HDV. The newest Panasonic DVC HD–DVC Pro 50 cameras can record directly to memory chips avoiding tape altogether. They also shoot to tape in DVC Pro. Because DVC Pro HD recorders always output an HD digital video stream without regard to the tape format being played, they can be used to "up rez." Tape-to-tape dubs can be made as 720p or 1080i.

Figure A3.5 AJ-HDC27 VariCam by Panasonic

HDV is the newest DV format and has become very popular after Sony entered the arena with several pieces of HDV equipment. HDV is a highly compressed HD format that is recorded in the MPEG4 format. The amount of data recorded on the tape is virtually the same as DVCam, yet the picture information in HD is six times that of SD. This requires that the image be much more compressed than standard DVCam. In spite of this extra compression, the image quality is very good. As this was intended as a "prosumer" format, the early cameras were cheap and the image only fair. But the new Sony cameras demonstrate just how good the HDV image can look.

The Sony format is 1080i and lacks a real 24P format. The professional versions of the Sony cameras and recorders can also record and play in DVCam for standard definition projects. HDV is supported in versions Final Cut Pro 5 and above.

D-5, D-1, IMX, and Digital Beta

D-5 is the highest quality SD video format available. It is somewhat rare and very expensive. Although the frame size is still 720 × 480, it is recorded in 10-bit digital.

D-1 is one of the oldest digital formats, developed in 1986. It is similar to D-5 with the exception of being an 8-bit system and 640 × 480. The quality is nevertheless quite good, better than Digital Beta. There are also the D-2 and D-3 formats; however, these are not often used anymore. The quality of these formats is not nearly as good, closer to DV. D-1, D-2, D-3, and D-5 all record to a large $\frac{1}{2}''$ tape cassette. All digital formats were to be given a D number as a SMPTE standard, but not all manufactures have done this. DVC Pro, for example, is also known as D-7. The number 4 was skipped because it is considered unlucky in Japan, the word for four is the same as the word for death.

D-1 and D-5 are often referred to as "uncompressed." This is not exactly true. All digital video formats use compression; however, these formats are "lossless." With lossless, compression all compressed information can be uncompressed into its exact original form.

Digital Beta (Digi Beta) has become the broadcast format of choice. While not quite as high in quality as D-1, it is much more affordable and much more commonplace than D-5 or D-1. There is an offshoot format of Digital Beta called IMX. IMX format uses the same tape as Digital Beta but has an improved image quality.

DVD, Blue Laser Optical Disc, P2 Memory Card

Digital Versatile Disc (DVD) is a recordable consumer format, and while it looks great in your living room, it has few professional applications except as a "screener" format. Although the image is optimized to look good on SD video, the picture is highly compressed. There are also HD DVDs, some of which are recorded and played with a blue laser. Blue laser can record much more information onto the DVD.

Sony has released several cameras and recorders that record to optical disc using a blue laser. The format is called XD Cam. These devices record in either IMX, DVCam, or HD Cam. The signal is recorded just as it would be to tape; only in this case, it is recorded to optical disc. The advantage in recording to optical disc is having no need to log and capture before editing. This is a great advantage in Electronic News Gathering (ENG). The media can be transferred at high speed in just minutes to the hard drive, and is ready to edit while still being transferred. There are other features in these disc recorders that make them attractive to news producers. They can also shoot 24P.

There are high-end optical recorders intended for data storage that can be used to record many digital video formats. Some experimental formats record directly to optical or magnetic storage devices.

It is also possible to record to memory card, an example of which is shown in Figure A3.6. The advantage of this is that memory is extremely fast and can easy record high bandwidth digital video. The down side is it is expensive and fills up rapidly. The Panasonic AG-HVX200 P2 HD Camcorder can record to HDV tape or to P2 card that stores 16 gigabytes of data, or 16 minutes of 1080i high-definition video at 60 FPS. While it is possible to load up to five P2 cards in the camera, at more than $1,000 per card, many users load only two cards and download the video to drive periodically. Panasonic also sells a portable drive with P2 slots just for this downloading. It's also a very good idea to backup this video to a second drive as soon as possible, even on set, just as a safety backup.

Figure A3.6 Panasonic 16 gigabytes P2 memory card

HD D-5, HD Cam, HD Cam SR

HD D-5 is a very high-quality HD video format. It records at true 1,920 × 1,080 image in a moderately compressed 10-bit format. It uses a standard D-5 transport and can play SD D-5.

HD Cam and HD Cam SR are Sony's HD video formats, and are the most common HD formats. They record an 8-bit digital image at a variety of frame rates in either progressive or interlaced format. Because HD Cam is somewhat compressed, the colors are not as true as HD D-5 or HD Cam SR.

2 K, 4 K, 5 K

These are not really video formats, but rather tapeless, digital movie formats. The number refers to the number of horizontal pixels, approximately 2,000, 4,000, or 5,000. The codices used are Cineon and Digital Moving Picture exchange (DPX). These formats are normally created by scanning film and recording the resulting digital frames onto a computer drive or array of drives. While it is possible to record from a digital camera directly to 2 K and 4 K, this has been highly experimental and not in common practice until 2007 with the release of the new Red One camera that shoots to drive in 4 K DPX. These formats have been only used as intermediate steps in the production workflow. Very slow film scanners are used to scan film into 4 K and 5 K. 2 K can also be scanned, or a device called a datacine can "scan" the film in real time. These files can be shot back onto film for printing or they can be transcoded into HD. Film to HD transfers are sometimes made in this way. The film is scanned to 2 K, color corrected while in the 2 K format, and then transcoded to HD Cam, HD Cam SR, or HD D-5 and recorded to tape, all in real time. 4 K and 5 K are used exclusively for film intermediates and are generally shot back to film; however, they, too, can be transcoded to HD.

The Cutting Edge

Predicting the future is a risky business at best. In an area that is evolving as quickly as video and digital formats, it becomes impossible to even imagine how film will be shot and edited in ten years. What new digital formats will arrive? Which will survive? How will that affect filmmakers and the film industry?

There are new film scanning systems being developed that might soon make it possible to shoot film, develop, and "print" the good takes to digital and never go back to the negative, a system called "virtual negative." And, a new generation of digital cameras is able to shoot directly to this same "virtual negative." Some scenes could be shot digitally, others on film, and everything delivered to postproduction in the same format and edited together. And none of this is science fiction; it's six months from now, or next month, or now.

There are 2 K and 4 K projectors that can project this "virtual film" and remove "video" from the digital motion picture image. And could 6 K be far behind?

There are several new cameras that represent a quantum leap ahead. Only with the new drive recorders and tapeless workflow have these cameras really been ably to show what they can do.

The Panavision Genesis 262, shown in Figure A3.7, is a giant step up from their version of the Sony HDWF 900 Cine Alta. The Genesis is a custom made camera that uses a single 1,920 × 1,080 CCD

Figure A3.7 Panavision Genesis 262

that is the size of a super 35 mm film frame, making it possible to now use the full line of Panavision 35 mm lenses, and creating an image with the same depth of field and other image-to-focal length parameters as 35 mm film cameras. It's an HD video system, and records in HD Cam SR using a camera mounted Sony recorder. The chip captures in a fourteen bit mode, which is transformed into a recordable ten bit using the "Panalog 4" transform curve resulting in a ten stop contrast range.

The Arriflex D20, shown in Figure A3.8, uses a 2,880 × 1,620 pixel custom-made, single-chip CMOS sensor that is the exact size of a super 35 mm frame. CMOS is similar to the CCD chips used in most cameras, but the CMOS has the processor built right into the chip making it possible to do extra image processing in the chip without needing to send the data through the camera to the processor.

Figure A3.8 ARRI D20

Like the Genesis, this allows for use of Arri's existing line of lenses. Here, too, the depth of field and image size to focal length exactly matches their 35 mm cameras. Arri Group bills this as a "film style digital camera." It operates in two modes. In "video," it records to several HD formats including HD Cam SR. In "film," it sends a "film stream" of uncompressed image at frame rates up to 150 FPS. This data can be recorded, but must be processed and compressed before it is usable. The amount of data recorded per hour of "film" is huge. Moreover, the processing is extremely time-consuming, making feature filmmaking in this mode highly problematic.

The Viper by Thomson is similar to the Arri D20 and the Genesis except it uses 3 custom CCDs that also are the same physical size as a 35 mm frame. Using a system similar to the Genesis, the image is captured in 12 bit and processed down to 10 bit using a compression that mimics a film characteristic curve. The camera is, therefore, able to reproduce a huge contrast range that exceeds film. Like the D20, the Viper also operates in either a "film stream" mode or a "video" mode. Here, too, the data stream in the film mode is huge and needs to be processed before it can be used.

Figure A3.9 The Red Camera

The Red Camera is the newest offering in this area. The camera shoots only in the 4 K Redcode format. It records to onboard drives that can hold a surprising amount of "film." While this 4 K can be transcoded into HD or any other video format, it was designed for transfer to 35 mm film or be projected directly. The image is incredible, some claiming it looks better than 35 mm film. The image can be projected directly in 4 K from the Sony 4 K projector and looks shockingly good.

Like the ARRI D20, the Red uses a single, custom CMOS chip. However this is a full 4 K CMOS, similar to the 10 mega pixel chips used in high-end still digital cameras. Where it differs is speed. A 4 K still camera can only record one frame in about two seconds, far from usable as a motion camera. The 4 K CMOS in the Red processes this data into Redcode, which is smaller than DV video data and making it possible to record this 4 K data and edit it natively in final Cut Pro, even from a removable drive.

Because it is the same physical size as a 35 mm frame, it can use a variety of existing lenses and has the exact same depth of field as 35 mm film. The camera can be configured in dozens of ways for hand-holding, jib mounting, or just about any configuration needed. Perhaps the most shocking feature of the camera is the price, less than $20,000 without lens. The first 100 cameras have been sold and are now being delivered.

The question on everyone's mind is, what impact will this camera and others to follow have on 35 mm film? Why shoot 35 mm if this looks better, can be released to theaters on 35 mm, 4 K or HD, when the cost of this camera is less than raw film for a feature? So far these questions have gone unanswered because the camera is just too new. Most of what is known about it comes from rumors and factory tests. Now that these cameras are out there being used, we will soon have a much better picture of how the camera performs.

The workflow for this camera will be similar to shooting DVC Pro HD to P2 cards. Only, in this case, the Redcode is imported from the removable camera drive to the editing drive, which can even be a firewire drive. The 4 K can be seen on the computer screen, but there is no video format equivalent to this 4 K and, so, it cannot be displayed on a video monitor. It is possible to send a 720P HD image to an HD monitor in real time from the Redcode without affecting the native Redcode in any way. In this case, the 720P in encoded with the Redcode to serve as a video proxy for the 4 K. Unlike other proxy videos, this is part of the Redcode and the native media need not be replaced in online. It simply allows the Redcode to be viewed in 720P while editing.

Appendix 4
Current Film Formats

Super 8

Super 8 is an archaic film format created for use in "home movies" in the 1960s. The format was based on an even earlier format, 8 mm. Super 8 differs from 8 mm in frame size. The super 8 sprocket hole is smaller and subsequently has a larger frame area. Although no cameras are being made, thousands are still around and film and processing are available. Other services are also available, including telecine. Some people love the grainy look of this format and it is occasionally used as a shooting format in music videos and other productions where its down-and-dirty look is a plus.

16 mm

Also intended as a "home movie" format, 16 mm is a shooting and projection format that soon evolved into a professional format and became a low-cost distribution format. It was used for years in schools for educational films and distributed to independent or "underground" theaters. Before videotape and portable video cameras, it was used for the distribution of television shows and commercials and was used in news cinematography and documentary filmmaking. True film lovers often had their own 16 mm home theater and collection of 16 mm prints. With the development of home video formats as well as affordable portable digital video formats, 16 mm has all but vanished. It is never used for news gathering anymore and rarely used in documentary production. 16 mm is still widely used as a professional shooting format for short films and commercials to be finished digitally or blown up to 35 mm; however, few people still use it as a projection format.

Super 16 mm

Super 16 mm is a shooting-only format. It cannot be projected because the area of the 16 mm frame normally used for the sound track in 16 mm is used for picture to increase the frame size. In the standard 16 mm camera, this sound track area is used for a second row of sprocket holes. So, while all projection prints in 16 mm are single perf, camera film has usually been double perf. But, because in super 16, this area is used for picture, it must be shot on single-perf film. The frame in super 16 mm is the same height as a 16 mm frame, but it is much wider. The aspect ratio of 16 mm is 1.33:1, where the aspect ratio of super 16 is 1.66:1. For more information, see Appendix 5 on aspect ratios. Because super 16 mm is a shooting-only format, it must be finished to digital video or blown up to 35 mm for projection.

When working with super 16 mm, there are many considerations. In conforming and printing, be aware that special printers need to be used, and not all labs can work with super 16 mm. Because the film is single perf, conforming and splicing is a bit more complicated.

35 mm 4 perf

The most common film shooting format is 35 mm 4 perf, and it is the standard film projection format. The 4 perf refers to the perforations running down both sides of the film edges. In this case, each frame is 4 perforations tall. This makes the aspect ratio 1.37:1. However, modern film is rarely projected in this aspect ratio; normally it is masked to 1.66:1 or 1.85:1. All 35 mm projectors are designed to project in 4 perf. Again, for more information, see Appendix 5.

35 mm 3 perf

In 35 mm 3 perf, only 3 perforations are pulled down making it a shooting-only format. The aspect ratio is approximately 1.77:1 and is often used for shooting 16 × 9 HD video. Because only 3 perforations are pulled down for each frame, film usage is reduced by 25 percent, and therefore represents a substantial cost savings. It can be optically printed at 4 perf for projection, but this is expensive and more than offsets any cost savings.

Super 35

Super 35 is another shooting-only format. In super 35, the entire frame area is used for picture. In standard 35 mm, a small area to one side of the frame is reserved for the sound track; however, in super 35 mm, this area is used for image. The format is most often used for wide-screen 35 mm in 2.35:1 aspect ratio. In this case, the super 35 negative is optically compressed to anamorphic and printed. It can be shot in 4 perf or 3 perf.

65 mm and 70 mm

The 65 mm and 70 mm are the same format; 65 mm is a shooting-only format that can be directly printed to 70 mm print stock. The 70 mm print is 5 mm wider to accommodate extra sound tracks. The format was developed in the 1950s for major motion pictures, but is not generally used any more.

IMAX

IMAX is a huge format using 65 mm film running horizontally. It is both a shooting and projection format. While several major motion pictures have been released in IMAX, for the most part, it is a specialty format. In projection, it uses a rotating optical system removing the need for a shutter. Each frame "wipes" on the screen replacing the previous frame. The image is therefore flickerless. This rotating optical system was used on many of the "flat bed" editing machines that came on the scene in about 1970 and more or less died by the twenty-first century.

Interestingly, this is also the oldest "film" projection system. In 1886 Charles-Émile Reynaud invented the théâtre optique, shown in Figure A4.1, a projection system for projecting his short animations. Reynaud drew his frames on gelatin squares that were approximately the same size as an IMAX frame. He then stitched his frames into thin leather bands that were perforated between the frames. The perforations engaged with sprockets on the projector. The strips were wound onto reels exactly like film reels. Just like the IMAX projector, the théâtre optique projector ran the strips horizontally and used a flickerless optical drum. It even looked something like an IMAX projector.

Figure A4.1 The théâtre optique

Other film formats have come and gone: 9.5 mm, 51 mm, VistaVision 8 perf, Techniscope 2 perf, and Cinerama to name a few. These days, few are asking what will be the next great film format or film stock, but rather, how much longer will film be around? The answer is likely to be for quite a while, at least as a shooting format. Digital projection may well push film out of most of the theaters soon, but digital cameras will need to come a long way before replacing film as the usual format for shooting movies.

Appendix 5
Understanding Time Code

Drop Frame Versus Nondrop Frame

There are several time code formats in use; however, they can be divided into two types: drop frame and nondrop frame. The following is an example of nondrop frame (NDF) time code:

12:45:22:27

The first set of numbers represents hours (12), the next are minutes (45), then seconds (22), and finally frames (27). It can be identified as NDF by the colon (:) in the last position. In this case, we are looking at a frame of NTSC video. We know it's not 24 FPS film because the frame number is 27. There would never be a number higher than 23 in 24 FPS. In NDF, this is a simple counter; every frame has a sequential number that identifies it. It's great for editing because you know exactly how many frames you have in a shot. This number represents 1,377,687 frames.

But as this is a frame of NTSC video, the clock is not time accurate. Because the frame counter is based on 30FPS and the real frame rate is 29.97 FPS, the clock is running .1 percent too slow. So if we need to know exactly how long the video is, or if we need to record the time of day, NDF will not work.

The following is an example of drop frame (DF) time code:

12:45:22:27

This can be identified as DF by the semicolon before the frames number. In DF, a frame number is skipped now and then to keep the clock time accurate. In nine out of every ten minutes, the 0 and 1 numbers are skipped. So, in this case, we know this video is exactly 12 hours, 45 minutes, 22 seconds, and 27 frames long. Or it may have been recorded at 12:45 P.M. plus 22 seconds and 27 frames (time code uses a twenty-four-hour clock). But we do not know the exact number of frames it represents. Keep in mind that the time code has no effect on the actual frame rate, nor are any frames skipped or dropped. Only numbers are skipped. Even though the frame rate is not controlled by the time code, it is necessary to know the frame rate to know when the frame column will roll over. The frame rate will also tell us if the speed is pulled down and whether the clock is real time or not. So time code is expressed with the frame rate.

Some common time codes are: 30 NDF, 29.97 NDF, 29.97 DF, 24 NDF, 25 NDF, 23.98 DF, and 23.98 NDF. There are also 30 DF and 24 DF formats where the counter runs too fast by .1 percent.

VITC, Subcode, and Linear Time Code

To better understand time code, we need to understand how it is recorded onto tape or imbedded in a media file. Time code written onto video can be recorded two ways. In one system, the time code for a particular frame is written into that frame. In analog video, it is written into the sync information between the frames, the vertical interval. This is referred to as vertical interval time code (VITC). There is a digital equivalent called subcode time code. In this case, the time code is written into the digital information or metadata after all the image information is recorded. In both cases, a frame number as time code is recorded as part of that frame. There is, therefore, a one-to-one relationship between frames and numbers. With metadata, it is also possible to record several different time codes into the frame at the same time.

It is also possible to record time code on a linear videotape track outside the video information. This information can be recorded and played with the tape running at almost any speed. It need not have a one-to-one relationship with the video frames as it is totally independent of the video. In fact, it can be recorded onto any tape or media, not just video. If linear time code is recorded onto videotape at the same frame rate as the video, there will be a one-to-one relationship with the video as every video frame will lie opposite a linear time code number residing in its own track. DV video uses subcode time code. DVCam and DVC Pro formats use both subcode and linear time code. In normal usage, the two tracks match exactly. The linear time code is used for high-speed shuttling as it can be read at almost any speed.

In video, it is necessary that the time code format match the video format. Therefore, NTSC video will always use 29.97 DF or NDF. In audio formats, there are no frames to match. However, if syncing is going to be done to the time code, the time code frame rate on the audio recording must match the frame rate on the video. Changing the speed of the recording will also change the speed of the time code. For example, time code can be recorded onto a DAT tape as 30 NDF. If this audio is "pulled down" or slowed by .1 percent, the time code becomes 29.97 NDF. For this reason, the time code formats usually used for audio recording are 29.97 NDF or DF for shooting on video, 30 NDF for shooting on film. Depending on the workflow, 30 DF, 24 NDF, and 24 DF can also be used for shooting on film.

Appendix 6
Aspect Ratios, Anamorphic Image, and Wide-screen

One of the earliest decisions you need to make before production is the aspect ratio of the finished project. There are several ways to make a motion picture wide-screen. Most film frames are one and one-third times wider than they are tall. This is an aspect ratio of 1.33:1. This is often called one-three-three. Another way of expressing this aspect is 4 × 3, in other words, four units wide for every three units high. This was the aspect ratio for the first forty years of motion pictures and has been the standard for television until recently. The easiest way to make the picture wider is to mask off some of the top and bottom. Wide-screen has become popular and today the average film in the United States has an aspect ratio of 1.85:1. If you were to look at the original negative, there would be a full 1.33:1 frame with an area at the top and another at the bottom that you were never meant to see. This area is sometimes masked off in printing, but more often it masked off right in the projector. In Europe, the 1.66:1 aspect has been more popular. But there, too, the real size is 1.33:1 with the rest masked in the projector. Various aspect ratios are illustrated in Figure A6.1.

There are even wider aspect ratios; 2.35:1 is often used, but at this point you are throwing away half the picture. In an effort to keep the film frame as large as possible, the anamorphic lens was developed. The anamorphic lens is only curved in one axis. The shooting anamorphic lens squeezes the image horizontally keeping the picture the same height but packing almost twice as much horizontal image onto the negative. The projection anamorphic lens unsqueezes the image, making the projected picture two-and-a-third times wider than tall while showing the entire frame.

Letterboxing

Wide-screen movies are often "letterboxed" on video. It's interesting to note that when watching a 1.85 motion picture letterboxed on a 4 × 3 television, you are seeing exactly what is on the film: a

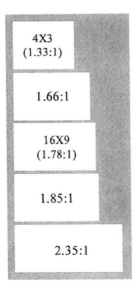

Figure A6.1 Aspect ratios

1.33 frame with the top and bottom masked off. Many of the new televisions now use a 1.78 : 1 aspect ratio, which can be expressed as 16×9. A 4×3 video displayed on a 16×9 screen is dramatically stretched horizontally.

When watching a letterboxed 4×3 movie on a 16×9 monitor, it is necessary to set the monitor to zoom in vertically so the entire image fills the wide-screen (see Figure A6.2 lower right). This is done by discarding 120 scan lines, 60 from the top and 60 from the bottom. This leaves a reduced-resolution, 360-scan line image. The display will be scaled up, it will likely be a 1080i HD display, but the image being scaled is still only a 360-line image. Notice also that because the 16×9 image is not as wide as the $1 : 1.85$ image, a small amount of letterboxing can still be seen on the full-screen image. The scaling is done right in the monitor, not in any postproduction workflow.

If we want to keep the resolution as high as possible, we need to borrow from the anamorphic lens idea. Like a projection anamorphic lens, the 16×9 television naturally stretches a 4×3 image to fit its wider size. All that is needed is to squeeze the image in production or postproduction.

In fairness to the film shooters out there, this is not a true anamorphic process, which is an optical process. But as it involves stretching the image in a similar fashion, it has been called anamorphic and the name is here to stay.

Many 4×3 digital cameras have a 16×9 setting and shoot an "anamorphic" image. But, just as with 16×9 monitors, they, too, achieve this by zooming in on the 4×3 chips, discarding 120 rows of pixels and, therefore, resolution. You can fit a 4×3 camera with a true anamorphic 16×9 lens adapter and squeeze the image optically, and as long as the lens is good and set up correctly it works well. However, many of these lenses are rather cheap and hard to use.

Figure A6.2 The frame at the top from Johnny Bishop's "False Prophet" is 1:1.85 letterboxed on a standard definition 480 scan line 4 × 3 screen. The frame in the lower left shows what happens when 4 × 3 video is displayed on a 16 × 9 monitor. The image is stretched horizontally. Images courtesy of Phantom Mullet productions

The best solution is to use 16 × 9 chips in the camera. When native 16 × 9 video is displayed on a 16 × 9 monitor, it looks normal; but, on a 4 × 3 monitor, the image is stretched vertically. This stretched image can be scaled vertically and letterboxed on the 4 × 3 monitor without loosing any significant image quality because all 480 scan lines are scaled and letterboxed. You can also shoot 4 × 3 on a 16 × 9 camera by zooming horizontally into the chips with no loss of resolution because all scan lines remain intact. Virtually all high-definition and some standard definition are shot this way.

Whether the digital video was shot with an anamorphic lens, on a 4 × 3 camera set to 16 × 9, or shot on a 16 × 9 camera, the 16 × 9 video is referred to as "anamorphic" in Final Cut Pro. 16 × 9 cameras and 4 × 3 cameras set to 16 × 9 "flag" the recorded video as anamorphic 16 × 9. When captured, Final Cut Pro also flags this media. There are 16 × 9 anamorphic settings in the sequence settings and the capture settings. These should be set before capturing video or creating the editing sequence in the time line. These can also be set with the "easy setup" feature. The flag can also be set in the browser window by clicking in the anamorphic column.

When you open an anamorphic sequence, the Canvas window resizes to 16×9. When you open an anamorphic clip, the viewer resizes to 16×9. As long as the two match, the anamorphic video is unaffected. If the two don't match, the sequence will require rendering and the new image will be stretched or letterboxed.

The flags do not make the video anamorphic, it already is. You are only flagging it as 16×9 so that the QuickTime image on the computer screen or any QuickTime exported for DVD authoring will have the proper aspect ratio. The image on the video monitor is not affected by the anamorphic flagging. If a 16×9 monitor is used to edit anamorphic video, the image will be normal with the flags set or not.

When playing 16×9 anamorphic video, the newer DVD players format themselves; these DVD players will automatically play an anamorphic movie wide-screen to a 16×9 television or letterboxed to a 4×3 television. In the examples illustrated in Figure A6.3, the $1 : 1.85$ film (top) has been transferred or "telecined" anamorphically to 16×9. When played from an automatically formatting DVD player to a 16×9 monitor (lower left), the image is full-screen. When this anamorphic video is played directly to a 4×3 monitor without formatting (lower center), the image is stretched vertically. However, as this video is "flagged" as anamorphic, the DVD player automatically letterboxes the video when displayed on a 4×3 monitor (lower right). This requires scaling the image, but all 480 scan lines are scaled keeping the image as sharp as possible. There is more on this in Chapter 1 in the section on anamorphic telecine.

Figure A6.3   Images at 16×9 on a 4×3 monitor

These DVD players will also "pillar" or "pill box" 4×3 video when viewed on a 16×9 monitor. Pillaring is the opposite of letterboxing. In this case, masking off the edges of the 16×9 image to 4×3. This only holds true if your DVD authoring software supports this kind of formatting. Without this special formatting, the anamorphic movie will always look squeezed on a 4×3 television. In this case for 4 × 3 viewing, you will want to reformat the film letterboxed. If your DVD authoring software doesn't support automatic formatting, you can burn an anamorphic version for full-resolution 16 × 9 and a letterboxed version for 4 × 3.

If you want to reformat an anamorphic 16 × 9 sequence to a letterboxed 4 × 3 sequence in Final Cut Pro, edit with the media and sequence 16 × 9 flagging set, then drag the 16 × 9 sequence in the browser into an empty 4 × 3 sequence in the timeline.

When shooting film for anamorphic telecine or letterboxing, make sure you have the proper viewfinder guide frame on the camera. It is extremely ill advised to shoot without a guide frame thinking the operator can frame the shot by remembering to frame for wide-screen.

Pan and Scan

Another way of displaying wide-screen images in 4 × 3 is pan and scan. In pan and scan, the edges are simply cropped off keeping some part of the center of the screen (see Figure A6.4). The system

Figure A6.4 The pan and scan process. The original 1 : 1.85 can be letterboxed on a 4 × 3 monitor, (lower left) or it can be "Pan and Scanned". The pan and scanned image on the lower right shows how the edges of the 1 : 185 image are cropped to make the aspect 4 × 3. The image can be shifted left and right to keep the action on screen, but this adds "camera moves" that were not intended by the filmmaker. Pan and scan can be done in the Color application

187

is widely used for video distribution, but is highly controversial. Many filmmakers are offended to see their compositions cropped, electronic pans and even edits added all in an effort to keep the action on the narrow screen. Some filmmakers have even called to have the practice outlawed.

The cropping is moved right and left to keep the action on the screen creating camera moves that were never there in production. Pan and scan can be done in Final Cut Pro with the motion controls, but is most often done as part of the DVD authoring, making it possible for the viewer to select between anamorphic 16 × 9, 4 × 3 letterbox, or 4 × 3 pan and scan in the DVD player's setup menu.

There was a time when 4 × 3 was thought to be the perfect aspect ratio and that there would never be a need for anything else. But soon filmmakers wanted wider and wider images, and audiences agreed. Today 4 × 3 has an archaic look, and while still quite common, it feels antiquated. Which is why it will no doubt make a strong comeback in twenty years when people long for "the good old days" of the twentieth century.

Appendix 7
Understanding File Architecture

Final Cut Pro, Cinema Tools, and Pro Tools

Final Cut Pro, Cinema Tools, and Pro Tools use a similar architecture. A central project file controls the entire project yet contains no actual media. It is simply a complex road map with links to scores of other files, often hundreds of files. In Final Cut Pro, this central file is referred to as the "project file." In Cinema Tools, it is known as the "database." In Pro Tools, it is the "session." The central file is small, perhaps a few hundred K. It contains hundreds of links to the actual media, which are often huge files, sometimes hundreds of gigabytes for a feature film.

If the link between the central file and the media is broken, either because the media has moved or been removed entirely, the media is "off-line" or "missing." The media can be relinked to the central file or sometimes recaptured from the original tapes or other media. The online media can even be relinked to different media, for example, the same shots with the same names, but at a new frame rate or a higher resolution.

As this architecture is simplest in Pro Tools, let's start with that. When a new session is created, a folder is created labeled with the name you have given the session. Inside this folder are the "session" file (the central file) and three more folders, the "audio files" folder, the "region groups" folder, and the "fade files" folder (see Figure A7.1). Any audio recorded to the session will be written into the audio files folder and a link between that media and the session file is created. Any automated fades created in the session will be written as a fade file into the fade files folder and again, a link connected to the session file.

If all we were doing was recording new audio, this simple architecture would suffice for the entire session. However, we also need to import our video and many new audio files from scores of other

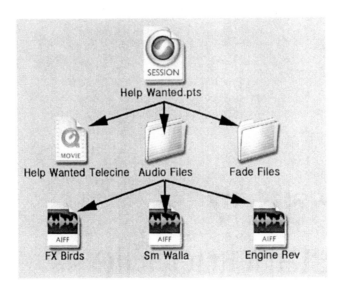

Figure A7.1 Pro Tools filing structure

sources. All of these (even the video file) can be copied into the audio files folder and linked to the session file. However, you may want to keep your audio files in several folders just for management, and you may want to keep your video on a separate drive just to improve performance. So, we may end up with several large media folders on multiple drives, all linked to the session file. Care needs to be taken keeping track of where the media is written so that linked media is not removed. This is especially true when taking the project from one facility to another on a portable drive or drives. In order to keep it as simple as possible, many editors keep all their audio media only in the audio files folder. They then make subfolders inside the audio files folder to facilitate file management.

It is very important to have subfolders in Pro Tools. The "region bin" in the Pro Tools interface is simply one large bin holding all of the audio media. There is no system for making subbins or any filing strategy to speed a search for needed media. If, however, all of the audio media is placed into subfolders, these folders can be searched from the Pro Tools "workspace" found in the windows menu. This shows the layout of folders, subfolders, and sub-subfolders created in the filing architecture. On large projects, it is highly advisable to use the workspace and subfolders for production sound, music, sound effects, or whatever the project requires. Using only the region bin will cost valuable time looking for wanted sound.

With Final Cut Pro, there are many more folders and links than with Pro Tools. When a new Final Cut Pro project is created, the software links to six separate folders based on the system settings. If these folders are not present on the selected drive, Final Cut Pro creates the missing folder as soon as it needs to write to it.

Within each folder, Final Cut Pro also creates a new folder named for the current project and writes all files to these folders. Final Cut Pro writes automatically to five of the six folders, only the "capture scratch" folder can be written to by the user. All captured media, sounds and video, are recorded there.

Imported files are simply linked to their current location. If titles and graphics are not organized into a logical filing system before being imported, you will have scores of links to files in scores of locations. The problem can become totally unmanageable if there is no plan on how to organize the files as the project is being built.

Different editors have different ideas on how to arrange their files. A good basic system is to use only a single, large portable drive for the film. Then, make a folder at the top level of the drive for Final Cut Pro projects. Set all scratch drive settings in the system settings to this drive. Final Cut Pro will now create its six folders, Audio Render, Capture Scratch, Render Files, Autosave Vault, Thumbnail Cache, and Waveform Cache. The folders will appear automatically over time as you edit and as Final Cut Pro writes to them.

All of the media files to be imported can be copied into the project's folder in the Capture Scratch folder. Or, several files can be created to hold titles and graphics, sound effects, and music. Inside each of these, an individual project folder can hold all of the corresponding media.

Keep all Pro Tools sessions and Cinema Tools databases on this drive in dedicated files as well. Keep daily backups of this drive on a second drive.

Find a system that works for you and stick to it. Many hours can be lost needlessly when looking for missing media, chasing broken links, or rerendering missing render files.

Figure A7.2 is an example of the basic Final Cut Pro file architecture. The project file for *Help Wanted* at the top has been created and based on the system settings and was automatically linked to the

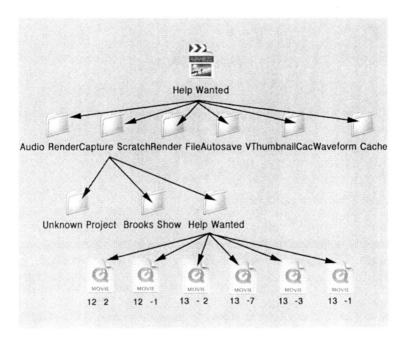

Figure A7.2   Final Cut Pro filing structure

basic six Final Cut Pro files. Six shots have been logged. This logging becomes part of the information-tion stored in the project file. When this logged media is captured, it is written into an automatically created new folder named for the project in the Capture Scratch folder. In Figure A7.2, there are two media folders already here for other projects, Brooks Show and Unknown Project (the default name for an unnamed project). The media for the six shots is captured into this project folder and links are recorded in the project file directing it to look here for these six shots.

Cinema Tools also uses this same architecture. However, instead of having its own media folders, it links to the same media folders as the Final Cut Pro project.

The Cinema Tools database for *Help Wanted* has been linked to the media in the Help Wanted folder in Final Cut Pro's Capture Scratch folder. In Figure A7.3, there are only three shots in the *Help Wanted* folder and both Final Cut Pro (black links) and Cinema Tools (white links) are linked to them.

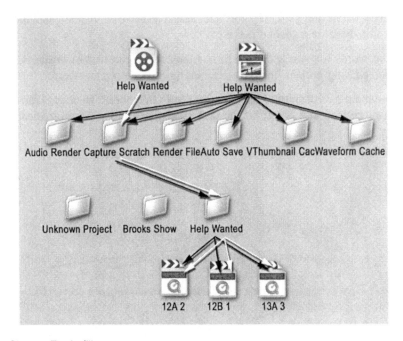

Figure A7.3 Cinema Tools filing structure

Many of the operations preformed during editing may cause Final Cut Pro or Cinema Tools to break or change these links. The editor may want to break the links and recapture the media at a higher resolution. In such a case, the old media would still be present on the drive, and the editor could link to either the high- or low-resolution media.

Some operations will even cause Cinema Tools to drastically change the filing architecture. The reverse telecine operation not only creates an entirely new set of shots at a new frame rate, it reorganizes the media and breaks the Final Cut Pro links to the media knocking it off-line.

Figure A7.4 is an example of the reverse telecine operation in Cinema Tools that has been applied to the three shots in the previous two figures. New media has been created at 24P, the original media being 29.97 FPS. The new media has the extension .rev added and has been placed in a new folder named "reversed." The original media has been moved to a new folder named "originals" breaking the links (transparent links) and causing the shots to go off-line. The Final Cut Pro links need to be redirected to the new "reversed" folder. Cinema Tools has automatically been linked to the reversed folder (white links).

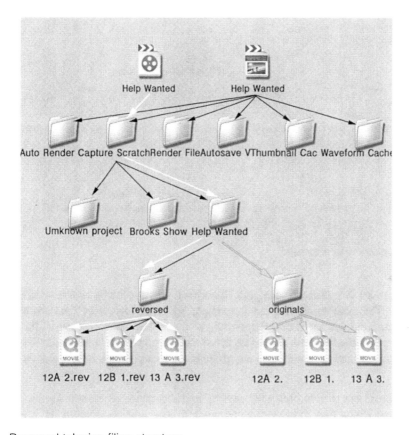

Figure A7.4 Reversed telecine filing structure

This is covered in detail in Chapter 1 on Cinema Tools and editing in 24P. For now, it's most important to understand how the filing system works and understand the importance of having a logical filing system.

Filing Strategies

Different editors have different systems of organizing their files. Final Cut Pro is designed to keep all projects together in one set of folders. While this may be confusing over time, it is a great system when working on several related projects at the same time.

A single, removable drive holds all the files and media. Final Cut Pro will automatically create the top row of six files shown in Figure A7.5 if all four of the Final Cut Pro systems settings are set to this drive. These settings should be checked at the beginning of every edit session and never set to any folder on the drive, only to the drive itself. Final Cut Pro will handle file management of these files, with the exception of removing old files. This needs to be done by the editor after a project is completed.

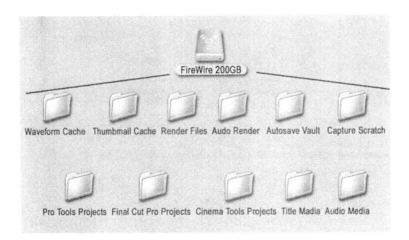

Figure A7.5 FireWire filing structure

Final Cut Pro uses the Waveform Cache and Thumbnail Cache directly and no management of these files is possible. They are small and can be simply ignored. The other four folders contain inner project folders, each named for the corresponding project. With the exception of the Autosave Vault, these contain large media files and should be removed after a project is finished. The Autosave Vault contains backups of all projects. As these are quite small, many people keep them on file after removing the media.

You create the lower row of five files when setting up the directories. Except for the Pro Tools folder, project folders inside the files also need to be created. You will also handle all management of the files and media in these folders.

You create the folder for Pro Tools Projects. When a new Pro Tools project is created, save it in this folder. Pro Tools then creates the project folder inside the Pro Tools Projects folder. Pro Tools also creates the session file, the audio files folder, and the fade files folder inside the Project folder, as seen in Figure A7.6. Management of the new media is also handled by Pro Tools. However, when importing media form other sources, you must be sure to copy the imported media to the audio files folder. Pro Tools will allow you to copy imported media to a separate folder. The simplest solution is to keep all of your audio in the audio files folder or in subfolders inside the audio files folder. The reference video for the Pro Tools session can be placed in the project folder as well. However, for improved performance, you may want to keep it on a second drive, preferably the hard drive. If you keep a backup of the reference video in the project folder as well, this makes the project totally por-

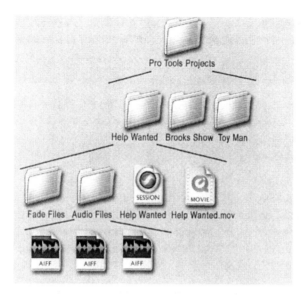

Figure A7.6   Pro Tools FireWire filing structure

table. It can be copied to any computer hard drive and reimported into the project when needed. Other files used in the audio edit may be stored here in the project folder, for example an audio OMF file.

Inside of the Final Cut Pro Autosave Vault folder, Final Cut Pro has created a folder for all of the current projects. These folders contain the backups of the project file. This exact same architecture is used in the Capture Scratch, Audio Render, and Render Files folders.

As Cinema Tools also uses this media, Cinema Tools may create new folders inside the Capture Scratch project folder. Final Cut Pro and Cinema Tools handle the importing of files and media to these folders, you only need to remove old files and media.

Cinema Tools databases can be saved in the Cinema Tools project folder. As Cinema Tools uses the Final Cut Pro media folders, all that will be saved in the Cinema Tools projects folder will be the databases.

The folders for title media and audio media should have individual project folders inside of them if multiple projects are being saved on the drive. Some people save their titles and graphics in the project folder in the Capture Scratch with the video; however, there are reasons to keep it in a separate folder. If you are going to online the project, you need to be able to quickly find and replace the titles and graphics and you will be slowed if you are sorting through scores of video files looking for your titles. Also, when the project is finished, you will want to remove all the video and render files to clear up drive space. If, however, you save the Final Cut Pro project file or the Final Cut Pro edit as an XML backup, the Cinema Tools database, the Pro Tools session, and audio media, the graphics and titles, as well as any imported audio files and the original shooting tapes, you can rebuild the entire project by simply recapturing the video and rerendering. The audio and graphic files can be somewhat large, but usually fit easily on a DVD-ROM. This DVD can be stored with the digital videotapes and, even years from now, the project can be rebuilt and reedited.

Titles, graphics, and audio media may come from a variety of sources or have been created with a variety of applications. However, they should all be placed here in these two folders.

The Final Cut Pro projects folder should have individual folders inside for each project. Along with the project file, you may have EDLs, XMLs, batch lists, cut lists, and other reports exported from Final Cut Pro.

Backing Up

It is essential to make backups of all critical files. When a drive crashes, it can destroy months of work and cost thousands of dollars if there are no backup copies. The entire project can be backed up to a second drive. However, as the project is huge, this will take a great deal of time. And this may lead to not backing up as often as needed. Not all files need to backed up all the time. Here are some general rules:

- Final Cut Pro Autosave Vault: This contains automatically generated backup project files. However, it will do you no good at all if it is saved on the same drive as the project file and that drive goes down. You can set Final Cut Pro up to save these backups to a different drive, but if you need the project to be totally portable you will want to make backups of the Autosave Vault and current project file often.

- Capture Scratch: This is a huge folder and can take a long time and use a large amount of drive space when backing up. As long as the original videotapes are stored in a safe place, these can be your backups. Even if the media are lost, it can be recaptured just as it was in the first place. Even reversed media can be recaptured and re-reversed.

- Various cache and render folders: These contain only media created by Final Cut Pro. They can be rendered; however, it may take quite a bit of time. It is not critical that they be backed up. In fact, anything exported from Final Cut Pro can be reexported as long as the project file is intact.

- Cinema Tools database: This is critical, and while it can be regenerated, it makes much more sense to make backups of it whenever you make any changes to it.

The entire Pro Tools project is critical, media as well as the session file. As recording in Pro Tools creates some of the media, this is the only copy of this media. Always back up the entire Pro Tools project, audio files as well as session files, any time you import or record any media.

Organization has always been key in postproduction. When movies were cut on film, an assistant editor was expected to find a one frame trim from a shot and do it in just a few minutes. The computer has made this simple, but has led to a new problem, lost media. File origination and backups are essential.

Appendix 8
Conforming Negative

Normally, a professional cuts negative. Much is at risk; a mistake can ruin a shot. If you have made an expensive motion picture, it's not likely you will want to risk the negative to save a few thousand dollars. However, if you are working on a shoestring, you may have no choice. Or, you may want to involve yourself in every aspect of making your film.

For the most part, this appendix addresses conforming 16 mm. If this is your first time cutting negative, it's reasonable to assume you are cutting 16 mm. Most people make at least one mistake their first time out, usually on their own student 16 mm film. A 35 mm film follows the exact same process with several exceptions:

- The leader lengths are different when measured in feet. The frame counts remain the same.

- 16 mm is always A-B rolled; 1.85 : 1 and 1.66 : 1 aspect ratio 35 mm is often conformed to a single roll with all effects done as opticals.

- When pulling shots, one-and-a-half frames are left at the head and tail for splicing. In 35 mm, only one-half of a frame is left at the head and tail.

- The maximum reel lengths are different: 35 mm reels should not exceed 2,000 feet; 16 mm should not exceed 1,600 feet. This can vary from lab to lab, so always check with the lab.

Super 16 mm

When working with super 16 mm, there are many considerations. In conforming and printing, be aware that special printers need to be used, and not all labs can work with super 16 mm. There is no projection format for super 16 mm as there is no area on the film for a sound track. Super 16 mm will always be finished digitally or blown up to 35 mm. Because the film is single perf, conforming and splicing is a bit more complicated. A good rule to follow is to use all single-perf leaders and film throughout the rolls.

Double-perf film is becoming somewhat rare, single-perf film is often used even on standard 1.33 16 mm projects. However, some filmmakers still prefer double-perf. 16 mm double-perforated leader should be used only if the entire negative is double perforated. If any of the original is single perforated, use single-perf leader in the same wind as your original to warn the lab not to attempt to print tail to head. While it is possible to mix single and double perf, this can be confusing for you and the lab.

A and B Rolling

There are two systems for building print rolls. In the first, you simply splice the negative into one roll. The splice can be seen in full-screen 1.33, but on 35 mm at 1.85, it can't be seen. With this system, other than fades to white, all effects, including fades to black and dissolves, become expensive opticals. Nevertheless, it is the system most often used on 1.85 35 mm projects.

The second system is called A-B rolling. With this system, two rolls of negative are cut. The first shot is cut into A, the second into B, the third into A, and so forth, as shown in Figure A8.1. The spaces between are filled with black leader creating a sort of checkerboard layout. Fades and dissolves are easy and there is no extra cost per effect.

Print

A Roll

B Roll

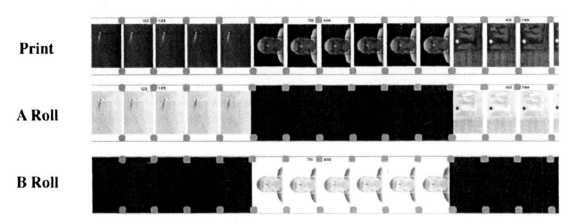

Figure A8.1   A-B rolls and print

Each roll is printed onto the print stock separately. The splices don't show using this system because the black leader covers the overlapping film. Because of the invisible splices, this is the only system that can be used for 35 mm full-frame and 16 mm. A-B rolling costs a lot more: the negative cutters charge more, the lab charges a lot more for printing, and the black leader is expensive. However, opticals are also expensive. The cost-saving of avoiding A-B rolling soon disappears if you have a lot of opticals. Count the number of effects and get prices.

On some films, a C roll is made as well. The C roll is used for extended superimpositions, often titles. As each roll is printed in a separate pass, many layers of image can be superimposed. Even a D roll or an E roll may be used if there are complex superimpositions. This is also how fades to black are made. By cutting clear leader into one roll, light can be passed through the clear leader gradually printing the image down to black. Optical sound will also be printed onto the print on a separate pass through the printer.

The Splice

A glue splice made with a "hot splicer" is used when splicing negative. The hot splicer has a heating element that warms the splicer. It is never "hot," just slightly warm to the touch. The heat helps the glue dry more quickly. Hot splicers heat slowly. Plug it in an hour or more before use, or place it under a lamp for a few minutes.

The glue splice is made by overlapping a small section of film. The emulsion must be removed from this area on the overlapping frame so that the glue splice is made base to base, never base to emulsion. The size of the overlap is small, and on 35 mm this overlap falls outside of a 1.66 or larger mask. So, unless the 35 mm is projected full frame, the splice will never show. On 16 mm, however, the splice reaches almost a third into the frame. The splice is quite visible unless the negative is A-B rolled and "invisible" splices are used.

The black leader used in A-B rolling covers the splice. Black leader is placed in the splicer on the right. One frame must extend past the splice line and will be lost when the splice is made. The leader is locked into the splicer emulsion up. The entire right section of the splicer is now rotated up and out of the way.

The negative is placed in the left section of the splicer and locked into position. Here, too, one frame extends past the splice line and will be lost. On 35 mm, only one-half frame is required.

With the negative locked into position, the scraper is used to remove the emulsion in the area of the overlap, as illustrated in Figure A8.2. The scraper must be aligned perfectly so as to remove all the emulsion without cutting into the base and weakening the splice. Carefully scrape away all of the emulsion in the overlap area. Care must be taken to not tear the sprocket holes.

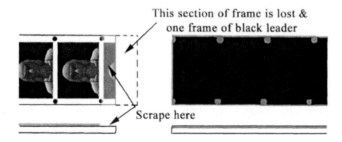

Figure A8.2   Scraping a cement splice

Using the small brush in the glue bottle, quickly brush on a good amount of cement and quickly close the splicer. This will trim away the remaining two-thirds frame of negative as well as one frame of black. Lock it in place and screw the lid back on the cement bottle. Never leave the cap off the glue after making the splice. Use only a small bottle and replace the cement daily.

Let the splice stand for thirty seconds or so, longer if the splicer is cool. Carefully open all the clamps on the splicer and check the splice. There should be no glue extending onto the picture and the splice should be strong. The black leader should totally hide the splice, as shown in Figure A8.3. This is true in bookend splices as well, where film is spliced at both ends of a negative, as seen in Figure A8.4. After a few minutes, you should be able to twist the film slightly without the corners coming up.

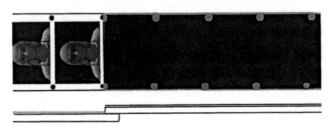

Figure A8.3 The finished splice

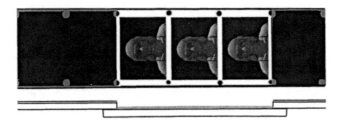

Figure A8.4 Bookend splices

The outgoing splice is a mirror of the incoming splice. The film can be placed in the splicer forming a large S shape coming off the reels, or you can make all the head splices in one pass rolling head to tail and all the tail splices in one pass rolling tail to head. But the picture is always in the splicer on the left and black on the right. Never scrape the black leader.

The standard practice is to conform the entire negative by taping the rolls together with paper tape stuck only to the area that will be lost in splicing. Then making all of the head splices rolling in from head to tail then reversing the rolls and winding back tail to head doing all of the tail splices.

The shots are pulled from the camera or lab rolls by winding into the shots and cutting out the shots with scissors. Because the splicer requires an extra frame at each end for scraping, standard practice on 16 mm is to cut through the center of the frame outside of the frame to be scraped. This means that one-and-a-half frames are lost. This is why the "cut handles" in Final Cut Pro are set to three frames in 16 mm, one and a half at the head and tail of every shot. On 35 mm, standard practice is to cut through the middle of the frame to be scraped. As noted earlier, 35 mm splicers only require one half of a frame for scraping. Here, too, this makes the cut handles in 35 mm only one frame.

Zero Cuts

Another way of making invisible splices when printing from A and B rolls is to extend each shot at least two frames past the point where you want the "cut." When these A and B rolls are placed in a synchronizer, the splices will have a four-frame overlap at the head and tail of each shot. These rolls must be printed on a printer that can make "cuts" by means of a fast shutter. Not all labs have zero cut capabilities, so check with your lab. This guarantees an invisible splice. Even if glue extends into the frame or if the splice causes a "bump" going through the printer, this is never seen as the first and last two frames in the shot are never printed. Also, if a frame is lost due to a torn sprocket or bad splice, there are two extra frames before losing a frame of the shot. There is, however, an extra charge at the lab.

When using zero cuts, it is necessary to set up the export film list in Final Cut Pro to a three-and-a-half frame "cut handle" for 35 mm or seven frames in 16 mm, to account for the two frame overlap and the lost frames. This way, any shot that extends into the overlap will be properly reported as a double use.

Before Cutting Negative

There are a few things to keep in mind before cutting negative:

- Set up a dust-free work area and keep the work area clean.

- Handle the negative only when wearing clean cotton gloves.

- Check the alignment on your splicer. Make several test splices. Test the splices by flexing and twisting the splice. Look for the corners to lift.

- Use only fresh film cement. Replace it daily. Keep the can lid on tight.

- Do not make any grease pencil marks on the original.

- Use standard leaders and never put more than one head sync or any other type of sync mark on any roll.

- All 16 mm film including the optical sound must be the same wind as the picture negative, usually B wind. This is only an issue in 16 mm.

- When you are finished, wind the rolls tightly, preferably on a tight-wind, not a split reel.

- Include cue sheets for fades, dissolves, and so on, as well as a continuity sheet with color correction, day for night, and such.

Pulling Negative or Work Print

In an effort to avoid problems, many filmmakers conform a work print to the Final Cut Pro cut list before cutting the negative. Others jump right in and conform negative to the cut list. Work print costs more money and takes longer. However, if you are not 100 percent comfortable with cutting your negative, conform work print first.

If your database is logged by camera roll only and not lab roll, you may want to start by breaking all of your lab rolls into camera rolls. Wind through each roll and locate the splices in the negative made by the lab to combine rolls before telecine or printing. If you have work print, you may also want to break it back into camera rolls. In 16mm, there may be several camera rolls per lab roll. More if you shot roll ends. In 35mm, some lab rolls may be full camera rolls. Label each roll with camera roll number and start and end key codes. If you keep the lab rolls together, label each lab roll with the camera roll numbers and the same key code information.

Using your pull list from Final Cut Pro, start pulling the shots used in the edit. The pull list will give you a roll-by-roll list, in order, from head to tail of the shots to pull. When pulling negative, *do not* cut on the frame lines: mark the frame with a small scratch between the sprocket holes and cut one-and-a-half frames before (head) or after (tail) the frame line. Add three-and-a-half frames for zero cuts. On 35mm, leave one-half frame only.

With 16mm, it is also possible to cut on the frame line with a splicer so that only one frame is lost. You will always need the extra frame to make the glue splice, but most conformers prefer to cut one and a half so that they can cut with scissors and tape the roll back together with paper tape. When pulling work print, mark the frame with a grease pencil then cut on its frame line with the splicer. Work print is tape spliced and no frames are lost in splicing.

In the example shown in Figure A8.5, the first frame of the shot listed in the cut list is 7659 6497 +4. The tiny dot above the K in KW80 indicates this is the key code frame. The actual frame is +4, so we count four frames past the key code frame and mark it with two scratches. The information is tiny; you will need a magnifier to see it. Count back toward head one frame for the lost frame and cut on the frame line with a splicer, or in the center of the next frame back with scissors. Proceed to the tail of the shot. Find the correct frame, add one for the splice and cut on the frame line or one-and-a-half frames and cut in the center with scissors. The marked shots will be in the finished rolls, so you should see the scratches on the first and last frame in each shot. Be careful to not scratch in the image area.

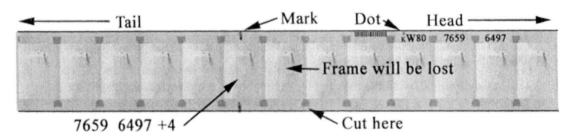

Figure A8.5 Marking a splice from key code numbers on 16mm film

Wind the shot onto a two-inch core, place in a small plastic bag, and label with the scene and take number, camera roll number, and the shot number from the construction order. Paper tape the camera roll back together, move on to the next shot, or rewind and return it to the shelf. Once you have all the shots pulled, you are ready to start building rolls.

If you are pulling work print, you can simply hang each shot on a hook in an editing bin. When all the shots are pulled, make up head and tail leaders and tape splice the roll together.

Always cut negative emulsion up. The splicer works this way, and the small marks you need to make between the sprocket holes need to be scratched into the emulsion. Work with emulsion down on the work print; the image should read backwards on both negative and work print. The key code numbers should be on the same side on both work print and negative.

The leaders used in conforming are actual film with emulsion. Plastic leaders are never used. The white leader is called "light struck," and is a clear base with a black-and-white emulsion that appears white. As the film is light sensitive, it turns dark over time. It is kept in a black plastic bag before use and the completed negative rolls must be kept out of bright sunlight. It is normal, however, for the head leader to become rather dark. The black leader is simply camera film that has been exposed to its maximum density (d-max) and processed to form a very opaque black leader.

Leaders

To prevent problems later, build proper head and tail leaders for your rolls before assembling the shots into rolls.

For work print, the proper head leaders can be built by following this workflow:

- Splice 18 feet of white leader to the head of a positive SMPTE Universal head leader.

- Place the Picture Start frame (frame before the first 8 frame) in the synchronizer and zero the counter.

- Back out to exactly 12 feet, 0 frames.

- Mark an *X* through this frame and label it Edit Sync. Punch a hole though the center of this frame.

- Roll back 6 more feet to the beginning of the leader. Label the leader with the title of the project and the production company. Indicate that this is the work print and head.

- Wind into the Edit Sync mark and reset the counter to 0 feet, 0 frames.

- Wind forward to 47 frames past the 2 on the countdown leader. This should be 16 feet, 31 frames. The first frame of picture will be 16 feet 32 frames. Mark and cut this frame line.

You can now start building the work print roll by tape splicing each shot in proper order into the roll.

At the end of work print roll, splice on the tail portion of the SMPTE leader. There should be 87 blank frames between the last frame of your film and the frame marked "Finish" in the SMPTE leader. To build the tail leader,

- Splice 16 feet of white leader to the SMPTE leader.

- Put the "Finish" frame in your synchronizer at 0. Roll forward 12 feet and mark this frame with an *X*. Label this frame "Tail Edit Sync."

- If you have included a tail pop in the mix, which is a good idea, the pop should be 48 frames from the last picture. Place the last frame of picture in the synchronizer and roll forward 1 foot 8 frames (48 frames). Write POP on this frame.

- Many people cut 2 feet of black leader on after the white as a very noticeable indication that this is the tail and not the head.

Working with 35 mm work print is virtually the same as 16 mm with a few exceptions. The head leaders remain the same; however, the lengths are different, as shown in Figure A8.6. The 6 feet of white before the edit-sync and printer start marks stays the same. The length between edit sync and the 2 frame on the SMPTE leader is now exactly 20 feet (19 feet, 15 frames between the frames). The distance from the 2 frame to the first frame of picture is 3 feet exactly (2 feet, 15 frames between the frames). In other words, with the counter set at 0 feet, 0 frames on edit sync, the 2 frame will be 20 feet, 0 frames, and the first frame of picture 23 feet, 0 frames.

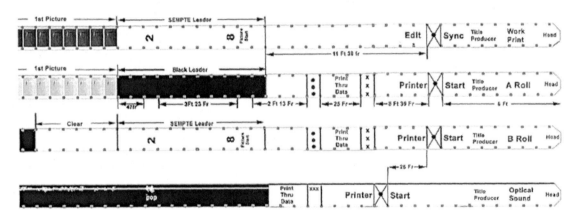

Figure A8.6 Leader layout in 16 mm

Also, 35 mm has 4 perfs per frame. Care must be taken to not cut into the frame but on the frame line.

Audio Leaders

Depending on your audio workflow, you may or may not have the optical sound when building the negative print rolls. With many workflows, the sound is not mixed until after the first answer print is made from the negative rolls. In this case, it is best to let the lab lay out the leader for the optical sound and put it in sync. If you have already mixed and have the optical sound when conforming, you can make your own optical sound leaders and set the 26-frame offset for sync. Once you have the head leaders built, you can remove the optical sound from the synchronizer and place it on the shelf. You will not be using it again until you are building the tail leaders.

Edit Sync Versus Printer Start

Edit sync is marked on the work print and any editorial sound rolls to indicate that the film is in editorial sync. That is to say, the audio and picture are exactly opposite each other. When placed on a flat bed or in a synchronizer, the picture frame in the synchronizer is lined up exactly with the corresponding frame of sound. Before printing, the sound must be "pulled up" by 26 frames. In projection sync, the sound precedes the picture by 26 frames so that the frame of sound will be arriving at the sound head on the projector at the same time the picture arrives at the gate. On rolls that have been pulled up (i.e., in projection sync), the start marks are labeled "Printer Start." Some filmmakers send their printing rolls to the lab in edit sync, clearly labeled edit sync with clear instructions that the lab needs to do the pull up. As always, commutate with the lab.

There are several grease pencil marks you want to make on the work print to indicate effects. These lines help you when conforming negative and, in conjunction with the cue sheets, they help the lab understand your intent. The following are some examples of these marks and the A-B roll negative cut needed to print the effect.

Laying Out and Marking Effects

A and B Roll Fade-in

This is marked by two straight lines forming a V shape, as illustrated at the top of Figure A8.7. The lines start at the beginning of the shot in the center of the frame and extend to the end of the effect, ending at the edges of the work print.

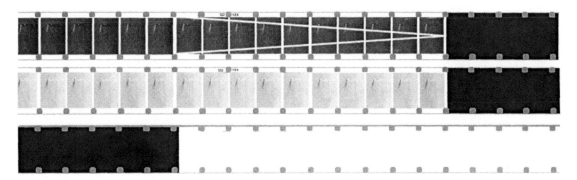

Figure A8.7   A and B roll fade-in

Fade-out

The fade-out negative cut is the reverse of the fade-in. In both cases, the point where the lines meet in the center indicates a black screen.

The top roll in Figure A8.7 is the work print with the grease pencil marks. On the A-roll negative, a fade to black is accomplished by cutting a length of clear, or orange, mask on color negative. The printer light can be faded up through the clear leader burning the print down to black. The example is a fade-out and fade-in. In this case, the two shots are cut together in the center. The splice will not show as the image is printed down to black covering the splice. Clear can be cut into either A or B roll, fading the shot on the opposing roll. Notice at the bottom of Figure A8.7 that the clear leader extends to the left past the end of the fade out by five frames. This is called an effect cut handle. Final Cut Pro has a setting in the Export Film Lists dialogue for effects handles. While it is possible to cut the effects without handles as seen in the example in the fade-in, normal practice is to have three frames of effect handle.

As the printer, not the position of the leader, controls the fade, the exact start and stop are not an issue unless they are too short. Many labs and Association of Cinema and Video Laboratories standards call for all fade leaders and dissolve overlaps to start and end five frames early and late. As always, check with the lab on their needs and suggestions. When cutting a series of fade-ins and fade-outs together, say a title series, it is easiest and proper to cut all the shots into one roll and clear through the entire section on the other roll.

Dissolve

When you come to a transition, like a dissolve, the splice will go in the center of the transition on the work print. A dissolve is a fade-in of one shot over a fade-out of a second. When marking a dissolve, the lines are the same as for the fades, but are on top of each other, as in Figure A8.8.

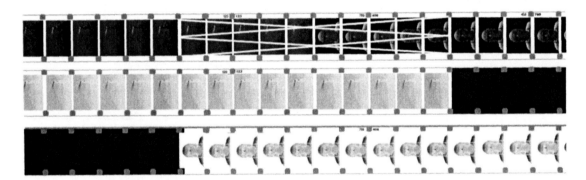

Figure A8.8   A- and B-roll dissolve

Final Cut Pro will warn of double uses and insufficient content to make a dissolve. It does not know, however, what that content is. In theory, if there is a visible problem, you will be able to see it in the Final Cut Pro edit. Just to be sure, however, when cutting the work print for a dissolve, make sure that the overlap of the dissolve does not contain a slate, odd action, or flash frame so there will be enough clean negative to make the overlap. For example, if you have a 48-frame dissolve, the splice in the work print is at the center of the dissolve. You need least 24 clean frames after the end of the outgoing shot and 24 clean frames before the incoming shot to complete the total 48-frame overlap.

Forty-eight frames is the most common length for dissolves, 24 for fades. Many labs also make fades and dissolves 16, 32, 64, and 96 frames long. Check with your lab.

Superimpositions

A wavy line running the length of the super indicates titles and other superimpositions. Cutting a few frames of the superimposed shot also indicates the start of the super. The insert for the super must include at least one key code number.

Unintentional Splices

Anytime you cut into the work print in the wrong place and need to repair the cut by splicing it back together, indicate this splice as unintentional by marking two straight lines across the splice.

There will soon be a time when the only people cutting film in any form will be those who have no interest in changing, or who want to have this experience for anachronistic reasons. But until that day arrives, negative editing will be used because it provides excellent quality with a cost saving over the digital intermediate process.

Appendix 9
Deconstructing Several Films' Workflows

Success
by Glynn Beard

Success is an HD project by experimental filmmaker Glynn Beard as part of his *Ocean of Storms* series of films. Success was shot and finished on 1080p Sony HD Cam at 23.98 FPS. Although the film is anything but conventional, the workflow was, for the most part, a classic Final Cut Pro HD workflow similar to Basic Workflow 4 in Appendix 10. The film was shot with Sony CineAlta HDW-F-900 at 23.98 FPS.

Audio was recorded double system on a Nagra 4.2 to achieve a "warm" analog quality.

Down conversion of the HD video to DVCam video was done at Digital Film Tree who also advised on the workflow. Digital Film Tree has been one of the louder voices in Hollywood promoting Final Cut Pro. They are an Apple development partner and have helped design the Final Cut Pro workflow on many films including the Oscar-winning *Cold Mountain*.

The pull-down pattern was 3:2. The DVCam tape received two window burns. One was for 24 NDF time code from the original HD tape, the other 30 NDF time code recorded onto the DVCam tape with zero frame "A" frame. A cycle identifier was added to the HD time code window burn.

The DVCam tapes were logged and captured. The Final Cut Pro batch list was exported. A Cinema Tools database was created and the Final Cut Pro batch list was imported into the database and the media linked. The media was then batch reverse telecined.

Figure A9.1 Poster from *Success*

Production audio was transferred to DVCam tape and batch captured. There was no need to pull down as the shooting and edit frame rate was 23.98. Audio was sunc to the sticks in the timeline and each shot was exported to a new directory for editing. This is an unusual system for syncing, but is 100 percent dependable and avoids both the merge clip and link clip functions. It does require more drive space, but some filmmakers prefer it just for its reliability. A 23.98 sequence was created and the project was edited.

Most interestingly, the footage was captured to the hard drive of a G4 laptop. The entire project was then portable and could be edited wherever and whenever the filmmaker felt the urge.

Often, when editing on a laptop, many editors will use the photo JPEG capture settings to save drive space. In this case, the capture was done with the DV capture settings to keep the edit image as clean as possible. There were even several test screenings in a high-definition theater directly from the laptop and the DV image looked quite good. While editing, an optical mouse and keyboard, seventeen-inch monitor, and NTSC video monitor were used with the laptop.

The sound edit and mix were also done in Final Cut Pro on the laptop. Reference monitors were attached to a DVCam deck for audio monitoring. The final mix was astonishingly good in spite of being done in Final Cut Pro on a laptop.

The HD titles and graphics were made, also on the laptop, using Photoshop at 1,920 × 1,080.

The online HD editing and color correction were done at Digital Film Tree. Media Manager was used in Final Cut Pro to eliminate all of the footage not used in the edit and to create an off-line sequence. The project file and HD tapes were taken in and all of the media recaptured at 1,920 × 1,080 to the online drive array. The laptop was connected to the online system and the titles and sound mix transferred to the array.

Color correction consisted of stripping away all the color to monochrome and crushing the blacks. Each shot was adjusted to get a consistent look. The transitions and "color" correction were rendered, and the project recorded back to HD Cam tape, still at 23.98 FPS. There is a plan to shoot the HD to black-and-white film in the future. This will be a simple process if the audio is encoded only to Dolby® LCRS. As this is an analog audio process, the optical sound can be shot at 23.98, sync will match, and when projected, even though it will be playing .1 percent faster at 24 FPS, it will look and sound fine. If the projection prints will use digital audio (i.e., DTS), the sample rate will need to be converted so that the sample rate is correct at 24 FPS.

Figure A9.2 *Help Wanted* poster

Help Wanted
Directed by Ryan Mooney
Written by Albert Santos

Help Wanted was a film made by students at the Brooks Institute as part of the Kodak student film-maker program. It was shot and finished on 35 mm with a Dolby LCRS sound track. Production audio was recorded on a PD6 digital recorder with smart slate for much of the shoot. The sample rate was 48,048 Hz. Some audio was also recorded with a Nagra 4.2 with "dumb slate," common clapper sticks.

The workflow that should have been followed was the standard film-to-film workflow, Basic Work-flow 5 in Appendix 10. However, because of the inexperience of the postproduction crew, several mistakes were made. There were several other problems in the telecine logs. But, the mistakes and problems were as much of a learning experience as making the film. Even though the mistakes were "large" mistakes, because of the flexibility of the workflow, in the end everything turned out fine and the problems not only did not find their way to the screen, but they proved easy to repair. Here are the workflow, the mistakes, and the solutions:

- Footage was telecined with zero frame "A" frame and with field "1" dominance. NTSC NDF time code was used with burn windows for:
  - Time code
  - Key code with pull-down cycle identifier (for example, "A" frame) following the key number
  - Audio time code on PD 6 shots, blank window on Nagra shots
- Each tape was given a different hour code.
- A telecine log was made.
- PD 6 footage was sunc in telecine. As the PD 6 records directly to an optical disc, the files were transferred to DA 88 tape and the audio sample rate set at 48 K achieving pull down.
- Nagra footage was sunc later, transfers being done in Pro Tools with a stripped house sync video reference creating the pull down.

This was the first mistake, pulling down in telecine and transfer. As there was a smart slate, it seemed reasonable to sync to it. In telecine the digital audio was transferred at 48 K, which is standard practice as transferring at the lower sample rate creates the pull down. However as this was to be a film-to-film workflow, there was no plan in place on what frame rate would be used, 23.98 or 24. Later, a plan was made to reverse to 24 FPS avoiding the need to pull down and back up, but also precluding the ability to be in sync before the shots were reversed to 24 FPS. Even using 48,048 Hz in the pro-duction recording was unnecessary. It was possible to sync in telecine without pulling down; which is say, shoot and transfer at 48 K. The shots on the telecined video would drift out of sync until they were reversed later.

However, the 29.97 video was dead in sync as would be expected. If the project would have been reversed to 23.98 and the audio pulled up in transfer to optical after the film was finished, everything would have been fine. But the next mistake was to not reverse at all, but edit the 29.97 footage. This mistake was not caught until the edit was locked. In export to Pro Tools, it was noticed that the frame rate was 29.97. This appeared to be a total disaster; however, the fix was reasonably painless. The captured footage had never been linked in Cinema Tools. However, the database from the telecine log was intact. The footage was linked to the database and reversed to 24.

This backward workflow is actually used on some projects. When using an edit system that does not support 23.98 or 24 but only 29.97, often the project is edited at 29.97 and, after the edit, the added frames are subtracted mathematically. This system is called "match back" and is highly problematic. In match back, one frame in five is simply ignored. Without matching the pull-down pattern, the resulting 23.98 is unplayable. But this is only used to generate a film cut list; the video will never be used. The problem is that rarely does the mathematical edit land on a true film frame line. The extra subframe is rounded off and sometimes, about one edit in five, it is off by one frame. Projects that use match back must check the negative cut and resync audio that no longer matches the errant negative edit.

Help Wanted had reversed telecine after editing and, true to form, some edits moved one frame. But the audio edit was not affected and the new 24 FPS edit played fine, so problems were easy to find, and fix, and proved to not be a real problem. And, yet, the audio was now out of sync. This is because the reverse was done at 24, knocking all the pulled-down audio out of sync. There were discussions on relinking and rereversing, digitally pulling the audio up in Pro Tools and even exporting and re-importing the audio at a new speed. It was also noted that the mix would be done with machine control to a 29.97 videotape, so the project needed to stay pulled down through the mix. Once more, this seemed to be a disaster, and again the solution was fairly simple.

In spite of the audio being out of sync, the work print and negative were cut and, after the silent first answer print was made and telecined, the 29.97 video was imported into the Pro Tools session. The speed of this pulled down video matched the pulled down audio but were positionally out of sync. The production takes were lined up visually to the new picture. This is certainly not the best practice, but in a pinch, it may be all you can do. The music and effects also needed to be realigned with the new 29.97 picture.

When lip syncing in Pro Tools, it is easy to select the audio and set up a loop playback. Now, use the nudge to move the line one frame at a time until it appears in sync. Keep moving it. You will find there is a "window" of "acceptable" sync about three or four frames wide. Place the audio in the center of this window.

Another problem had appeared back when the first double use report was exported. There were three double uses. Two were fixed by reediting and removing the double use. The third was not a double use at all, but an unintentional edit that was throwing off the double use report. All were easily fixed and the audio tracks reworked around the reediting.

During reverse telecine, several problems were also found in the original telecine log. This caused major concern as they threw several shots totally out. When the problem was found to be in the telecine log, the problem was solved by entering the proper information into the time code fields in Cinema Tools. This kind of problem comes up from time to time, but is found and fixed before the picture is edited. In this case, the picture had already been edited and it caused two days of total confusion. The giveaway was that the reversed footage did not have a clear pull-down pattern identifier after the footage was reversed. The Cs were all printed over with Ds. A frames were found to not be on 0 time codes. As the edge code window and videotape did contain the proper information, the time code information in the database was changed to match the videotape. The shots were re-reversed and the problem vanished.

The cut list was carefully compared to the key code window burn and was found to be perfect. However, because of all the problems, the decision was made to edit a work print to the cut list for insurance before cutting the negative. This proved unnecessary as the cut list was perfect.

The negative was cut as the titles were put together and shot. The project was delayed waiting for titles because the producer's credits were not accurate and ready on time. The title negative was cut into the negative rolls. A-B rolls were used to avoid opticals, and because the good people at Kodak were willing to supply black leader as part of the grant.

Finally, Foto Kem pulled the first answer print with no sound. This was telecined and used as a syncing guide in the errant the Pro Tools session. A temp dub was made and transferred to 35 mm mag stripe film pulled up to 24 FPS. This was interlocked with the first answer print and projected. Everything was in sync and the first attempt at color correction was fair. Changes were made to the color settings in preparation for a second answer print.

The final mix was made at Mix Magic. Machine control was used to lock the Pro Tools session to a Beta SP videotape with time code matching the Pro Tools session, 01:00:00:00 at Picture Start. The Pro Tools session was duplicated and all levels and filters removed from the tracks so that Mix Magic would have a clean start.

After the mix, the Dolby LCRS encoded mix was recorded to DA88 at 29.97. The optical sound was shot to 35 mm by NT audio with pull up as the Pro Tools session had ended up at video speed after resyncing to the 29.97 video. A second answer print was made with sound. To everyone's surprise and joy, the colors looked great, the Dolby sound track was incredible, and it was dead in sync.

Three release prints were made as well as a low-contrast or "low con" print. This was telecined to Digibeta, captured, and compressed on Apples Compressor software. This was matched to the original non-Dolby encoded comp mix audio. DVDs were authored using DVD Studio Pro.

The project was a great learning experience for everyone involved. Even the mistakes proved a great learning experience. Some of the lessons learned:

- Plan out the workflow and discuss it with the entire postproduction crew. Make sure everyone is on the same page.

- Never put off ordering titles or opticals. Have a schedule and stick to it. Schedule all telecine, mixing, and transfer ahead of time and then be ready to go at the scheduled time.

- Check the database against the window burns. Don't assume the logs are correct.

- Check for double usage as you go. Don't end up reediting after picture lock just because of a double usage.

- When problems come up, don't panic. Keep your thinking creative and outside the box. A simple fix may be staring you in the face.

- Understand the reasons for the work flow, not just the steps. This is critical when problems come up or work-arounds are necessary.

- Reverse to 23.98 not 24. The "simpler" 24 FPS workflow is not simpler. It only sounds simpler.

Lost Hope and More
Directed by Carmon Cone and Isaiah Mcamini
Written by Jessie Griffith

Figure A9.3 *Lost Hope and More* poster

Lost Hope and More was another student film made by students at the Brooks Institute as part of the Kodak student filmmaker program. It was shot and finished on Kodak 35 mm with a Dolby LCRS and Dolby 5.1 sound track. Production audio was recorded on a PD6 digital recorder with smart slate.

The workflow that was followed was the standard film-to-film workflow, Basic Workflow 5 in Appendix 10.

- Foto Kem labs pulled circled takes from the camera negative and spliced in into "selects" rolls.

- Work print was printed from the selects rolls.

- Silent work print was projected to look for problems.

- PD6 audio was transferred to DA88 tape by Laser Pacific. Clappers were logged by time code.

- Footage was telecined by Laser Pacific to DVCam with zero "A" frame and with field "1" dominance. NTSC NDF time code was used with burn windows for:
  - Time code
  - Key code with pull-down cycle identifier
  - Audio time code

- HD Cam was also recorded at the telecine for DVD authoring.

- Each tape was given a different hour code.

- A telecine log was made.

- Audio was sunc in telecine to the clapper logs.

- The telecine logs were imported into a new Cinema Tools database and a batch list was exported.

- The batch list was imported into a new Final Cut Pro project at 29.97 FPS.

- A batch list was also opened in Excel to create a cutting log.

- The DVCam footage was captured.

- The shots were linked to the database in Cinema Tools.

- All shots were batch reversed to 23.98 FPS.

- The 23.98 FPS shots were linked to the Final Cut Pro project.

- A 23.98 sequence was created in the Final Cut Pro project.

Several problems were found in checking the database. Several slates were mislabeled. These were noted in the cutting log and database. As the editing moved forward, a major problem was encountered. When the first film list was exported to check for double uses, several double uses were reported. Yet these were not double uses, they weren't even from the same camera rolls. At first, it looked like the almost impossible had happened, that there were two camera rolls with the same key code numbers. This turned out to not be the case.

When the selects rolls were telecined, a splice had passed through the telecine without the colorist noticing. The telecine machine cannot read every key code number; many are interpolated from known key code numbers. When a splice goes through the telecine, if the new number is not entered, it will continue with the numeric sequence from the previous roll, logging the wrong key code information into the telecine log.

Close examination of the database showed that four shots had key code numbers from a different camera roll. Several fixes were discussed; the consensus was that the shots should be retelecined. As it turned out, the fix was much more simple. The negative editor rolled into the selects rolls and found the shots with the wrong key code numbers. She wrote down the key code numbers for sticks close on the slates of the four shots. These key code numbers were entered into the Cinema Tools database on the corresponding sticks close frames. The key code information for the entire shot came online and the double use reports were cleared up. The window burns remained erroneous, but the database and film lists were accurate.

Once the edit was locked:

- The edit was exported as a QuickTime at 23.98 FPS.

- The audio was exported as an OMF.

- The edit was recorded onto DVCam tape for Foley picture.

- The OMF was opened in Pro Tools using Digi Translator.

- Foley and effects were cued.

- Foley was recorded at Film Leaders.

- ADR was cued and recorded.

- The score was recorded at two studios using MIDI and live instruments.

- Sound effects were recorded and edited.

- Film lists were exported including:
  ○ Double use list
  ○ Dupe list
  ○ Pull list
  ○ Cut list
  ○ Optical list

- Work print was pulled to the pull list and conformed to the cut list.

- A temp dub was made and recorded to DA88 tape.

- The temp dub DA88 was interlocked with the work print and projected.

- Negative was pulled for the optical effects.

- The negative for the opticals was printed to IP.

- Titles and opticals were made at T and T Effects using the IP.

- Camera negative was conformed and A-B rolled.

- Color was timed and the silent, first answer print was made.

- The answer print was telecined to DVCam and Beta SP for use as the dubbing picture.

- All levels and EQ used in the temp dub were removed and the final dub was preformed at Mix Magic.

- Dolby LCRS was encoded to DA88 tape.

- The mix was remixed to 5.1 at Sunset Screening Room.

- Dolby 5.1 was encoded to DA88 tape.

- Audio from the DA88s was recorded to optical film at NT audio.

- A second answer print was printed with sound and screened.

- Final color corrections were made and a third answer print made.

- Three release prints were made.

- An off-line sequence was made with media manager in Final Cut Pro.

- Titles and effects were telecined to HD Cam at Match Frame Video.

- The original HD Cam tapes and the HD Cam of the opticals were taken to Match Frame Video for HD online.

- The HD online and color correction was preformed at Match Frame Video.

- HD and SD QuickTimes were exported for HD and SD compression and DVD authoring.

Geography of the Imagination
Written and Directed by Jan Andrews

Figure A9.4 *Geography of the Imagination* poster

Geography of the Imagination is a very unusual 16 mm film that followed an equally unusual workflow. The film was made in the late 1980s when workflows like this were somewhat commonplace, but even for its time, this film used some exotic sound mixing workflow that was somewhat esoteric (and the brain child of this author).

This was more or less the way films were made from 1930 to the late 1980s with the exception of the sound mix. In this era, most films were mixed by loading all of the magnetic or optical tracks onto individual playback machines that were interlocked together. It could take more than fifty playback machines, or "dubbers," in order to perform such a mix.

For *Geography of the Imagination,* most of the film was shot on black-and-white reversal film. Some was shot on super 8 color film that was projected on a screen and rephotographed in black-and-white reversal film. This produced a very flickery, contrasty, and unstable image that was exactly what the filmmaker had in mind. Other shots were printed from stock footage.

All footage was work printed and edited on a Steenbeck flatbed editor. The film has no sync sound so that was not an issue. All sounds were transferred to 16 mm mag stock and the sound design created right on the flatbed editor.

The work print key code information was logged and printing cue sheets prepared. All original camera reversal film was pulled to the key codes and glue-spliced into A-B rolls.

Preparation for the mix is where the workflow became somewhat exotic and is the reason for mentioning it here. Even though the mix was going to be preformed to video, there was to be no pulling up or down. The mix would be done at 24 FPS. At the time, true 24 FPS workflows were thought to be the superior system and are still used and promoted as a simpler system. A quick review of the workflow on *Help Wanted* will show some of the potential pitfalls of a 24 FPS workflow.

For *Geography of the Imagination,* all of the sound tracks were transferred two at a time from two playback dubbers. The dubbers were locked to 60 Hz line sync to ensure 24 FPS playback, and they were then locked together by means of a "servo interlock," a system that is still used to lock multiple machines together. This way, when one machine moved forward or backward they both moved together in sync.

The system works like this: every machine has an "optac," short for optical tachometer. This sends a signal whenever the machine moves forward or backward. A servomotor that can move forward or backward drives each machine in very small and controllable steps. Each machine also has a computerized controller. When the master machine moves forward some number of steps, its optac sends this signal to all other machines that in turn are moved forward by their controllers until their optac informs the controller that they have moved exactly the same number of steps in the same direction. Any number or size of recorders or projectors or whatever can be locked together this way.

The master machine was "line locked' to the incoming 60 Hz line current (in other words, the electrical power from the wall plug). Electric clocks use this reference and, while it is not as accurate as the house sync, in this case, it is the best reference. The house sync is a video reference and is intended to keep 29.97 FPS devices in sync. If the dubbers were locked to this, they would run at 23.98 FPS, just like a telecine machine. Because this is a 24 FPS workflow, the dubbers needed to be locked to a 60 Hz reference and so line power was used.

The optac output was also sent to a time code generator that generated 30 NDF when the system was moving at 24 FPA. The plan was to use 30 NDF as the mixing and delivery time code to help identify this as a 24 FPS film speed workflow while avoiding 24 NDF because not all equipment can be locked to 24.

The NDF time code was sent to 2 DA88 digital recorders that were put into a "chase" mode. In chase, a recorder sees incoming time code and then "chases" it until it is in sync with it. It can chase forward or backward.

This meant that whenever the main dubber was rolled forward or backward, the other dubber rolled forward and backward matching every movement as well as the DA88s also rolling forward and backward also matching every move.

The "edit sync" point used was 01:00:00:00. This way, if DA88s were parked on 01:00:00:00 and two sound tracks threaded to their respective edit sync marks everything was in sync. Every 16 mm magnetic sound track could now be loaded two at a time and transferred to the 16 channels of the two DA88 recorders until all sound tracks were transferred in sync with each other to the DA88s.

The work print was "telecined" on an Elmo film chain locked to house sync. This pulled down the film speed to 23.98 FPS. As this would now drift out of sync, the video playback deck was locked to the 30 NDF time code and 60 Hz reference, causing it to run at 30 FPS and pulling the video back up to the original film speed.

This was the exotic part of the workflow; video recorders do not like to run at 30 FPS. The 30 NDF time code was sent to a video sync generator that could cause a video recorder to run off-speed. While this worked, it looked horrible; the video was tearing and had color banding, which is exactly why NTSC video uses a 29.97 frame rate. As this was only a mixing video reference, the poor image was forgiven and used.

The film was mixed to a remaining track of one of the DA88s and this DA88 tape sent to Film Leaders for quality control. They in turn sent it out to be transferred to 16 mm positive optical sound film, ready to be printed with the camera original reversal A-B rolls.

Like the workflow for *Help Wanted*, the 24 FPS workflow actually added complexity. While the sound was never pulled up or down, sync was solid and the workflow straightforward. Yet, using a video reference picture and forcing it to run at film speed was problematic.

The film could have been mixed at video speed. Had the dubbers been locked to the house sync instead of line power, they would have run at 23.98 FPS, pulling the tracks down as they were transferred to the DA88s. The DA88s could have been referenced to 29.97 NDF from the time code generator locked to the optac.

The picture and sound would now play at video speed, 29.97 FPS and the mix could have been done at this speed with good picture. The DA88 tape could have been pulled up to 30 FPS in the transfer to optical film and the optical would be back in sync with the camera original.

So, here again, pulling down and then pulling back up may seem like the more complicated workflow, in reality, it is not. Postproduction at video speed is always simpler and the better choice.

And not to sound like a stuck record, everything would be simpler and, therefore, better if 24 FPS simply went away. Shoot and display all video, digital media, and motion picture film at NYSC video speeds, 23.98 FPS or 29.97 FPS. Of course, now we would need to talk to our PAL friends. . . .

Zodiac

Directed by David Fincher

Written by James Vanderbilt (screenplay), Robert Graysmith (book)

Zodiac marked the first time a major motion picture was shot without the use of film or videotape. The film was shot on the Viper camera by Thomson, but not to videotape. Rather, the camera was in the "film stream" mode, raw data from the camera was recorded directly to drive. Parts of feature films and short films have been shot this way in the past, but the processing required to turn the data into workable and viewable "footage" made the process too cumbersome for a major, feature-length film. New products and faster computers have now made this workflow possible.

Zodiac was shot in uncompressed 10-bit 4:4:4 1,920 × 1,080/24p FilmStream mode with a 2.37:1 anamorphic aspect ratio. Zeiss DigiPrime lenses were used to help ensure a razor-sharp image. Industry standard DPX data from the Viper camera was recorded on one of 20 D.MAGs (digital magazines) removable hard drives loaded in DFRs (Digital Film Recorders) made by S.two of Reno, Nevada.

The drives were transported to the edit room where they were downloaded and backed up to data tape. This was done with S.two's A Dock, which also allows for checking the backup data for problems. With as many as six cameras rolling on some scenes, the amount of data being downloaded challenged the workflow, but with twenty "magazines" the system worked well. Well enough that Fincher has stated he will never shoot film or video again. He just started his next feature, and he is back using the Viper and S.two data recorders.

The data was rendered and processed to usable image media that was stored on 40TB of Apple Xsan storage. At one point, the rendering became a bottleneck with more footage coming in than could be rendered on the Xsan. Rather than bringing in a second Xsan, the postproduction team opted to buy a collection of Mac minis and let them help out with the rendering. Good bang for the buck.

The media was cloned and down converted to the DVCPRO HD format and transferred to Xsan drive array. The DVCPRO HD shots were imported into Final Cut Pro for editing. The project was also kept on FireWire drives and made available to the postproduction team via the Internet so that everyone had access to the media without being restricted to the edit room. While this presents a security issue, good encryption is more secure than a locked door on an editing room.

As the rendered media from the Viper has not been "timed," the look is very bland. Several temporary looks were decided on for each scene, and the DVCPRO HD shots were color corrected using Apple's

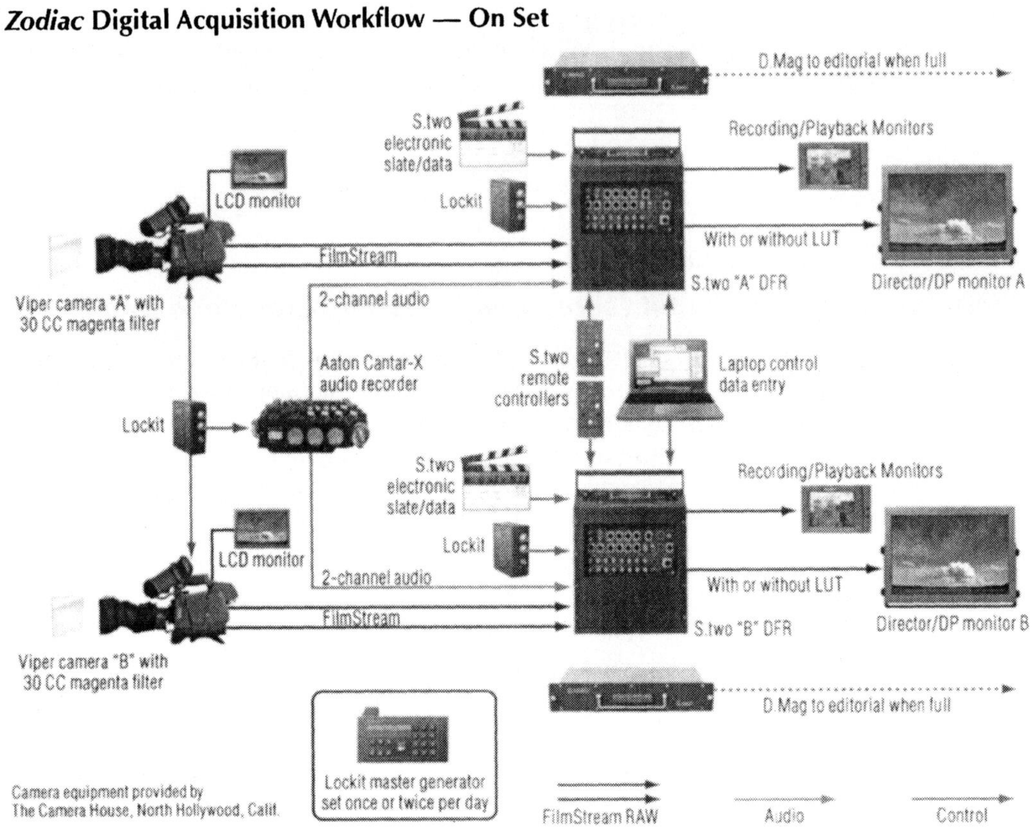

Zodiac Digital Acquisition Workflow — On Set

Figure A9.5 *Zodiac* on-set data recording. Image courtesy of Thomson

Shake compositing software. This way, the editors could get the feel of the scene by seeing the, more or less, "proper" look.

The shots had no physical slates. Slates were added into the first and last frames of the shot automatically. The slate information was also written into the metadata, which even contained the f-stop, focal length, lens height, and other information that may be helpful to the effects and sound people. It was estimated that the production saved twenty minutes per day by not needing to slate (see Figure A9.6 regarding on-set recording).

Once the picture is locked, the sound is handled in exactly the same way as other video workflows. The 2 K DPX media is put online with the edited timeline, and the 2 K is ready for color correction. This is exactly the same process as a 2 K digital intermediate workflow. In this case, the 2 K is not a film scan, but the 2 K camera data.

The finished 2 K can be down converted to HD video, SD video or shot to 35 mm film. It can even be projected with a 2 K digital projector.

Zodiac **Editorial Workflow — Post Dailies**

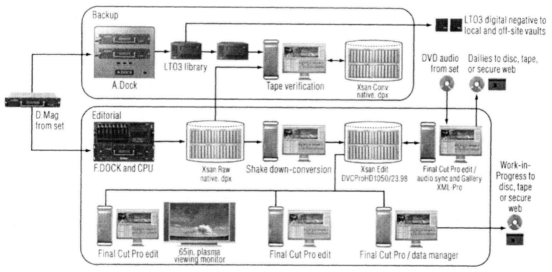

Editorial equipment and custom inhouse software provided by Rock Paper Scissors, West Hollywood, Calif.

Figure A9.6 *Zodiac* postproduction workflow chart

While this workflow, illustrated in Figure A9.6, may look complicated (and it is), the complexity is in the functioning, not the operation. Once a person understands the steps and learns the tools, the workflow is actually very straightforward. The look of 2 K DPX recorded to film or in direct 2 K digital projection is great, rivaling a direct film 35 mm release print. For more information on this workflow, see Appendix 10, number six on shooting on data recorder.

Appendix 10
Example Workflows

Basic Workflow 1

Shooting on 29.97 NTSC low data

(Mini DV, DVCam, DVC, DVC PRO 50)

Finish on 29.97 NTSC low data

This workflow is proper for all 29.97 low-data formats. Even 24 P, when not reversed and left at 29.97 FPS, follows this workflow. Because the data rate is low, the video can be stored on a standard FireWire 400 drive. And because this is low data, there is no need to online, the off-line edit being full resolution.

Most often, single-system sound is used with this workflow, recording audio directly on the camera tape. However, some projects use double-system sound, recording sound on a sync sound recorder. In this case, as there will be no pull down, the sample rate for recording digital audio should not be a "30 FPS" film speed sample rate such as 48,048 Hz, but rather, a "29.97 FPS" video speed sample rate. 48 K is ideal.

The aspect can be cropped to any size, but the native aspect ratios are 4×3 and 16×9. 16×9 finish can be anamorphic or letterbox.

Many "basic" projects shot on these formats edit and mix sound entirely in Final Cut Pro. This example workflow uses Pro Tools, which has huge advantages. However the sound can be mixed in Final Cut Pro.

- Log and capture all footage.

- If the footage is anamorphic, set up the capture and sequence to anamorphic.

- If the project is going to be cropped to another aspect ratio, capture using the shooting aspect ratio 4 × 3 or 16 × 9. Cropping will be done later.

- If using double-system sound, import or transfer all audio.

- Sync all takes using the merge clip function.

- Create finished titles and graphics *or* edit in slug or scratch titles.

- Edit the project to a locked cut, the length and sync must be exact including end credits.

- Cut in a Cinema Tools head leader (29.97 FPS).

- Organize and split off all sound tracks.

- Export the movie as a QuickTime.

- Export the audio as OMF.

- Open the OMF as a Pro Tools session using Digi Translator.

- Import the QuickTime movie and guide track into the Pro Tools session.

- Record and import all sound effects, ADR, Foley, and music.

- Edit the sound tracks and create the automated mix.

- Export the mix with the "bounce to disc" function.

The next three steps can be performed before, during, or after the sound edit and mix. These steps can be done in any order.

- If scratch titles and graphics were used in the edit, create the finished versions and cut them into the project. Use care to not change the length of the title, it needs to be a straight replacement. NTSC graphics should be 720 × 480 pixels.

- Go through the project shot by shot and color correct using the Final Cut Pro plug-ins (i.e., color corrector three way), or use second-party plug-ins.

- If cropping to another aspect ratio, crop the project using the motion tab controls.

- Make a copy of the sequence in the timeline and delete all of the sound tracks. Do not use the original edit; use a copy.

- Import the mix into Final Cut Pro, drag it into the new sequence and line up the 2 pop.

- If the project is full-screen 4 × 3 or letterboxed 4 × 3, the project is finished. Print to tape and/or export the QuickTime for burning to DVD.

- If the project is anamorphic, you can record the anamorphic version to tape or export for DVD; however, if you need a full-screen letterboxed version, drag your 16 × 9 sequence from the browser window into an empty 4 × 3 sequence and render. This will give you a letterboxed version.

Basic Workflow 2

Shooting on 24 P NTSC low data

(24 P cameras such as the SDX 900, DVX 100, and XL-2)

Finish on 24 P DVD, HD or Film

This workflow is the Holy Grail, the Northwest Passage. The promise of this workflow is the cheapest system ever devised to put a motion picture into theaters. Several films have done this; *28 Days Later* used a similar workflow with the XL-1 camera. No doubt if the XL-2 had existed when the film was made, they would have used that. The film *November* was shot on the $3,500 DVX 100, and went on to not only play at the 2004 Sundance Film Festival, it won Best Cinematography.

Developments are happening almost daily with this workflow, new cameras, new up-convert systems, and new ways of thinking. Opinions differ wildly on how to up-convert and finish, but the capture and edit is simple and straightforward.

Just as in the first workflow, the shooting data rate is low, so the video can be captured and stored on a FireWire 400 drive. There will be no real online, but rather some type of up-convert of the full-resolution off-line edit.

Because we are trying for the best possible result, projects generally use double-system sound. There will be no pull down, as we are shooting at 23.98, a "video speed." The aspect should be 16×9 anamorphic. HD finish will also be anamorphic. Although the cameras can shoot 3:2 or advanced, use the advanced cadence, 2:3:3:2.

- Set up Final Cut Pro for 24 P NTSC anamorphic. This can be done from capture and sequence settings or with an "easy setup."

- Log and capture all footage at 23.98 FPS.

- As this footage uses advanced 2:3:3:2 pull down, simply set the capture rate to 24 P in the capture window.

- If using double-system sound, import or transfer all audio.

- Sync all takes using the link clip function.

- Create finished titles and graphics *or* edit in slug or scratch titles.

- Edit the project to a locked cut, the length and sync must be exact including all credits.

- If you are planning a film-out, divide the show into proper reels. Even if you are not planning a film transfer, if your film is long, you may want to divide it into ten-minute film reels just to keep the project more manageable.

- Cut in a Cinema Tools head leader (23.98 FPS) on every reel.

- Organize and split off all sound tracks.

- Export the movie (reels) as a QuickTime (they will be 23.98 FPS QuickTimes).

- Export the audio for the reels as OMF.

- Open the OMF as a Pro Tools session using Digi Translator.

- Import the QuickTime movie and guide track into the Pro Tools session. Pro Tools will support the 23.98 FPS rate.

- Record and import all sound effects, ADR, Foley, and music.

- Edit the sound tracks and create the automated mix.
    - If you are making a feature, or want to open up more distribution options, you will want to make stems. Do not mix dialogue, effects, or music in the same tracks.
    - Copy the 2 pop from Pro Tools track 1 into one effects track and one music track. In export, every stem needs a 2 pop.

- Export the composite mix with the "bounce to disc" function.

- Mute the effects and music tracks and export the dialogue stem with the bounce-to-disc function. Do the same for the effects stems and the music stems.

- Create the finished HD titles and graphics. Graphics should be made at $1,080 \times 1,920$ pixels. If you are using Final Cut Pro titles, and you are up-converting by rendering instead of going tape-to-tape, they do not need to be redone. They will automatically be rendered at high definition in the HD render.

The finishing and up-conversion can follow several workflows. All have advantages and disadvantages. The simplest and most straightforward system is by rendering to HD.

- Take the finished project on FireWire drive to an HD online facility.

- They will copy your project onto the facilities high-speed drive array.

- Make a new sequence with HD settings. Copy or drag your sequence (picture only) into this sequence.

- The new sequence now needs to be rendered. The render is quite long; however, most facilities do renders after hours at a greatly reduced rate.

- Do some test renders. Often problems come up, don't dive in and render everything only to find problems need to be addressed in the standard definition before rendering. Often, problems come up in bright reds. Reds tend to blow out in the HD render. You may need to use the Final Cut Pro color correction tools to pull down some colors before the HD render. These can be restored after the render in final color correction.

- If scratch titles and graphics were used in the edit, the finished versions are now cut into the project. Use care to not change the length of the graphic or title, it needs to be a straight replacement.

- Import the mix into Final Cut Pro, drag it into the new sequence, and line up the 2 pop.

The project is now ready for final color correction. There are several ways to do this, which are discussed later in this appendix.

Another way to convert the project to HD is tape-to-tape. Panasonic offers recorders, the AJ-HD1700 and AJ-HD3700B, that can input standard definition formats while converting and recording to HD.

In this case, the project is simply recorded directly to 720p, 1080i, or 1080p. While this process seems incredibly simple, there are several problems that need to be addressed. Getting the video out of Final Cut Pro and into one of these recorders is a bit more complicated than simply playing it out via FireWire.

Find a facility that can make this up-conversion. Each will have different equipment and interfaces and may, therefore, want to follow a different workflow. Some will simply load your project into their Final Cut Pro and record to tape via Serial Digital Interface (SDI). Others may not even use Final Cut Pro and want to do the up-conversion from an NTSC tape. This seems odd, yet some of the best up-conversions have followed this workflow, including the film *November*.

In this case, the project is recorded to an NTSC tape, usually Digibeta. As this is a 29.97 FPS format, the project can be recorded with $2:3:3:2$ advanced cadence or $3:2$, depending on the needs of the transfer house. It may seem that taking the project back to 29.97 defeats the reason for editing in 23.98 in the first place, but it does not. Before reversing, each shot had a different zero A-frame reference. It is not possible to reverse the edited sequence without causing the edits to move or the video to become unstable. With the shots reversed to 23.98, the entire edit can be recorded back to 29.97 with one zero A-frame reference. Now the 29.97 tape can be captured or transferred in real time at 23.98 with advanced removal and the project is back, frame-for-frame, to 23.98.

If titles were edited into the original standard definition sequence, these have been up-converted as well. These will look much better if they are replaced with true $1,080 \times 1,920$ HD titles and graphics. These can be recorded to HD tape and replaced one at a time with a tape-to-tape edit. This even works for superimposed titles. If you are using superimposed titles, do not edit in a scratch or standard definition version in the original edit. These will be up-converted and be impossible to remove or replace.

The project is now ready to add the mixed sound track and color correct. The sound can be recorded to tape and sunc to the 2 pop with a tape-to-tape edit. Many recorders have eight tracks and support 5.1 surround mixes.

Final color correction should always be done in HD. There is more control in HD and this is the final step: what you see is what you have. There are many fine systems for color correcting HD. Here, too, many projects will color correct tape-to-tape, going through the project one shot at a time, correcting and recording to a second tape.

You may feel that these tape-to-tape dubs are costing image quality. After all, the final tape is several generations down from the shooting tapes. However, this is not the case. These formats are, for all intents, lossless. You would need to be down scores of generations before seeing loss of quality in Digibeta or HD.

Film output from this HD tape is simple, but good film-outs are expensive. As the HD project is recorded at 23.98, the film-out will speed this up to 24 FPS. This will also speed up the audio and change the sample rate. For digital audio film prints in DTS or SDDS, the sample rate will need to be converted to keep the sound in sync. This is all part of the film-out process and is handled by the facility doing the film-out. Depending on their method, they may want to go back to the composite mix master and perform a pull up.

Basic Workflow 3

Shooting on 24 P HD low data

(HDV, DVC Pro HD)

Finish on 24 P HD low data

This workflow is proper for the HD 24 P (23.98 FPS) low-data format. These formats are extremely new and may replace Basic Workflow 2 just as HD will surely replace SD. Because the data rate is lower than formats like HD Cam and HD Cam SR, the video can be captured and stored on a FireWire 400 drive. Just as in the NTSC workflow, there is no need to online, the off-line edit being full resolution.

Just as in the NTSC workflow, single-system sound is often used with this workflow, recording audio directly on the camera tape but here, too, some projects use double system sound. Here, too, there will be no audio pull down; the production sample rate should be a video speed sample rate.

The aspect is 16×9 anamorphic. HD finish will also be anamorphic.

- Set up Final Cut Pro for 24 P HD anamorphic. This can be done from capture and sequence settings or with an "easy setup."

- Log and capture all footage at 23.98 FPS.
  - As this footage uses advanced $2:3:3:2$ pull down, simply set the capture rate to 24 P in the capture settings.
  - If using double-system sound, import or transfer all audio.
  - Sync all takes using the link or merge clip function.

- Create finished titles and graphics *or* edit in slug or scratch titles.

- Edit the project to a locked cut; the length and sync must be exact including end credits.

- Cut in a Cinema Tools head leader (23.98 FPS).

- Organize and split off all sound tracks.

- Export the movie as a QuickTime. (It will be a 23.98 FPS QuickTime.)

- Export the audio as OMF.

- Open the OMF as a Pro Tools session using Digi Translator.

- Import the QuickTime movie and guide track into the Pro Tools session. Pro Tools will support the 23.98 FPS rate.

- Record and import all sound effects, ADR, Foley, and music.

- Edit the sound tracks and create the automated mix.

- Export the mix with the "bounce to disc" function.

The next four steps can be performed before, during, or after the sound edit and mix. These steps can be done in any order.

- If scratch titles and graphics were used in the edit, create the finished versions and cut them into the project. Use care to not change the length of the title; it needs to be a straight replacement. Graphics should be made at 1,080 × 1,920 pixels.

- Go through the project shot by shot and color correct using the Final Cut Pro plug-ins (i.e., color corrector three way), or use second-party plug-ins. You are working in an HD color space; however, it is a very compressed color space. You will have no more control than if you were in NTSC.

- If cropping to a wider aspect ratio than 16 × 9, crop the project using the motion tab controls.

- Make a copy of the sequence in the timeline and delete all of the sound tracks. Do not use the original edit, use a copy.

- Import the mix into Final Cut Pro, drag it into the new sequence and line up the 2 pop.

- Print to DVC Pro HD tape.

This workflow is similar to Basic Workflow 1, and is really being seen as a direct replacement of that SD workflow. But, it will likely also be a replacement for Basic Workflow 2.

Basic Workflow 4

Shooting on high-bandwidth 24 P HD

(HD Cam, 1080i, 1080p, 720p)

Finish on 24 P HD, optional 35 mm film

This is the classic HD workflow. This is not a single workflow; there are so many options along the way, it is almost a family of workflows. There are many frame rates and different but related formats, yet they follow similar workflows. There are many options along the way, different ways to accomplish each step. The results can be fantastic. Many feature films have been made this way, including the huge-budget *Star Wars 2* and *3*. In these cases, the reason for using this format was not cost savings, it was chosen for its ability to seamlessly integrate digital effects and maintain a consistent look.

There are several cameras that shoot these formats. Most commonly used are the Sony Cine Altas, the HDW-F-900, and the HDC-950, as well as the Panasonic Varicam. While these cameras shoot several frame rates, the most common is 23.98 FPS. This simplifies conversion to 29.97 FPS video and makes a great film out at 24 FPS by simply speeding up the frame rate. By keeping the entire workflow at a 23.98 FPS rate, there are no pull-up or pull-down problems until and unless there is a film out for 35 mm release.

Double system sound is often used with "video speed" sample rates. As there is no need to pull down, the playback and transfer sample rate is simply the same as the recorded sample rate.

The video data rate of these formats precludes the use of portable drives. The video can only be played from an array of drives through a high-speed data bus into the computer. Even capturing video from tape is a slow process. The data rate is so high that even with a serial digital interface, video can only be captured in small "chunks" one or two seconds long. The video can then be played from the array in real time.

231

Because of the high cost of an HD online facility, it is necessary to do an off-line edit at standard definition and then online with the original HD video. This requires a down conversion of the HD video to SD video. The SD video can then be edited slowly at the editor's pace without worrying about being "on the clock" at several hundred dollars per hour.

There are several good ways to down-convert and capture into the off-line system. The first requires down-converting the video on the fly from the original HD tapes and recording onto SD NTSC videotape at 29.97 FPS. This is done tape-to-tape usually to a DVCam tape.

- The HD tape is played on an HD recorder and recorded to DVCam tape with matching time code formats.

- As the video is down-converted, it also receives a 3:2 or 2:3:3:2 frame rate conversion to 29.97 FPS.

- The DVCam tape receives two window burns. One displays the time code from the original HD tape, the other the time code recorded onto the DVCam tape.

- The two time codes must be the same general type, drop-frame or nondrop-frame. Usually this is nondrop.

- Although the two time codes display different frame rates, the zero frames must line up. And there must be a zero A-frame reference between the two.

- A cycle identifier is added to the HD time code window burn.

- When played, the DVCam tape 30 NDF time code window burn will count normally, but the 24 NDF with cycle identifier will lurch along with some numbers and letters unreadable.

- The DVCam tape is now logged and captured. If the down converts are 2:3:3:2, the capture can be done at 24P (23.98) by simply checking the check box in the capture window.

- Be sure to clearly name your tapes in capture and label both the HD tapes and down-converts with the same names.

- Down-converts with 3:2 cadence will need to be reversed in Cinema Tools to 23.98.
  - Export the Final Cut Pro batch list.
  - Open Cinema Tools. Create a new database. Now import the Final Cut Pro batch list. Link the media.
  - Batch reverse telecine.

- Captured and reversed footage will now show normal counting in the 24 NDF time code window, and the cycle identifier will show clean A, B, C, and D, but the 30 NDF will be missing one frame number in every five. (For a more detailed look at this workflow, see Appendix 9 on match backs.)

On some projects, down-converts have been made by rolling dual recorders in production. HD and SD DVCam tapes are recorded simultaneously whenever the camera rolls. This has proven to be problematic. It is tricky enough to get good down-converts with proper time code and window burns without attempting to do this in "video village" on the set or in camera.

Another way to down-convert and capture is to capture directly from the camera HD tapes at low resolution. In this case, the log and capture is done in a high-definition facility directly to portable drive. The capture settings in Final Cut Pro are set to Photo JEPG 23.98 and all the footage is logged and captured. Because of the low-data rate, capture can be done in real time. This is slower and, therefore, more expensive than down-converts to tape, mostly because of logging time. If the batch capture list is made by logging blind from the camera reports before going in to capture, this can be almost as cost effective as tape-to-tape down-converts. And because capture is done at 23.98, there is no need for matching time codes, dual window burns, or reverse telecine.

Just as with the other workflows, if the project is destined for film-out, split the edit into ten-minute or less reels, and slug for missing titles or effects. After the off-line edit, when the edit is locked, the project is ready for sound and online edit. Sound is handled exactly like the other workflows.

- Cut in a Cinema Tools head leader (23.98 FPS) on every reel.

- Organize and split off all sound tracks.

- Export the movie (reels) as a QuickTime (they will be 23.98 FPS QuickTimes).

- Export the audio for the reels as OMF.

- Open the OMF as a Pro Tools session using Digi Translator.

- Import the QuickTime movie and guide track into the Pro Tools session. Pro Tools will support the 23.98 FPS rate.

- Record and import all sound effects, ADR, Foley, and music.

- Edit the sound tracks and create the automated mix.

- Export the composite mix with the "bounce to disc" function.

- Export the stems.

- Create the finished HD titles and graphics. Graphics should be made at 1,080 × 1,920 pixels. If you are using Final Cut Pro titles, they will automatically be rendered at high definition in the HD render.

You are now ready for the online HD edit and color correction. There are a few steps in getting ready for the online.

- Make sure that all of the video is in V1 unless it is a superimposition. Many people edit by layering shots simply to facilitate moving shots around. This becomes extremely confusing in online. Keep all of your shots in V1.

- Use "Media Manager" in Final Cut Pro to make an off-line sequence of the locked cut. Media Manager will eliminate all of the footage not used in the edit. All of the edited footage needs to be recaptured, but there is no reason to capture footage not used in the edit.

The project file is very small, only a few hundred K, yet this is the map to the finished online. Have your online facility check the project file before going in. They can load it in onto the HD online Final Cut Pro system and look for problems. And, as it is very small, you can simply e-mail it to them as an attachment.

What you should bring with you to the online:

- Your mix, on a portable drive

- Any HD titles or graphics that will be replaced

- Your original HD tapes

- Your project file, if it has not been e-mailed in, also on portable drive

What to expect in the online:

- The off-line project file will be opened on the HD online system. All of the media will be off-line (missing). The exception will be any Final Cut Pro titles that are part of the project file.

- The HD tapes will be batch captured to the high-speed drive array. If you have a long project, it makes more sense to leave the HD tapes with the online facility and let them perform this capture before you arrive. It is a slow process.

- Import your mix into the project. Line up the 2 pop.

- Replace any titles and graphics that are missing with the new HD titles on your portable drive.

At this point, you can start color correction on the online system or render and record to tape for color correcting tape-to-tape, as in Basic Workflow 2. Tape-to-tape is often less expensive, but many prefer to color correct now, in online. Much will depend on costs and the type of color correction equipment available in the online facility. Whether you render effects and titles now and color correct later, or color correct now and then render color, effects, and graphics, you will need to render before recording out to the master tape. The render is extremely slow, especially if rendering color correction. Most facilities render after hours or on dedicated machines at greatly reduced cost.

Just as with Basic Workflow 2, a film-out from the color-corrected HD tape is simple, yet very expensive. Here, too, the HD project is recorded at 23.98, the film-out speeding up to 24 FPS. This is handled by the facility doing the film-out. Depending on their method, they may want to go back to the composite mix master to perform a pull up.

Basic Workflow 5

Shooting on film (35 mm or 16 mm)

Finish on 35 mm or 16 mm film by cutting the camera negative

The film finish workflow is complicated, with many steps and, as always, there are options along the way. The film can be shot on 16 mm, super 16 mm, 35 mm with 4 perf pull down or 35 mm with 3 perf pull down, super 35 mm, and this list could go on and on.

It is necessary to choose the editing frame rate before beginning. This can be 23.98 FPS or 24 FPS. For most projects, 23.98 works better. The disadvantage of 23.98 is that the audio must be pulled down before syncing and pulled back up before printing the optical sound. But this is simple and generally more accepted. Video output from 23.98 is simple and audio can be sunc in telecine.

At 24 FPS, the film runs at the true film speed and this seems to be a tremendous advantage. With 24 FPS, there is no need to pull up or down, but syncing in telecine is a trick as the audio will be out of sync until the footage is reversed to 24 FPS. Most projects will choose to sync after reversing. This makes managing an audio EDL more complicated as the time code must be entered by hand instead of importing it with the telecine log. Also, video exports from 24 FPS are tricky and run at a different speed as the original media.

For this example, we will assume 23.98 as this is much more common. We will also assume that a DAT audio recorder is being used in production, sample rate at 48.048 K, 30 NDF continuous time code, and Smart Slate. Also, 35 mm film is being shot at 24 FPS 1 : 1.85 aspect 4 perf pull down.

- At the end of every shooting day, the camera negative is processed and telecined to DVCam tape, zero frame A-frame transfer with field 1 dominance and NTSC nondrop-frame time code. Window burns are made for time code, key code with pull-down cycle identifier, and audio time code. Different hour codes for each tape are used and a telecine log generated often as a FLX file. Syncing is done in telecine using the numbers from the smart slate and, therefore, adding the audio time code to the telecine log and window burn. The playback DAT is set to 48 K, pulling the audio down to video speed. Little color correction is used as this is only an editing print.

- A copy of the telecine log is made and imported into a new database in Cinema Tools. A batch list is exported.

- The batch list is imported into Final Cut Pro and the DVCam footage is batch captured. A second copy of the batch list is opened in Text Edit and used as a cutting log.

- The Cinema Tools database is reopened and the captured footage linked to the database. The footage is reverse telecined to 23.98.

- The Final Cut Pro project is reopened and the shots in the project are relinked to the new 23.98 footage. A new sequence is created at 23.98 and the picture edited. At the end of each day, a Cinema Tools film list is exported with only Dupe List and Warn of Duplicates selected to ensure that no footage is being used twice. Edit only to V1 with any superimpositions in V2.

- When the picture is locked, a complete Cinema Tools film list is exported and checked against the window burns on the picture. The negative is cut to the cut list. A work print may be cut first as insurance. Opticals and titles are ordered and added into the negative.

- Just as with the other film finish workflows, split the edit into twenty-minute or less reels, and slug for missing titles or effects.

Sound is handled exactly like the other workflows.

- Cut in a Cinema Tools head leader (23.98 FPS) on every reel.

- Organize and split off all sound tracks.

- Export the movie (reels) as a QuickTime (they will be 23.98 FPS QuickTimes).

- Export the audio for the reels as OMF.

- For those planning to recapture audio from the production DAT, an audio EDL is exported and used to batch capture audio to the digital audio workstation. Several digital recorders and theater sound formats now support very high sample rates, 96 K at 24 bit. Pro Tools HD is also capable of these sample rates. So, rather than convert the OMF derived from the 48 K 16- or 24-bit Final Cut Pro edit, audio is recaptured from the original production tapes.

- Open the OMF as a Pro Tools session using Digi Translator.

- Import the QuickTime movie and guide track into the Pro Tools session. Pro Tools will support the 23.98 FPS rate.

- Record and import all sound effects, ADR, Foley, and music.

- Edit and sync the sound tracks.

With the expense of a film production and film finish, few projects will mix their own tracks, but rather, take the project to a reputable mixing house. You can mix in Pro Tools just as with the other workflows, but the mix will need to be pulled up, checked against the negative for sync, Dolby encoded, and shot to optical sound.

When the negative is cut, a first answer print is made without sound. This is the first step in color correction and serves as a sync reference for the sound edit and mix. If any errors were made in the negative cut, they will show up in the first answer print. Project the print and make notes on the first attempt at color correction. The Pro Tools session can be recorded to magnetic film at 23.98 and interlocked with the print to check sync and act as a temp dub, a trial to see if all the sounds are working with the picture or if any effects or other sounds will need to be redone.

Telecine the first answer print to DVCam and capture the video to Final Cut Pro. In the mix, the video will likely be played from an interlocked videotape player rather than from QuickTime. This system, machine control, is more accurate when looking at sync. Find out what tape format the sound mixing house uses and telecine to this format as well as your DVCam. Most sound houses will want the time code to match between the Pro Tools session and the videotape reference. The Picture Start frame, which is the first frame on the countdown leader, should be the first frame of the project and should be at 01:00:00:00 in the Pro Tools session. If not, set this in the Session Setup window. Make sure the Picture Start frame on the videotape is also at 01:00:00:00.

Export the 29.97 capture of the answer print from Pro Tools and import it into the Pro Tools session. Because both the 23.98 QuickTime and the 29.97 QuickTime of the answer print both play at video speed, the sync should match. If there are any problems in the negative cut, any sync problems can be repaired now as this video reference is derived from the cut negative.

In preparing for the mix, remove any level changes and filters you have added to the Pro Tools session. If you are concerned about losing your "temp dub" levels and EQ, you can make a copy of the session or, what is often done, make copies of every track directly under the existing track. Remove all levels and filters from the new tracks and mute and hide the originals. Now you have access to "clean" tracks in the mix and you can still bring up the temp dub to check what levels were used there. As always, follow proper track layout to speed mixing and facilitate recording the stems.

At the end of the dub, the Dolby representative will be called in and the final mix encoded to Dolby SR. This will be recorded to DA88 at 29.97 FPS. The tape is delivered to the facility that will be shooting the optical sound negative. The optical sound negative is shot with the DA88 set to 30 FPS and delivered back to the lab where a second answer print is made, this time married to the optical sound.

The second answer print may need further color adjustments and a third, or even fourth, answer print will be made. When the picture looks as good as possible, an interpositive is printed. This looks almost exactly like a projection print, but is made on low-contrast stock. This is printed to an inter-negative, or several internegatives, and release prints are printed on high-speed printers.

Basic Workflow 6

Shooting on film (35 mm or 16 mm)

Finish on 35 mm film and/or video using digital intermediate

As always, there are many variations on this workflow. In its most basic form, it is like the negative cutting workflow with the exception that the pulled negative is scanned to DI and the final conforming, color correction, and cleanup are done to this DI, not to the film directly. The DI is then shot to film and release prints made. There is also the "virtual digital intermediate" that is much more like the high bandwidth 24 P HD workflow.

In either case, the workflow is as follows.

- For true DI, at the end of every shooting day, the camera negative is processed and telecined to DVCam tape. Zero frame A-frame transfer, with field 1 dominance and NTSC nondrop-frame time code. Window burns are made for time code, key code with pull-down cycle identifier, and audio time code. Little color correction is used as this is only an editing print.
    - For virtual digital intermediate, all of the footage is datacined to HD Cam or D-5 at 24 or 23.98 FPS. Down-converted clones are made to DVCam with window burns for 29.97 NDF and 23.98 NDF.

- A copy of the telecine log is made and imported into a new database in Cinema Tools. A batch list is exported.

- The batch list is imported into Final Cut Pro and the DVCam footage is batch captured. A second copy of the batch list is opened in Text Edit and used as a cutting log.

- The Cinema Tools database is reopened and the captured footage linked to the database. The footage is reverse telecined to 23.98.

- The Final Cut Pro project is reopened and the shots in the project are relinked to the new 23.98 footage. A new sequence is created at 23.98 and the picture edited. With DI and VDI, double uses are fine so there is no need to make a daily double use report. Edit only to V1 with any superimpositions in V2.

- For DI: When the picture is locked, a complete Cinema Tools film list is exported and checked against the window burns on the picture. The negative is pulled to the pull list. The entire shot is pulled from flash frame to flash frame; the DI will be conformed to the edit later.
    - For VDI: You are ready to head to the HD online. The rest of the finish will be an HD high-bandwidth finish with the exception of the 23.98 or 24 FPS HD video being shot back to film and audio pulled up to 24 FPS on 23.98 projects.

- Just as with the other film finish workflows, split the edit into twenty-minute or less reels, and slug for missing titles or effects.

For DI and VDI, sound is handled exactly like the other workflows.

- Cut in a Cinema Tools head leader (23.98 or 24 FPS) on every reel.

- Organize and split off all sound tracks.

- Export the movie (reels) as QuickTime (they will be 23.98 FPS QuickTimes).

- Export the audio for the reels as OMF.

- For those planning to recapture audio from the production DAT, an audio EDL is exported and used to batch capture audio to the digital audio workstation. Several digital recorders and theater sound formats now support very high sample rates, 96 K at 24 bit. Pro Tools HD is also capable of these sample rates. So, rather than convert the OMF derived from the 48 K 16- or 24-bit Final Cut Pro edit, audio is recaptured from the original production tapes.

- Open the OMF as a Pro Tools session using Digi Translator.

- Import the QuickTime movie and guide track into the Pro Tools session. Pro Tools will support the 23.98 FPS rate.

- Record and import all sound effects, ADR, Foley, and music.

- Edit and sync the sound tracks.

- The DI conform and color correction are handled in a DI color correction suite. All of the pulled footage is slowly scanned one frame at a time to a drive array in 2 K or 4 K DPX.

- The show is then assembled to construction order matching the Cinema Tools cut list.

- Any cleanup and restoration needed is preformed at this point. Many scratches can be removed as can dust and unwanted movement in the gate.

- The show is now color corrected in the DI color correction suite. As there is no tape format for DPX files, color correction must be done in online, not later as it often is in video finishing.
  - In VDI color correction is often preformed tape-to-tape after the HD online.

- The finished audio mix is brought in to the online. For film prints, the audio is also encoded and shot to optical sound track to be matched to the film interpositive.

- The DPX DI or HD video is now shot onto 35 mm film on a film recorder.

- Internegative is made with the optical sound and release prints are made.

Basic Workflow 7

Shooting on tapeless data recorder

Finish on 35 mm and/or video

The tapeless workflow is the newest workflow, and while still somewhat experimental and often expensive, could be the prototype workflow for future filmmaking.

Several cameras and recording systems can use this workflow. The Panasonic AG-HVX200 3-CCD P2/DVCPRO HD Format Camcorder can record in several formats to P2 cards. These can store about one minute of HD video per gig of size. They come in two-, four-, and eight-gig, and much larger ones are on the way. There are many options, but since the P2 cards are PCMCIA cards, they can slip right into your laptop on set and you can download them. Panasonic also makes a five-slot docking bay that can mount in a $5^1/_4$-inch drive bay on your desktop editing system. There is also

Panasonic's new portable HD bank, which has a single P2 Slot and a hard drive that you can use to transfer an entire P2 card in about four minutes.

The format can be DCV Pro, HDV, 720p, or 1080i PVC Pro HD and the frame rate can be 23.98 or 29.97.

There are also several systems for recording to drive in HD Cam, HD Cam SR, or even raw data. S.two of Reno, Nevada, makes the digital magazine (D.MAG) removable hard drive that is hot loaded into their Digital Film Recorder (DFR). This is a fairly large device that defiantly does not mount on the camera. The raw "film stream" data from the Thompson Viper can be recorded via a dual data link to the camera. Unwanted takes are deleted to clear up drive space. When the D.MAG is full, it is transported to the edit room and downloaded to an array of drives. It is also backed up before the D.MAG is cleared and reused.

Once the media is delivered to the edit room, the data is simply imported, a database created, and the project is ready for editing. On broadband video formats such as HD Cam or raw DXF data from the Viper camera, this requires editing right on the main editing system with a disc array. Or, the media can be down-converted to a narrower video format such as DVC Pro HD that can play directly from a hard drive or even a FireWire drive.

This is where the Red Camera workflow could change everything. The Red has a small, swappable drive right onboard the camera. Once full, the drive is swapped out and downloaded. So, while this is very similar to the AG-HVX200, and the Viper with the D.MAG, the differences are stunning.

The resolution of the Red One is claimed to be 4 K, not 2 K like the Viper and the AG-HVX200. Both Viper and the Red One can record 10-bit uncompressed data to drive, which needs some processing before it can be edited. The AG-HVX200 records a compressed 8-bit digital format, DVC Pro HD. The drives for the Viper are huge and require an even larger device to operate, the Digital Film Recorder. The Red drives are tiny, light, and mount right on the camera. And the biggest difference, the Red is less than $20,000, and the basic drive system is less than $1,000. Cheaper than the rental of the DFR.

And, tapeless does not necessarily mean filmless. It is possible to shoot 35 mm and then scan all selected takes to 2 K or 4 K DPX data just like the output of the Viper. While high-speed scanners are not as good as slower, pin-registered scanners, they are, nevertheless, very good. In this case, the camera negative would be sent to the lab for processing and scanning, and it would then be vaulted and never touched again. The reason this is not done now is simply the costs. It is so much cheaper to edit first and then only scan the footage used in the film, but this does add much more work to the workflow. If tapeless workflow becomes the norm, and scanning continues to get cheaper and faster, this "virtual film" workflow could become commonplace. That is provided that filmmakers still want a "film look" and the digital processing does not ever truly look like film.

Finishing a tapeless project is no different than finishing a project shot on tape or scanning film to a DI. DVC Pro HD can be finished right on the editing system and then recorded to tape. Color correction can be done in Color before recording to tape or it can be done tape-to-tape after the show is recorded to tape.

Many 2 K and 4 K projects will be edited to down-converted DVC Pro HD. After the picture is locked, the HD media is taken off-line and the edit is relinked to the DPX media on the drive array. The Red code media from the Red One can be edited in 720 P DVC Pro HD without ever taking the Redcode off-line. In this unique workflow, both formats are delivered from the Redcode media; there is no need to online or even relink to the original media.

This is color corrected in a DI color correction suite and the final media is shot to 35 mm film, and/or rendered for direct projection and/or down-converted to HD video.

In terms of the computer recourses and technology, this is the most complicated system ever devised for making movies. But, in terms of use, it is one of the simplest. No edge code numbers, no capture, no telecine, no reverse telecine, no frame rate conversions, no pull up or pull down, no database other than a basic edit log showing what scenes and takes are on the drive and basic notes. True portability where editors don't need to be in the same room together; they don't even need to be on the same continent.

Basic Workflow 8

Shooting on any HD or SD video format

Finish on any HD or SD video format using ProRes 422

This very new (2007) workflow requires an I/O device such as the AJA ioHD as the capture input device. The HD or SD video is captured from tape by connecting the recorder to the ioHD. ProRes 422 is created in hardware in the ioHD and sent to Final Cut Pro via FireWire 800. Tapeless media is imported and transcoded into ProRes 422.

The ProRes 422 is monitored in edit through the ioHD to an HD monitor and audio monitors. Editing, color grading, compositing, and even sound can be preformed in ProRes 422 in Final Cut Pro, Motion, Color, and Sound Track Pro or Pro Tools. The final project can be recorded to tape in any format by connecting the proper digital recorder to the ioHD.

While this seems like the simplest workflow ever devised, and in many ways it is, it does not represent any advantage over native capture and editing in any of the DV formats. It requires extra hardware, and because all formats edited with this workflow are transcoded into ProRes 422, there is a potential for loss of quality and artifacts. However, on projects that require some type of transcode anyway, say an HD finish of an SD shoot, mixed formats in one project, or any format that would normally require an online (i.e., Digitalbeta, HD cam, D5, and so on), this is the easy solution. And, while the ioHD may not up-rez SD to HD as well as the Teranex Xanthus, at $3,500, the ioHd is something that most editors can afford.

There are many workflows, and there are always choices to be made. The key is to have a plan in place before the production even begins shooting. Changes to the plan need to be made with caution, knowing the potential for creating problems,

Index

24PA video
  capture settings in Final Cut Pro, 27
  mixing with 24P video, 29
  output cadence settings in Final Cut Pro, 28
  reverse telecine, 27
2 K, 173
2:3:3:2 cadence, *see* 24PA video

A
A and B roll
  A-B rolling, 198–199
  fade-in, 205
Adobe Illustrator, title generation and import, 120–121
ADR, *see* Automatic dialogue replacement
Alpha channel, titles, 124–126
Anamorphic finish, film, 70–71
Anamorphic telecine, overview, 4–5
Answer print, definition, 59
Arriflex D20, 174–175
Aspect ratio
  letterboxing, 183–187
  overview, 183
  pan and scan, 187–188
Audio, *see also* Sound design
  film pull down, 37
  music, *see* Music
  online editing, 87
  recorders
    analog versus digital, 35–36
    digital capture, 41
    tape capture, 41–42
  Sound Track Pro, *see* Sound Track Pro
  sound effects, *see* Sound effects
  syncing
    Final Cut Pro workflow, 47–48
    hard lock versus soft lock, 37–38
    time code as reference, 36
    time code locking to smart slate, 38–41

  track management in Pro Tools, 42–47
  workflow examples, 48–49
Automatic dialogue replacement (ADR)
  cueing, 101
  editor, 101
  mixer, 101
  recording in Pro Tools, 101–102
A wind, film, 59–60

B
Background sound
  overview, 105–106
  walla, 106
Batch list
  edit logs, 11–13
  importing from Cinema Tools, 8–9
Betacam, 167
Beta SP, 167
Blue laser optical disc, 172
B wind, film, 59–60

C
Checksum error correction, 158–159
Cinema Tools
  file architecture, 192–193
  inked edge code number support, 10–11
  Picture Start frame, 98–99
  reverse telecine
    file checking, 15–16
    sequence settings, 16
  telecine logs and database, 6–10
  vertical timeline editing problems, 52–53
Color compression, 160–161
Color grading
  definition, 133
  film or video when finishing on compressed video
    Color FX, 137
    color rooms, 136
    geometry/pan and scan, 138
    overview, 134–135

    primary out, 139–140
    render cue, 141
    secondary, 136–137
    setup, 138
    still store, 140
    working with color, 135–136
  film or video when finishing on uncompressed video or digital intermediate, 141–142
Color timing
  definition, 133
  varying red, green, and blue, 133–134
Compression
  color compression, 160–161
  DVD markers, 148–149
  lossless, 159–160
  MPEG, 160
  spatial versus temporal, 160
Compressor, DVD distribution, 146–147
Conforming
  digital intermediate, 74
  edit sync, 205
  laying out and marking effects
    A and B roll fade-in, 205
    dissolve, 206
    fade-out, 205–206
    superimpositions, 207
    unintentional splices, 207
  negatives
    A-B rolling, 198–199
    leaders
      audio leaders, 204
      workflow, 203–204
    preparation, 201
    pulling negative or work print, 201–203
    splicing, 199–200
    super 16mm, 197–198
    zero cuts, 201
  work print, 67–69
Contact printing, film titles, 130–131
Cut list, export in Final Cut Pro, 63–64

D

D-1, 171
D-5, 171
Dailies
 adding to picture edit
  digital, 52
  film, 51–42
 virtual negatives, 75–76
DI, *see* Digital intermediate
Dialogue
 automatic dialogue replacement,
  101–102
 clean-up, 102–105
 splitting off production tracks, 99–101
 stems, 111–112
Digital Beta, 171
Digital intermediate (DI)
 capture and preparation examples
  Son from the Ocean, 34
  Success, 33–34
 dailies adding to picture edit, 52
Digital S, 167
Digital video (DV)
 finishing
  workflow overview, 71–72
  titles, 72
  scanning, 72–74
  resolution, 73
  color correction, 74
  virtual digital intermediate workflow,
   76
 ProRes 422 capture, 31–32
 Redcode, 33
 shooting guidelines and workflows
  high-definition video, 29–31
  standard definition video at 24P, 26
  standard definition video at 29.97
   FPS, 23–25
 tapeless capture, 32–33
 24PA video capture, 26–28
Digital video
 finishing
  high-definition video, 87–88
  off-line edit, 82–83
  online edit
   audio, 87
   color correction, 87
   edit decision list export and uses,
    84–85
   historical perspective, 83
   Media Manager, 85–87
   printing to tape, 87
   time base matching, 87
   XML export, 85
  overview, 81–82
  standard definition conversion to
   high-definition, 88–91
 titles, *see* Titles
 workflow examples
  ProRes 422 HD or SD video formats,
   240
  tapeless data recorder, 238–240
  24P HD high bandwidth, 231–234
  24P HD low data, 230–231
 formats
  overview, 154–155, 168–171
  tape cassettes. 169–170

Digi Translator plug-in, 96–97
Dissolve, 206
Distribution
 digital media, 144–145
 DVD, 145–149
 film, 143
 videotape, 145
 Web, 150
Dolby
 film finishing, 112, 114
 LCRS encoding on film, 113
Double use list, 64–65
DV, *see* Digital video
DVCam, 168, 170, 172
DVC Pro 50, 168, 170
DVC Pro HD, 168, 170
DVD distribution
 burned DVD playability, 149
 compression markers, 148–149
 Compressor, 146–147
 duplication, 149
 DVD Studio Pro, 146
 mastering, 149
 player options, 145

E

Edit decision list (EDL), export and
 finishing, 84–85
Edit log, batch lists, 11–13
EDL, *see* Edit decision list
Emulsion, film, 58

F

Farnsworth, Philo T., 151–152
Files
 architecture
  Cinema Tools, 192–193
  Final Cut Pro, 190–192
  Pro Tools, 189–190
 backing up, 195
 FireWire filing structures, 193–195
Film
 anamorphic finish, 70–71
 audio pull down, 37
 composition, 58
 costs, 1
 cut list export in Final Cut Pro, 63–64
 cutting of negatives, 69–70, 76–77
 dailies adding to picture edit, 51–52
 distribution, 143
 editing historical perspective, 57–58
 finishing with digital intermediate
  color correction, 74
  resolution, 73
  scanning, 72–74
  titles, 72
  virtual digital intermediate workflow,
   76
  workflow overview, 71–72
 formats
  IMAX, 178–179
  70mm, 178
  16mm, 177
  65mm, 178
  35mm 3 perf, 178
  35mm 4 perf, 178
  super 16mm, 177

super 35, 178
 inked edge code numbers, 10–11
 key code, 61–62
 Lost Hope and More capturing and
  preparing, 20–22
 negative editing of *Lost Hope and More*,
  77–79
 optical printers, 60–61
 print types, 59
 projection print components, 113–114
 recording, 74–75
 reel length, 62–63
 resolution, 1
 speed, 4
 telecine transfer, *see* Telecine
 titles, *see* Titles
 virtual negatives, 75–76
 wind types, 59–60
 work print pulling and conforming,
  67–69
workflow
 basic workflow, 17
 examples, 234–238
 finishing step
  film finish, 19–20
  film-to-digital, 18–19
  overview, 17–18
 historical perspective, 16–17
Final dub, 110–111
Finishing
 digital video
  high-definition video, 87–88
  off-line edit, 82–83
  online edit
   audio, 87
   color correction, 87
   edit decision list export and uses,
    84–85
   historical perspective, 83
   Media Manager, 85–87
   printing to tape, 87
   time base matching, 87
   XML export, 85
  overview, 81–82
  standard definition conversion to
   high-definition, 88–91
 film
  anamorphic finish, 70–71
  cut list export in Final Cut Pro, 63–64
  cutting of negatives, 69–70, 76–77
  digital intermediate
   color correction, 74
   resolution, 73
   scanning, 72–74
   titles, 72
   virtual digital intermediate
    workflow, 76
   workflow overview, 71–72
  double use list, 64–65
  negative editing of *Lost Hope and
   More*, 77–79
  optical list, 66–67
  pull list, 66
  recording, 74–75
  virtual negatives, 75–76
  work print pulling and conforming,
   67–69

FireWire, filing structures, 193–195
5 K, 173
Foley, 106–107
4 K, 173

G
Geography of the Imagination, workflow deconstruction, 218–221

H
Hard lock, syncing, 37–38
HD Cam, 172–173
HD Cam SR, 173
HD D-5, 173
HDV, 168, 171
Help Wanted, workflow deconstruction, 212–215

I
IMAX, 178–179
IMX, 171–172
Inked edge code numbers, Cinema Tools support, 10–11
Interleaving, pixels, 159
Internegative print, definition, 59
Internet, *see* Web
Interpositive print, definition, 59

K
Key code, film, 61–62

L
Leaders
  audio leaders, 204
  workflow, 203–204
Letterboxing, 183–187
Liths, *see* Photolithographs
LiveType, title generation, 126
Lord of the Rings, 109
Lost Hope and More
  capturing and preparing, 20–22
  editing to locked cut, 54–55
  negative editing, 77–79
  sound design example, 115–117
  workflow deconstruction, 215–218

M
Media Manager, online editing, 85–87
Metadata, digital videotape, 158
MIDI, 107–108
MPEG, compression, 160
Music
  MIDI tracks, 107–108
  recording, 107

N
National Television Standards Committee (NTSC) video
  color format and titles, 124–125
  frame fields, 152
  frame rate, 151
  historical perspective, 151–154
  television lag, 153
  workflow examples
    24P low data, 227–229
    29.97 low data, 225–226

Negative
  conforming, *see* Conforming
  cutting, 69–70, 76–77
  editing of *Lost Hope and More*, 77–79
NTSC video, *see* National Television Standards Committee video

O
O Brother, Where Art Thou?, 134
Optical list, 66–67
Optical printer, film, 60–61
Optical printing, film titles, 129

P
P2 card
  features, 172
  tapeless capture, 32–33
PAL, *see* Phase Alternate Line
Pan and scan, process, 187–188
Panavision Genesis 262, 173–174
Phase Alternate Line (PAL)
  encoding system, 163, 165
  frame rate, 163, 165
  sound, 165
Photolithographs (Liths), film titles, 127–128
Photoshop, title generation and import, 120–123
Picture edit
  changes after edit is locked, 53–54
  dailies adding
    digital video, 52
    film, 51–52
  initiation, 51
  Lost Hope and More editing to locked cut, 54–55
  vertical timeline editing problems, 52–53
Picture Start frame, 98–99
Pro Tools
  advantages in audio capture and sound design, 93
  audio import from Final Cut Pro
    Digi Translator plug-in, 96–97
    file conversion, 98
    formats, 95–96
    Picture Start frame, 98–99
    sound design, 96
  audio track management, 42–47
  automatic dialogue replacement recording, 101–102
  control surfaces and automation, 111
  file architecture, 189–190
  final dub, 110
  sample rate support, 96
  sound design, *see* Sound design
  temp dub, 109
  virtual track switching, 103–104
ProRes 422
  color grading, 142
  high-definition video capture, 31–32
  standard definition conversion to high-definition, 91
  workflow example using HD or SD video formats, 240
Pull list, 66
Pulling, work print, 67–69

R
Red Camera, 175–176
Redcode
  Final Cut Pro support, 33
  Red Camera, 175–176
Reel length, film, 62–63
Release print, definition, 59
Reverse telecine
  Cinema Tools
    file checking, 15–16
    sequence settings, 16
  filing structure, 193
  frame rate selection, 14–15
  rationale, 13–14
  24PA video, 27

S
Scanning, film to digital intermediate, 72–74
SECAM system, *see* System Electronic Colour Avec Memore (SECAM) system
Slate, time code locking to smart slate, 38–41
Soft lock, syncing, 37–38
Son from the Ocean, capture and preparation, 34
Sound design
  dialogue
    automatic dialogue replacement, 101–102
    clean-up, 102–105
    splitting off production tracks, 99–101
    stems, 111–112
  elements, 99
  final dub, 110–111
  Lost Hope and More example, 115–117
  music, 107–108
  optical sound
    prints on film, 113
    projection print, 114–115
    pull up, 112–114
  Pro Tools advantages, 93
  sound effects, 105–107
  temp dub, 108–110
Sound effects
  backgrounds, 105–106
  cueing, 15
  editing, 105
  Foley, 106–107
  listing, 105
Sound Track Pro
  audio interfaces, 94
  loop editing and management, 95
  workflow overview, 93–95
Splicing
  overview, 199–200
  unintentional splices, 207
Stereo, export and finishing, 112
Success
  capture and preparation, 33–34
  workflow deconstruction, 209–211
Superimposed titles, film, 128–129
Syncing, *see* Audio
System Electronic Colour Avec Memore (SECAM) system, 165

T

Tapeless capture, digital video, 32–33
Telecine
　anamorphic process, 4–5
　Cinema Tools database, 6–10
　conversion of 24 FPS film to 29.97 FPS
　　video with 3:2 pulldown, 3–4
　logs and databases, 5–6
　Lost Hope and More capturing and
　　preparing, 20–22
　playback speed changes, 3–4
　principles, 1–3
　retelecine, 13
　reverse telecine
　　Cinema Tools
　　　file checking, 15–16
　　　sequence settings, 16
　　frame rate selection, 14–15
　　rationale, 13–14
　take-by-take transfer, 6
　window burns, 6
Temp dub, 108–110
Thomson Viper, 175
3:2 pulldown
　conversion of 24 FPS film to 29.97 FPS
　　video, 3–4
　removal with reverse telecine, 13–14
Time code
　drop frame versus nondrop frame,
　　181–182
　linear time code, 182

subcode, 182
syncing
　locking to smart slate, 38–41
　reference, 36
vertical Interval Time Code, 157–158,
　182
Titles
　digital video
　　Adobe file import, 120–123
　　alpha channel, 124–126
　　color formats, 124–125
　　design considerations, 126–127
　　Final Cut Pro title generator, 119–
　　　120, 126
　　moving titles, 125–126
　　video format size chart, 124
　film finishing
　　contact printing, 130–131
　　digital intermediate, 72
　　optical printing, 129
　　photolithographs, 127–128
　　superimposed titles, 128–129
　pixel versus vector-based graphics, 119

U

U-matic, 167

V

Vertical Interval Time Code (VITC),
　157–158, 182

VHS, 167
Video speed, definition, 4
Videotape
　digital video cassettes, 158, 169–170
　distribution, 145
　historical perspective, 156
　metadata, 158
　tape transport systems, 157
Virtual track switching, Pro Tools,
　103–104
VITC, *see* Vertical Interval Time Code

W

Walla, 106
Web, film distribution, 150
Window burn, video work copies, 6
Wizard of Oz, The, 133
Work print
　definition, 59
　pulling and conforming, 67–69

X

XML, export in Final Cut Pro, 85

Z

Zero cuts, 201
Zodiac, The, workflow deconstruction,
　221–223

LaVergne, TN USA
09 December 2010

208131LV00003B/16/P